Supply Chain Disruption

Supply Chain Disruption

Aligning business strategy and supply chain tactics

Steve O'Sullivan

Publisher's note
Every possible effort has been made to ensure that the information contained in this book is accurate at the time of going to press, and the publishers and authors cannot accept responsibility for any errors or omissions, however caused. No responsibility for loss or damage occasioned to any person acting, or refraining from action, as a result of the material in this publication can be accepted by the editor, the publisher or the author.

First published in Great Britain and the United States in 2019 by Kogan Page Limited

Apart from any fair dealing for the purposes of research or private study, or criticism or review, as permitted under the Copyright, Designs and Patents Act 1988, this publication may only be reproduced, stored or transmitted, in any form or by any means, with the prior permission in writing of the publishers, or in the case of reprographic reproduction in accordance with the terms and licences issued by the CLA. Enquiries concerning reproduction outside these terms should be sent to the publishers at the undermentioned addresses:

2nd Floor, 45 Gee Street	122 W 27th St, 10th Floor	4737/23 Ansari Road
London	New York, NY 10001	Daryaganj
EC1V 3RS	USA	New Delhi 110002
United Kingdom		India

www.koganpage.com

© Steve O'Sullivan, 2019

The right of Steve O'Sullivan to be identified as the author of this work has been asserted by him in accordance with the Copyright, Designs and Patents Act 1988.

ISBNs

Hardback   9781789660104
Paperback   9780749484101
Ebook   9780749484118

British Library Cataloguing-in-Publication Data

A CIP record for this book is available from the British Library.

Library of Congress Cataloging-in-Publication Data

Names: O'Sullivan, Steve, author.
Title: Supply chain disruption : aligning business strategy and supply chain
   tactics / Steve O'Sullivan.
Description: 1 Edition. | New York : Kogan Page Ltd, [2019] | Includes
   bibliographical references and index.
Identifiers: LCCN 2019017731 (print) | LCCN 2019019217 (ebook) | ISBN
   9780749484118 (ebook) | ISBN 9780749484101 (pbk.) | ISBN 9781789660104
   hardback)
Subjects: LCSH: Business logistics. | Management–Technological innovations.
   | Risk management.
Classification: LCC HD38.5 (ebook) | LCC HD38.5 .O885 2019 (print) | DDC
   658.7–dc23
LC record available at https://lccn.loc.gov/2019017731

Typeset by Integra Software Services, Pondicherry
Print production managed by Jellyfish
Printed and bound by Ashford Colour Press Ltd.

For Sonja

CONTENTS

Foreword xi
Preface xiii
Acknowledgements xix
List of participants xxi

01 **An introduction to supply chain disruption** 1
Corporate supply chain disruption 5
Exponential supply chain disruption 10
Insurgent supply chain disruption 12
Humanitarian supply chain disruption 14
Supply chain disruption and ecology 15
References 25

02 **Supply chain strategic friction** 29
Historical context 30
Carl Von Clausewitz: friction 34
Strategy: an evolution 36
Strategic management as a process 41
Strategic management and the top management team 44
Strategic alignment 48
Globalization 56
References 69

03 *Ad omnia paratus* – **prepared for anything** 77
Chartered Institute of Logistics and Transport and the Irish Defence Forces 78
Nordic Battle Group: Irish Defence Forces rotation 80
United Nations Interim Force in Lebanon 86
Supply chain disruption: Irish Defence Forces 92
References 96

04 The art of responding to disruption through the physical supply chain 97

Lean inventory strategies and organizational failure to prepare for annual events 99
Cyber security, Government of China factory closures, dangerous goods policy implications 107
Super ocean carriers and seaport congestion, and the threat of ecommerce on the 3PL sector 110
Protectionism and trade wars, and non-tariff policy measures 115
Loss of containers at sea, and the Calais refugee crisis impacting road haulage 118
Mitigating disruption through change-adaption, and policy controlling oil prices 122
Conclusion 126
References 129

05 The challenges of humanitarian logistics 131

LogAid Humanitarian Logistics Consultancy – Supply chain disruption in Afghanistan and East Africa: a military and humanitarian perspective 133
Emergency Logistics Team: Responding to the ISIS crisis in the Republic of Iraq 143
The Irish Emergency Logistics Team in Yemen 147
Conclusion 150
References 153

06 Corporate supply chain disruption 155

Aligning business strategy and supply chain tactics 155
Demonstration of the Gattorna Dynamic Aligment™ model in action: Schneider Electric 161
Justification for borrowing dynamic business to information systems strategic alignment academic literature: Zoop Mobility Network Inc 167
Thoughts on evolving corporate supply chain disruption 173
Conclusion 179
References 183

07   China: supply chain disruption in the geographical heart of globalization   185

The challenges of globalization   185
Supply chain relational risk (SCRR)   187
Contemporary China   192
Collective understanding of the intricacies of Chinese Customs practices as a means of mitigating disruption   196
The power of sudden government environmental regulations to disrupt industries   198
China initiatives to reduce transit times to Europe, minimizing the demand challenge of globalization, and location as a critical factor in risk mitigation   199
The enforcement of 'mother-ship' control over subsidiaries disrupting cultural integration, and the challenge of the localization of globalization   200
Conclusion   203
References   206

08   Engaging in the process of business to supply chain strategic alignment   207

Categorizing supply chain management through the philosophy of determinism   208
The historically cyclical nature of supply chain disruption   209
Policy: historical source of supply chain disruption   212
Policy: empirical source of supply chain disruption   217
Supply chain category of determinism: External policy, beyond supply chain management   218
Supply chain category of determinism: Supply chain industry policy   219
Supply chain category of determinism: organizational policy, the TMT strategic renewal process   220
The autonomous supply chain category, impeded by strategic friction   221
Dynamic business to information systems strategic alignment: interchangeable with supply chain management   223
Supply Chain Disruption: research   225
Conclusion   237
References   238

Index   239

FOREWORD

It is not hard to find examples of disruptions to our enterprise supply chains, day by day, anywhere in the world. Typically, we have come to understand that such disruptions can come from practically any source, natural or man-made, and appear unexpectedly over the horizon like Exocets.

However, Steve O'Sullivan has dug deeper than this, and has come to the conclusion that 'policy', be it at government, military or business levels, is the underlying source of disruption to contemporary supply chains, and he has produced plenty of evidence to support his case.

If this insight is true, it implies that human behaviour at all levels and locations along supply chains has become distorted through the cultures embedded in the guilty organizations. And one of the biggest influences on the formation of internal culture is organization design – the structure that we put people to work in.

Steve's research is particularly interesting because he makes little or no distinction between the type of organization caught up in supply chain disruptions – be it business, military, or humanitarian. While acknowledging that each of these spheres can learn lessons from each other, he zeros in on the common cause, people in organizations making policy, consciously or unthinkingly, that in effect sets up conditions for a major or minor disruption to take place.

I think Steve is onto something very powerful here, because if we can understand how to make better policy in the future, cognizant of the potential impacts on the supply chains that are omni-present in our lives, then the effort and corresponding cost of retrieval will reduce significantly. Which is a good thing in an operating environment already punctuated with high levels of volatility.

John Gattorna
Global Thought Leader, Supply Chain Management
Winner of 2018 CSCMP Distinguished Service Award

PREFACE

FOUNTAINSTOWN in Cork, Ireland, my coastal birthplace, and home to one shop, three dogs, a tennis club and roaring sea, has provided much inspiration to me, and may indirectly provide the clue as to why I have such an ongoing passion for the profession of supply chain management. This passion has remained throughout two decades of corporate supply chain positions, a pending career shift to military logistics, both a Master of Science and the pursuit of a doctorate in this discipline. This same passion has always been a mystery to me because of the seismic shift from my previous incarnation, but with writing a book comes self-reflection. My predominant background is tennis, and the skills I honed on the Fountainstown courts brought me national titles and a subsequent coaching sojourn. So why this love for logistics? One thing I have learned is that supply chain management is about people and how they respond to situations, more than physical infrastructures and processes. Tennis is no different.

Akin to the strategic planning of a military commander, a tennis coach uses rhetoric and reason to prepare his player for a tournament or to face a particular opponent. The logistics of nutrition, practice and gym sessions, racquet stringing to the right tension (consistent across all racquets), replacement grips, appropriate footwear and other bag essentials brings the player to courtside. Once on court, however, although armed with the strategic intent of the coach, the player must face a myriad of disruptive friction that results in ever-changing tactics on the front line of battle. The technical side of his game has been shaped in practice (natural talent means nothing without hard work), and physical conditioning has provided stamina and endurance. But this is the same for all players. Given that a single event (point) can dramatically change the match outcome, regardless of the score, what sets a player apart from others is the ability to respond to largely unpredictable disruptions such as weather conditions, playability of different courts within a tournament venue, the evolving tactics of the opponent, ball types and condition, umpires and ball-boys at the latter stages of a tournament, injuries to themselves or their opponent, distractions from nearby courts, mental state, fear of victory in the sense of the emotional resolve needed to win, marginal bad luck, and so forth.

The player re-shapes the strategy of their coach to align with situational needs while simultaneously having sufficient faith and respect not to play outside the coach's overall vision. The speed of response to these disruptions can depend on the degree of preparations based on the coach's knowledge and the shared understanding between player and coach, in particular the coach's level of match-play experience. The player may adjust quickly to conditions or continuously battle through five-setters that should never have gone the distance. Tennis has no specified time and therefore excessive match durations can be described as a *gap of pain*. Overcoming these disruptions, more often than not, breeds success and passion. I have found huge similarities in the daily life of a supply chain manager, hence the transference of passion, but it would be remiss of me to completely credit tennis for this, given that Fountainstown also guards the second largest natural harbour in the world, and the regular sightings of naval and container ships were a thing of beauty and romance to me.

Perhaps this is why the recent attainment of a first dan black belt in shotokan karate was very satisfying and rewarding but did not fuel the same passion in me due to the repetitive, linear and defined nature of the movements. Other than occasional sparring confrontations, for me the art lacked the dynamic and disruptive attributes of tennis and supply chain management. I have always described tennis as boxing without contact, and a recent spell in white-collar boxing reminds me now of Mike Tyson's famous quote that 'everyone has a plan until they are punched in the mouth', which is really apt for the concepts explored in this book. Shotokan karate does, however, have its origins in Okinawan feudal times and it is to such historical references that I will turn my attention in due course, in order to understand the evolution of strategy and how logistics directly and significantly influenced its development.

So, let us look at a logistician in a small to medium sized multinational organization. Senior management strategic intent could perhaps include the implementation of a European central warehouse in Holland that would support products shipping from a manufacturing base in China, or an RFQ (request for quotation) process to identify a single third party logistics provider solution in support of a global logistics network. Whilst the logistics manager is specialized in such projects, progress is routinely hampered due to relentless and unplannable daily disruptive friction that dooms management to disappointment prior to strategic implementation: a less than container load (LCL) container from Hong Kong is held because it shares another firm's products that are under inspection, necessitating customs negotiation for its release; a second is held by Polish customs because the declared weight on the bill of lading does not match the weight check carried out at the port, and this can only be resolved if the co-loading shipping company in Los Angeles agrees to amend the paperwork.

Meanwhile, another container, already delayed due to Chinese New Year, is bumped at Shanghai because Apple Inc have just launched the latest iPhone and have taken all capacity at the port; a United Parcel Service shipment arrives at a customer back door with missing or damaged boxes, simultaneously requiring a replacement shipment, return material authorization, claim procedure and customer appeasement; a EUR-1 certificate cannot be provided for a shipment to Israel because the manufacturer cannot complete a long-term supplier declaration, resulting in the payment of customs duties that would otherwise be exempt due to preferential origin status; a discovery has been made that a Mexican contract manufacturer has been sending products on pallets (containing as few as two boxes) to US customers by FedEx next-day-air, and separate road shipments are being sent to two US addresses that happen to be within the same building, both scenarios significantly increasing freight costs, for which instructions need to be sent to both the US freight agents and the manufacturer to implement new procedures; a customer in France has been waiting for products since 7am but the driver has not arrived, and there is a scramble for his mobile number.

Elsewhere, a truck has come to collect five pallets from another manufacturing site in Czech Republic, but there was a miscalculation and there are in fact six pallets, thereby requiring the immediate sourcing of a second truck; one irate customer is complaining that her products were just delivered by truck when she specifically requested air freight (true story), and, before you know it, the clock says 10am and it is time to have a coffee. Ten logisticians reading this would have 10 varying challenges, but you get the idea. Strategic implementation is against the backdrop of this friction and the aim of this book is not only to recognize this friction as a form of supply chain disruption, but also to demonstrate that senior management is in many cases a source of such disruption.

The friction described thus far is largely at a micro or front-line level and can be addressed autonomously by supply chain professionals without negotiation with the top management team. However, the role of policy makers should be to acknowledge this friction during the strategic renewal process so that it can be triumphed over, as Carl von Clausewitz alluded to in *On War* (1832). On a wider or more macro scale, I have seen many policies leading to more significant disruption to supply chain networks. The geographical shift in manufacturing bases in search of reduced labour costs can often be to the detriment of supply chain cost efficiencies through increased logistical complexities. One company example was a $0.10-unit labour cost reduction through the transfer of a portion of product assembly from a base in southern to northern Suzhou, China. The final impact was a $0.25-unit cost increase due to consolidating shipments of all products from two facilities prior to sending to Shanghai Port.

Another example from China was the consignment of the manufacturing of certain products to suppliers in various regions, all of which comprised one end-product bundle. Instead of prior full container loads, LCL ocean containers were now split between Shanghai, Shenzhen and Hong Kong ports, before the product bundles were later combined in Europe. Supply chain metrics subsequently deteriorated with increased costs and lead-times, and lower container utilization rates. In both instances, the supply chain divisions were charged with improving these metrics, but it was policy making without their prior consultation that led to the situation. Any solutions leading to metric improvements require negotiation with the top management team in order to align with business goals, and to ensure that any actions stay within the core competencies of the organization. This suggests that policy is a source of supply chain disruption in the guise of strategic friction and network inefficiencies. Engaging in the process of dynamic business to supply chain strategic alignment would mitigate such disruption. Strangely, supply chain management literature is relatively silent in this respect.

Supply chain disruption has been prolifically explored by prominent academics and practitioners. Chapter 1 aims to summarize this body of work and includes the business, military and humanitarian domains, as it is my assertion that all are connected, and lessons can be learned from all perspectives. This research, predominantly within the scope of supply chain risk management, remains critical. My objective is not to expand on this specific area, but to complement it, by going to the heart of disruption, namely policy. Chapter 2 introduces this concept as various elements are pieced together to add policy to an already acknowledged supply chain disruption taxonomy of crises, disasters and breakdowns. This evolving jigsaw commences in 1800, a period that introduced a 'perfect storm' of true globalization, a technological revolution, and the founding of modern strategy, influenced by supply chain and logistics, through the development of physical infrastructures and cartography.

Great advances indeed, but ones that caused major disruption on a global scale through policy. In 1944 it was policy again that reversed this disruption and led to a golden age, when again in the early 1980s policy shifts resulted in a repeat performance of the chaos seen a century before. Throughout my text, supply chain and logistics are terms used interchangeably, as they are in practice. My stance is that logistics is a function within supply chain management. However, I also want to appeal to a wider readership outside our profession, who would relate more to the term logistics. A child of five would understand this. 'Send someone to fetch a child of five' (Groucho Marx). From Chapter 3 onwards I use case studies to demonstrate my concept that policy is perhaps *the* source and snake's head of supply chain disruption, first from a military perspective, and then within the humanitarian and business domains. 'Why military?' I hear many ask. Firstly, because the origins of the concept I am introducing lie within the military, secondly because supply chain management is about people, soldiers are people, and therefore their experiences are no less applicable, and thirdly because a book based on Napoleon is more romantic than supply chain disruption caused by a DAF truck breaking down on the M50 (Carl von Clausewitz, *On War*).

ACKNOWLEDGEMENTS

First of all, I must thank Grainne Lynch, the then Chairperson of the Chartered Institute of Logistics and Transport in the Southern Section of Ireland, who started me on this path of researching supply chain disruption in the military domain, through her invitation to publish an article on the Nordic Battle Group in the CILT professional journal, *LinkLine*. Then of course my Kogan Page team of Julia Swales, for facilitating this publication, and Ro'isin Singh, a very talented and patient development editor, who made each instalment better. A special thank you to my doctoral supervisors, Claudia Wagner (Cork Institute of Technology) and John Gattorna. Claudia taught me the significant value of framing research (and indeed any project) with aims and objectives before commencing, and this has been my guide throughout. The great genius of John is that our 20-minute Skype calls invariably included one crucial word to point me in the right direction. *Disruption* was the first such word.

The Irish Defence Forces are a source of personal pride and it was a great honour for me to have Commandant Robert Moriarty share his insights into the Nordic Battle Group and Lebanon missions. David Duddy was such an engaged participant and his 'No seat at the Big Boys' table' captured the entire essence of this research. Thank you too, William Holden. Our conversations recently led me to the Kurdistan Region of Iraq for a Human Capacity Development Program, and when I return soon, (Irish) Inshallah, you can be found again by *taking the second right after the Virgin Mary*. From an invisible nation, to an invisible profession, I am so grateful to the nine participants from the transport and distribution sector, whose art of physical supply chain connects the global commercial market, but also enables humanitarian and military machines to respond to disruption. Unsung heroes for sure.

Thank you, Heidi Larsen, for sharing your experiences and knowledge of doing business in China, and notwithstanding their organizational anonymity due to the Golden Shield, it must be acknowledged that our China participants were very generous (and brave) to give their perspectives on such a sensitive topic. John Gattorna is a global icon in supply chain management, and to be permitted to include the Dynamic Alignment™ model was wonderful. This gratitude extends to Stuart Whiting, Esther Lätte and Jon Bumstead for their demonstration of John's extensively proven model in action.

Acknowledgements

Fountainstown bookends this publication. This is my tribute to my parents and brothers. My father knew long before me that tennis was not going to pay the mortgage and covertly signed me up for an evening degree program in 1987, starting my passion for academia, ultimately leading to this research. Finally to Robynne, Ross and Madelyn, for supporting their Dad.

LIST OF PARTICIPANTS

Commandant Robert Moriarty, Logistics Branch (Army), Irish Defence Forces

David Duddy, Managing Director, LogAid

Will Holden, Managing Director, Emergency Logistics Team

Eduardo Vargas, Regional Director Los Angeles, US Southwest and Mexico, Morrison Express Corporation

Jeroen van Beek, District Manager, Netherlands, Morrison Express Corporation

Kevin Brady, Managing Director, Woodland Group Ireland

Michiel van Berkel, Sales Manager Netherlands, Royal Rotra Group

Paul Aerts, Benelux Logistics Manager, Royal Rotra Group

Ian Truesdale, Global Senior Vice President of Logistics and Innovation, Kuehne + Nagel

Shane Bradley, Business Development Manager, Crane Worldwide Logistics

Gerry Hall, Regional Logistics Manager, Crane Worldwide Logistics

Frank Kilbride, Country Manager for Ireland, Aramex

John Gattorna, Gattorna Alignment, Supply Chain Management Global Thought Leader

Stuart Whiting, Senior Vice President, Logistics and Network Design, Schneider Electric

Esther Lätte, Field Operations Manager at ZOOP Mobility Network Inc.

Jon Bumstead, Director, Nisomar Ventures

Heidi Larsen, Global Supply Chain Consultant, Founder Plus7

Li (Lucia) Huang, Global Supply Chain and Project Manager, Shanghai

Chunming Gu, Supply Chain Manager, Suzhou

Emily Yan, Global Supply Chain Manager, Guangdong

Raymond Gao, Supply Chain Manager, Research and Development, Beijing

Additional resources can be downloaded at koganpage.com/SCD

An introduction to supply chain disruption   01

It could be argued that the origins of supply chain management as we know it today lie with the ruthless and allegedly villainous Henry Ford, who in 1911–12 began to develop the concepts of mass production and the assembly line, which within two years resulted in the quadrupling of output and the reduction in labour force and costs of manufacturing. Alas it also later led in 1927–45 to the death of one worker per day, on average, on the banks of an Amazon tributary where Ford, the then world's richest man, produced rubber as a means of deflating the European monopoly of this commodity through their Asian colonies, a commodity more important to America than oil at that time according to the 31st President Herbert Hoover (Grandin, 2010). The term 'supply chain management' itself was invented in 1982 by a Booz Allen Hamilton consultant, Keith Oliver, to describe the 'overall process of planning, implementing, and controlling what goes on in the supply chain in order to satisfy customers' needs in a quick, efficient manner' (Harland, 1996). 'What goes on' is not very informative.

In 2010, I posited that the expansion of the British Marketing Institute's depiction of their own discipline to include *through the optimization of all known channels* provides as good a definition as any: supply chain management is the management process responsible for identifying, anticipating and satisfying customer requirements, at a profit, through the optimization of all known channels. In suggesting that supply chain management is a management process, I again took the lead from marketing, a science that has facilitated organizational evolution from the traditional production or sales orientation to holistic customer orientation, made possible only through multi-functional management coordination. As markets emerge and grow, challenges will arise and, accordingly, companies need to plan, organize, develop, communicate and control in an integrated way (Rogan, 2011).

Supply chain management also recognizes that the customer drives the organization and that this must involve participative or collaborative management to encompass the vast network of activities or functions across the entire business. These functions include buy, make, move, store and sell, which were developed by Professor Edward Sweeney, Aston University. Prior to the Beast from the East dumping copious amounts of snow on the United Kingdom and Ireland in March 2018, the general public may have thought that bread and milk came from the supermarket. Not so. This collaboration should be expanded, so that, where possible, knowledge of the customers' supply chain should also be gathered, as ultimately it is their process that the company needs to fit. The sell function of the company may be the buy function of the customer. Packaging redesign, container strategies, demand analysis, order management restructuring or enterprise resource planning (ERP) implementations, as examples, should all have the aim of satisfying (strategic) customer requirements.

A more recent and holistic definition is 'any combination of processes, functions, activities, relationships and pathways along which products, services, information and financial transactions flow in and between enterprises, in both directions, end-to-end' (Gattorna, 2015). The latter reflects the fact that the complexity of supply chain management has been compounded by the force of globalization along the dimensions of replenishment, time and distance (Christopher and Towill, 2002), in addition to technology and climate change, all of which are accelerating beyond our ability to adapt (Friedman, 2016). Increasingly, organizations are finding themselves at the centre of unplannable events that interrupt and threaten their global supply chains. Vulnerabilities to disruptions have increased and these can be categorized as crises, disasters and breakdowns (Gattorna, 2015).

Supply chain disruption has been prolifically explored by prominent academics and practitioners. In this chapter I aim to summarize this body of work and include the domains of business, military and humanitarian, as it is my assertion that all are connected, and lessons can be learned from all perspectives. This research, predominantly within the scope of supply chain risk management, remains critical. Why so? Many organizations have adopted a lean approach, such as increased product variety, new product introduction with a greater rhythm of speed, cost reductions through a reduced supply base, just-in-time inventory systems, vendor-managed inventories, and reduced assets through outsourced manufacturing. In a stable environment, these strategies are extremely effective (Tang, 2006). We do not operate in a stable environment. In the event of supply chain disruption, the results can be devastating:

- The World Trade Centre in New York, and the 350 companies that occupied it, was bombed in 1993. One year later, 150 of these companies were out of business. Arabian Peninsula based terrorists sent camouflaged bombs through express parcel service in 2010 that were designed to explode over major cities in the United States. A severe acute respiratory syndrome (SARS) epidemic in China in 2003, and ash omissions from the Icelandic volcano Eyjafjallajökull in 2010, dealt severe blows to the air freight industry (and of course had a wider impact on airlines, tourism, global business).

- The revenues of Dole, the largest producer of fruit and vegetables in the world, declined in 1998 after Hurricane Mitch destroyed banana plantations in Central America. Similarly, droughts across Canada in 2000 and 2001 resulted in a $3.6 billion reduction in agricultural production. A 2011 drought in Texas cost the agricultural sector $7.63 billion and the forestry sector $669 million. Manitoba's 2011 flooding cost the Canadian economy $936 million.

- A Philips semiconductor plant in Albuquerque, New Mexico, caught on fire in 2000 after a lightning strike, leading to a loss of €400 million for Ericsson in Sweden. Nokia in Finland was also significantly disrupted by this ten-minute blaze. A 2011 flood in Thailand reduced Intel's quarterly revenue target by $1 billion.

- In March 2011, an earthquake and tsunami in Japan caused Panasonic to post a US$469 million second quarter loss, compared to a 2010 second quarter profit of $674 million. Renault reported a loss of $218 million. Toyota had an immediate drop in production of 78.4 per cent, while Honda's domestic production fell by 53.4 per cent in the days after the disaster. This was called a 100-year event, a Black Swan. The event also damaged commercial nuclear plants (the TEPCO Daiichi catastrophe), and ocean operators refused to pick up shipments in Tokyo and Yokohama for quite some time due to a fear of radiation-contaminated containers.

- A key supplier of Land Rover became insolvent in 2001 and they had to make 1,400 workers redundant. Operations at a United States west-coast port in 2002 took six months to return to normal after a longshoreman strike disrupted trans-shipments to domestic firms.

- A study of 827 companies reporting supply chain disruptions between 1989–2000 found that their stock returns were up to 40 per cent less than industry standards for two years after an event. Cisco Systems Inc wrote off inventory valued at $2.5 billion resulting from communication issues among its downstream supply chain partners.

(Tang, 2006; Hendricks and Singhal, 2005; Craighead *et al*, 2007; Wagner and Bode, 2008; Aggarwal and Bohinc, 2012; O'Riordan *et al*, 2013; Simchi-Levi *et al*, 2013; Hamner *et al*, 2015)

My objective is not to expand on this specific area, but to compliment it, by going to what I consider to be the heart of disruption. Policy. This is both in relation to the resulting impact of policy on supply chain network design, and its failure to acknowledge the existence of strategic friction, petty circumstances and blind natural forces that impede strategic implementation.

The Preface broached the subject of strategic friction through the lens of a logistician in a contemporary small to medium sized multinational organization, a concept that is attributed to Prussian General Carl Von Clausewitz from his observations of the Napoleonic campaigns. During the American Civil War, in December 1862, under ideal weather conditions, Union General Ambrose Burnside planned an ambitious move to entrench and massacre Robert E Lee's confederate troops against the Rappahannock river. This would have perfectly positioned Burnside to then march against Richmond, the ultimate goal of the Union. However, upon execution of the strategy, a winter cyclone suddenly descended, turning roads into 'deep muddy tracks', and to the delight of Lee's jeering soldiers, resulted in 75,000 hapless Burnside troops 'bogged down and their equipment demobilized'. Retreat to Falmouth was the only option for them. Friction turned a potential enemy massacre to self-humiliation (Brady, 2015).

It persists today, such as Desert Storm (1991 Persian Gulf War). Many F-111F air missions had to be aborted due to the fact that fuel tankers for pre-strike replenishment were nowhere to be found (a serious lack of coordination between strike and support aircraft), a further 82 target and time-on-target tactical changes were made once in flight, air-crews faced equipment malfunctions and sub-standard mission-planning materials, intelligence relating to enemy positions and defences was inconsistent, there were sudden adjustments to pre-war tactics, unfavourable weather conditions, latent bomb damage assessments and a general lack of understanding of what senior command was attempting to accomplish on any given day (Watts, 2004).

Chapter 2 explores this concept as various elements are pieced together to add policy to an already acknowledged supply chain disruption taxonomy of crises, disasters and breakdowns. This evolving jigsaw commences in 1800, a period that introduced a perfect storm of true globalization, a technological revolution, and the founding of modern strategy, influenced by supply chain and logistics, through the development of physical infrastructures and cartography. Great advances indeed, but ones that caused major disruption on a global scale through policy. In 1944 it was policy again that reversed this disruption and led to a golden economic age, when again in the early 1980s policy shifts resulted in a repeat performance of the chaos seen a century ago. From Chapter 3 onwards I use case studies to demonstrate my concept that policy is perhaps *the* source and snake's head of supply chain disruption, first from a military perspective, and then within the business domains. In the meantime, let me summarize the accepted academic wisdom within the domain of supply chain management.

Corporate supply chain disruption

Business breakdowns are at the operational level of disruption. Such disruptions can include uncertain customer demand, quality issues, transportation delays, poor supplier performance, equipment malfunctions, inventory and capacity issues, information system (IS) breakdowns, increasing competitive intensity, and human-centred issues from strikes to fraud. These result in severe stock and operating under-performance and should be a high priority for senior management and shareholders (Kleindorfer and Saad, 2005; Sylla, 2014; Roh *et al*, 2014). Costs and other consequences such as damage to a brand can be even more challenging than terrorist acts because they have a greater cumulative effect over time and have a disproportionate effect on demand (Sylla, 2014; Sheffi, 2001).

Recent tangible events have promoted supply chain management to critical importance. In the business domain, during 2008 a liquidity crisis in the United States triggered the collapse of financial institutions and property markets, the bailout of banks by national governments, and downturns in stock markets around the world. This global financial crisis changed the world in a precipitous way (Gattorna, 2009). This led to a volatile operating environment, but the most responsive organizations mobilized their supply chain networks to mitigate greater demand uncertainty, higher risk and increasing competitive intensity. The collapse of the Soviet Union in December 1991 resulted in the creation of 15 separate countries, and the Russian Federation faced unparalleled environmental discontinuity, instability, complexity and 'concomitant uncertainty' (May *et al*, 2000). Another major disruptive event of similar proportion commenced on 28 March 2017, when the United Kingdom invoked Article 50 to withdraw from the European Union (EU) by April 2019. The full impact of 'Brexit' is pending negotiations and, of course, of critical importance to supply chain professionals is how trading relationships will be impacted by the final decision on single market and customs union access.

Never before has a collaborative approach been so critical to survival. The management guru, Peter Drucker, once remarked that 'every 200 or 300 years, there is a very short period when the world suddenly changes. This is one of those periods when the old solutions no longer work' (Drucker, 1992). This was in reference to the international challenge facing organizations that needed to adapt to changes resulting from globalization in order to maintain strategic advantage. Subsequently, the Asia-Pacific region was to become the engine room of world economic growth. It was forecast that Asia's economies would account for 45 per cent of global gross domestic product (GDP), significantly more than the United States and Europe combined. Governments were becoming increasingly powerless as multinationals were now the masters of the world. In Europe the introduction of the euro currency in 2002 and expansion of EU member states in 2004 had increased trade in the eurozone. Of course, the collapse of the communist world bringing an end to the Cold War had also been a major factor, with new investment and trading opportunities being opened up (*Economist*, 2006).

It was widely assumed that continuous growth of the world economy was inevitable. However, as pointed out by Professor Thomas N Baldwin (University of Michigan Business School), such growth was not sustainable in the long term due to 'threats to the integrity, productivity, and resilience of our natural and social life support systems' (Venables, 2006). Charles Handy declared that we were entering an age of unreason, an era of rapid and highly discontinuous change (Handy, 2002). The economic explosion brought about dramatic changes not only in the geographical landscape of the business world but consequently also in the behaviour of consumers who came to expect and demand more and more to the point of unsustainable growth. This almost frenzied materialism, buoyed by dangerous levels of credit, finally culminated in an economic tsunami that suddenly engulfed the globe with immeasurable damage and duration (many nations today remain within an era of economic stagnation).

Consequently, in April 2009 Asia, the so-called economic engine room, had suffered a 21 per cent drop in trade with Europe (a relatively lower 9 per cent with USA), 303 container ships were anchored redundantly in ports, while 400,000 containers were sitting empty and idle in Shenzhens' Yantian terminal and in Hong Kong. There were 800,000 twenty-foot container equivalent units (TEUs) that represented excess capacity due to low trade volumes, compared to 150,000 in October 2008, and the price to send a container from Asia to England was $0 as a result of 'negative freight' (Chaina, 2009). Some commentators would argue, however, that this capacity situation was artificially created by freight companies in order to maintain costs and protect rates. Of course, one transparent reaction from these companies was the strategy of 'slow steaming' whereby a 10 per cent reduction in speed effected a 30 per cent reduction in costs, a strategy that increased the challenge of supply chain professionals, as it added three days to the transit time of containers from China to Rotterdam (Europe's premier sea port).

More challenging these events may be, but by the same token more exciting because it is in such times that we can have the most impact through supply chain excellence. John Gattorna, the acknowledged global supply chain thought leader, maintained that in 'the last sixteen years of high growth (1991–2007), we have learned little or nothing' due to such seemingly endless prosperity covering the many operational cracks in the business world. One needs to look no further than the banking crisis in Ireland and the failures of state-owned companies to illustrate this point. Gattorna may not have predicted the crash but does agree with Baldwin that it was inevitable, and also suggests that the pre-2007 business models have outlived their usefulness (Sweeney, 2009). However, I am of the opinion that the nature of supply chain management (SCM) is optimization and cost reduction, neither of which is a contributing factor to business collapse.

The manner in which an organization manages and strategically responds to supply chain disruptions has a direct impact on its reputation, consistency in earning and ability to increase shareholder returns (Rajesh *et al*, 2015). The traditional role of supply chain management is that of execution, and the prevailing age of accelerating forces of globalization, climate change and technology demand a more responsive and agile approach. Faster clockspeeds (Gattorna, 2018). Emerging from this, providing the tools, practices and efforts for reducing disruptions and building resilient supply chains, is the nascent sub-domain of supply chain risk management, which has been defined as 'the implementation of strategies to manage exceptional risks along the supply chain through continuous risk assessment with the objective of reducing vulnerability and ensuring continuity' (Rajesh *et al*, 2015; Sodhi *et al*, 2012; Schlegel and Trent, 2014).

Generic corporate supply chain strategies can include *collaborative*, where all parties work together to manage demand, reduce costs and improve lead-times, *lean or efficient*, a focus on removing waste while maintaining alignment with customer value sets when demand is predictable, product life-cycles are long and product profit margins are low, *campaign*, which is the management of major capital projects, and *fully flexible*, an ability to provide extreme customer solutions. However, in the context of supply chain disruption, an *agile strategy* is required, being responsive to customers in unpredictable demand situations, and when limited suppliers are unreliable (Wu et al, 2014; Gattorna, 2015).

Yossi Sheffi of the Massachusetts Institute of Technology suggests that organizations must add disruption consciousness to their culture and views a preparation phase as a form of insurance, a trade-off between the cost of just in case and the lean nature of just in time. One of the main tenets of military preparedness is the investment in redundancy and Sheffi advocates the use of both offshore suppliers for the bulk of procurement volume and local suppliers to offset disruption. The incremental cost of doing so is a premium paid for reduced risk and the insurance value depends on the probability of disruption. Maintaining strategic emergency inventory is another form of redundancy that is adopted by organizations such as hospitals that keep a stock of key medicines, and oil reserves held in that industry.

A third form of redundancy is knowledge back-up, through the standardization of processes and practices. Managing supply chains under increased uncertainty includes measures such as shipment visibility (new technologies: radio-frequency identification, and tags communicating with low-earth-orbiting-satellite systems), improved collaboration given that the long-term fate of an organization is intertwined with suppliers, customers and even competitors (Toyota has invited researchers and competitors to visit their plants and study their systems) and improved aggregate forecasting through the risk pooling strategies of postponement (build to order), product variability reduction and centralized inventory management (Sheffi, 2001).

Yang and Xu (2015) found that disruption may occur in any links of the supply chain from upstream to downstream and can cut off cash flows that halt entire operations whilst increasing consumer demand through panic. The modes identified are disruptions in supply, transportation, internal production facilities, communication flow, human resource capacity and freight breaches. Mitigation or contingency strategies that enhance general supply chain strategies include multiple sourcing, inventory management, product substitution and back-up suppliers. Resilience needs to be developed so that organizations, whether it is systems and processes, or resources and skills, have the ability to either return to their original state or evolve to a new and more desirable state after being severely disturbed. The characteristics of resilience include robustness against initial disruption, redundancy, resourcefulness and rapidity of the recovery process.

Kleindorfer and Saad (2005) maintain that designing alternative supply chain options is critical to building efficiency and robustness against various sources of disruption and advise that the foundation of disruption risk management is to continuously practice tasks which they presented within the SAM model: Firstly, the sources of risks and vulnerabilities, such as operational breakdowns, need to be *specified*, and appropriate strategies need to be formulated such as sourcing and inventory models, and emergency response capabilities. Secondly, there must be *assessment* of probable risk using fault and event trees. This should include vulnerability assessment and decision analysis. Thirdly, *mitigation* of disruption involves having visibility of risks across the entire supply chain, establishing appropriate incentives, including non-performance penalties, across all participants, and the implementation of supply chain disruption management systems. Specify. Assess. Mitigate.

Chopra *et al* (2007) determined that delays and disruptions are distinct and should have different supply mitigation strategies such as sourcing from less expensive, less reliable suppliers as recurrent risks increase (delays), and using more expensive, more reliable suppliers in the case of increasing interruptions (disruptions). Christopher and Peck (2004) suggest that many of the threats to the dynamic network of interconnected firms and industries are found outside the focal firm and the panoply of potential risks are summarized as firm internal (process and control), firm external (demand and supply) and network external (environment). In order to address supply chain vulnerability, exposure to serious disturbance, arising from risks within the supply chain as well as risks external to the supply chain, it is important that resilience is designed in when creating the supply chain, there must be a high level of collaboration across the network, supply chains must be agile, and a risk management culture must be nurtured.

Critical paths in the supply chain have been characterized as long lead-times, single sourcing, linkages where visibility is poor, and high levels of identifiable risks such as supply and demand. A further strategic approach to mitigating against disruptions is the triple-A supply chain, which suggests that competitive advantage requires the three elements of all supply chain partners aligning their interests, collectively adapting to political change and evolving economic conditions, using new technologies to enhance their effectiveness and building agile and resilient networks that can respond to sudden disruption (Lee, 2004). Sodhi *et al* (2012) are in agreement and propose increasing collaboration with partners including risk sharing, increasing demand, supply and process flexibilities, and building buffers or redundancies across supply chains. Finally, multi-dimensional integrations, including socio-technical collaboration with strategic suppliers and customers, and techno-process integration such as advanced manufacturing technologies, all toward time-based outcomes represent the most important characteristics of a responsive supply chain strategy (Roh *et al*, 2014).

Exponential supply chain disruption

Another emergent disruptive threat is that technology is doubling down as discovered in 1964 by Gordon Moore, the Intel Corporation co-founder (Friedman, 2016). Organizations in, most notably, but certainly not limited to, information-driven industries such as software and financial services face obsolescence from the resulting disruption of exponential organizations, a new breed of corporations that are accessing resources that they do not own, and using information as their best asset (Ismail, 2014). New organizational techniques that leverage accelerating technologies enable their output to be disproportionally larger, at least ten times, compared to traditional organizations. Perhaps 'any company designed for success in the 20th century is doomed to failure in the 21st' (Rose, 2014). Amazon is said to have created the exponential organization phenomenon with the launch of the cloud for small and medium sized businesses in March 2006. Perhaps this led Friedman to ask, 'What the hell happened in 2007?', a vintage year in history that saw the birth of the Apple iPhone, Google's launching of Android and purchase of YouTube, Amazon releasing Kindle, the global scaling of Facebook and Twitter, and the explosion of the mobile phone app industry, all of which prompted Michael Dell to return to the helm of Dell Computers Inc.

Motorola Inc launched a company called Iridium in the late 1980s that positioned a constellation of satellites that would provide mobile telephony across the globe for the one price of $3,000 per satellite phone and a $5 per minute usage fee. This subsequently failed at a cost of $5 billion, because Motorola did not change business assumptions at a time when the cost of installing mobile phone towers was falling significantly, network speeds were increasing, and handsets were getting smaller and cheaper (Ismail, 2014). The Iridium plan was also locked in place 12 years before it became operational, using linear tools to predict the future based on historical data. Albert Einstein observed that everything is connected and ironically simultaneous to the Iridium moment, there was growing evidence in the field of modern cosmology that the acceleration of the Universe was being driven by a cosmological constant or dark energy (Copeland *et al*, 2006) at a rate that is in conflict with gravity itself. It is beyond the scope of this research to link dark energy to Friedman's accelerating forces, but one can wonder.

Further Iridium moments continue. Kodak filed for bankruptcy in 2012, having rejected the digital camera that it invented, at a time when Instagram, three years in existence and with 13 employees, was bought by Facebook for $1 billion. Instagram is just one of a new breed of enterprise that is scaling at a rate never before seen by manipulating and using third-party owned information-driven resources, the exponential organization. Airbnb has a worth of $10 billion and is set to become the world's largest hotelier, without any physical assets, while Uber outsources private automobiles as taxis and has grown exponentially to a worth of $17 billion. Enabling this scalability is a completely different internal mindset in terms of performance measurements and business philosophies, but also in how they deal with and even embrace risk (Ismail, 2014). The exponential organization thinks big and is born from a massive transformative purpose that aims much higher than the traditional mission statement, such as Google's 'organize the world's information'.

Other attributes include interfaces that filter and match masses of Big Data into idea generation, and adaptable dashboards that involve employees from the bottom-up known as high-frequency objectives and key results (OKRs). OKRs ask the questions 'Where do I want to go?' and 'How will I know I am getting there?' Employees are encouraged to continuously experiment and innovate without the restraint of seeking permission, and risk mitigation increases as a result of this willingness to fail ('it is tinkering that allowed the Industrial Revolution'). Holacracy is adopted to 'increase agility, efficiency, transparency, innovation and accountability within an organization' as are social technologies that provide transparent and simultaneous sharing of information. The ultimate objective of the exponential organization is a zero-latency enterprise in which the time to market from idea generation and approval, through to development, launch or implementation, is almost in parallel (Ismail, 2014).

Such attributes are also applicable to organizations with physical assets. In the supply chain domain, United Parcel Service interfaces reduced the mileage of its American fleet of 55,000 trucks by 85 million through routing efficiencies, resulting in an annual cost saving of $2.55 billion. The exponential organizations' approach to speed, functionality and flexibility also has external characteristics but from a different perspective. They use their massive 'transformative purpose' to attract passionate talent, and harness creativity and innovation, in the form of communities and crowds, thereby increasing the agility of the organization through much faster idea generation. This enabled DIY Drones to build a $300 drone that is a 98 per cent replica of the $4 million US Military Predator drone.

Through machine learning that predicts future trends based on historical data, and deep learning where new patterns are discovered without the use of historical data, algorithms are continuously being improved upon. Google increased its revenues by a factor of 125 in the ten years since 2002 using the PageRank algorithm. A further characteristic includes leveraging assets such as Apple Inc, Hewlett Packard and Dell Computers using Foxconn and RR Donnelley as manufacturing partners (Ismail, 2014). With the embracement of risk, and continuous experimentation, the exponential organization has a greater capacity to respond to disruption through increased agility, also self-disrupting as a core strategy before others do so, unlike traditional firms that are rarely *structured* to counter unforeseen disruption.

In this context it is the garage entrepreneur that poses the most risk. Consider Craigslist, which overpowered the classified advertising model of the newspaper industry. Both internal disruptive innovation and external disruption takes place when a technology becomes information-enabled, costs drop exponentially, and access to the technology is standardized. This increased agility also reflects the discarding of traditional strategic planning. The future is changing so rapidly that any forward outlooks are most likely going to produce false scenarios and therefore this is 'death to the five-year plan' (Ismail, 2014). Smith (2016) supports this threat to traditional organizations. The once-favoured business model of outsourcing has seen satisfaction ratings drop from 80 per cent in 1997 to 54 per cent a decade later, and 59 per cent of companies (in 2007) needing to exit contracts before their full terms ended, due to poor supplier performance. This model is being replaced by the age of the networked company that can develop and sustain competitive advantage over the traditional asset-burdened and hierarchical linear organizations, with significantly less agility to respond to sudden change.

Insurgent supply chain disruption

Disruptions can also take the form of terrorist attacks (crises) resulting from the rise of purposeful agents such as Al-Qaeda. Quite often, how a government responds is the main cause of disruption rather than the actual attack or event, such as closing borders, shutting down air traffic, or evacuating areas (Sheffi, 2001). In the aftermath of the 9–11 tragedy, trucks loaded with components bound for US manufacturing plants such as Ford were delayed at the Mexican and Canadian borders, while steering sensors for Toyota were held at Frankfurt airport. In addition to physical disruption, there has been an increase in malicious cyber-attacks, prompting militaries to implement cyber brigades within their forces. Interestingly, crises are closely linked to the accelerating forces of globalization, climate change and technology in much the same way that the elements of computing power (processing chips, software, storage chips, networking and sensors) move forward as a group (Friedman, 2016).

Consider Syria, the geopolitical super-storm of the age of accelerations and the rise of the Islamic State of Iraq and the Levant. A combination of simultaneous factors such as a population explosion during the 1980s, President Bashar al-Assad's regulation of the agricultural sector to benefit large-scale farmers (who were also government officials) upon taking power in 2000, enabling the purchase of vast lands and water drilling rights, a catastrophic drought known as *jafaf*, and the subsequent migration of small deposed farmers and their families to cities such as Aleppo in search of food and jobs, politicized a young generation into civil war, whose cause grew exponentially through a global reach that was powered by technology (Friedman, 2016).

Supply chain disruption literature assigns a category to terrorism and applies mitigation strategies at firm level similar to those of corporate and humanitarian disruptions. However, the growing sophistication of insurgent organizations could potentially enable governments and militaries to manage direct mitigation. One example is the March 2004 Madrid bombings, sadly killing 192 people and injuring more than 1,600. Global Islamic media posted an Al-Qaeda strategy document in December 2003 in which there was a warning of 'painful strikes' against Spanish forces because of their involvement in the Iraq war, and that they would 'make the utmost use' of the upcoming Spanish elections in March. Another document appeared at the same time, a 'message to the Spanish people', informing of attacks on Spanish interests outside of Iraq. These strategic intents are of course not sufficient for mitigation without details of specific tactics (Lia and Hegghammer, 2004).

It is human nature and self-interest of corporate organizations to leave the security costs of mitigation to governments while they focus on operational efficiencies. This breeds inertia despite the fact that the immeasurable indirect costs of terrorism on the organization significantly outweigh and endure longer than the direct costs incurred by the government (Aggarwal and Bohinc, 2012). Indirect costs include the disruption of homeland defence (anti-terrorist measures) on the global transportation system and thereby the reliability of our supply chain networks. The rise in terrorism has been assisted by the transportation and communication systems that we have developed in our profession. Everything is connected. Pioneers such as Malcolm McLean who invented the container, and on 26 April 1956 sailed the first container ship from New Jersey to Texas (SS Ideal-X), could never have envisioned the collateral damage of terrorism that his business idea could enable, a business that doubles in traffic every seven years.

As a profession we can do more through public and private partnership. Sheffi advises that organizations should share information and concerns with local law enforcement and rescue agencies where vulnerabilities to nuclear or chemical attacks are known. A customs 'fast lane' can be created if the use of certified carriers and shippers increases in ocean and road transport similar to the FAA Directive 108-01-10 applied to air freight. In the United States there are 800,000 truck movements of hazardous goods (a target for terrorist groups) and the public and emergency services can and should be made aware of these through the emergency planning and community right-to-know act, easily identifiable through a labelling system employed by the US Department of Transportation. An air traffic control system for hazardous shipments would require trucks to file a 'flight plan' before departure. In 1986, US congress passed the Superfund Amendments and Reauthorization Act. This charges all communities to establish a local emergency planning committee to simulate the response to chemical attacks. These initiatives should be adopted more widely, such as European nations currently under threat.

Humanitarian supply chain disruption

There is much to learn from the humanitarian approach to disruption, or natural events (disasters), that could be applied to the business context, according to Sowinski (Kovács and Spens, 2007). Many cities are becoming more vulnerable as a result of high population density and poor adherence to planning and development protocols (Pettit and Beresford, 2009; Soneye, 2014). Global populations are set to rise by another 2.5 billion people and it is estimated that we will have 100 million climate refugees by 2050, with, among other consequences, sea level rising by up to 20 feet over the same period. This is considered largely 'anthropogenic' due to people consuming the Earth's natural resources 20 per cent faster than nature can renew them (Smith, 2016). It is forecasted that over the next 50 years, both natural and man-made disasters will increase five-fold. Notwithstanding the fact that only 58 per cent of humanitarian agencies have logisticians in their assessment teams despite logistics efforts accounting for 80 per cent of disaster relief, a phased approach to dealing with disruption has emerged in this domain.

The disaster management cycle (DMC) suggests that phases such as planning (preparedness), mitigation, detection, response and recovery necessitate different supply chain management practices as agencies urgently establish presence in disaster areas to reduce the '*gap of pain*' (Pettit and Beresford, 2009; Kovács and Spens, 2007; Heaslip and Barber, 2014). We were reminded in April 2010 that natural disasters are not limited to developing nations with the eruption of the Icelandic volcano Eyjafjallajökull.

Major economic and supply chain disruption was caused across Europe with up to 20 nations closing airspace to commercial jet traffic, affecting 10 million travellers, and restricting the delivery of critical componentry to manufacturing locations. These events are largely unplannable, but a preparation phase incorporates five supply chain elements of: implementing a disaster management framework, establishing logistic operations and process management, human resource management, knowledge management and preparing financial resources. The immediate response phase is determined by the nature of the event but should involve structured command and control systems coupled with appropriate asset capabilities. The reconstruction phase aims to bring the disaster under control and return all systems to a normal or better state (Heaslip and Barber, 2014).

The International Federation of Red Cross and Red Crescent Societies (disaster reduction program 2001–08) suggests a vulnerability and capacity assessment during the preparation phase to identify capacities and generate data that can be used for the planning, implementation and monitoring of activities (Center, 2009). Actions promoting resilience and risk reduction (response phase) most significantly include senior management ownership, the development of disaster management teams and redundancy support, and improving the longer-term situation by building up buffers that could help to absorb future stress. Gattorna (2015), guided by the doctoral research of Kate Hughes, describes a prequel phase of hedge and deploy by prepositioning supplies at strategic global locations before any catastrophic event, the adoption of a fully flexible supply chain during a search and rescue phase (survival response), an agile supply chain operating in an emergency response phase in the face of extreme disruption and re-establishing communities during the rebuilding and restoration phase.

Supply chain disruption and ecology

The research approach in this book is nothing if not eclectic and may encourage some to look outside our profession for clues to combat disruption. Take ecology. The concept of resilience was born in the physical sciences, and in his seminal 1973 text Holling defined resilience of an ecosystem as 'the measure of its ability to absorb change and still exist' (Annarelli and Nonino, 2016). Peterson *et al* (1998) ironically cited global transportation networks as one cause of disruption to ecosystems. Learnings and commonalities include:

- Interactions produce resilient ecosystems, and Charles Darwin found that an area is more stable if it is occupied by a large number of species, such as industry clusters. Increasing redundancy decreases the rate of stability increase. This suggests a redundancy threshold beyond which it is no longer effective, similar to excess inventory, but advocates supply chain collaboration.
- Functional overlap across scales can enable a system to persist, but loss of redundancy decreases the ability to withstand disruption. This compares to cross-training and shared understanding across the functions and levels of an organization as a form of redundancy.
- Drivers and passengers: Presence or absence of drivers determines the stability of a system such as the top management team influence on supply chain management professionals. In functional overlap, species with similar ecological impact are rivets, those with significant impact are drivers and others are passengers.
- Different species operate at different temporal and spatial scales. Interactions depend on the cross-scale organization of an ecosystem. Understanding how the top management team interacts across scales within a company can help supply chain managers reduce strategic misalignment.
- Contagious disturbance allows small-scale changes to drive large-scale changes in much the same way as supply chain disruptions have a disproportionate effect on demand. Systems are scale variant (such as a Mouse and a Moose), causing them to perceive or experience the environment differently. Bridging this scale is important to the alignment of business and supply chain goals.
- Resilience of processes depends upon the distribution of functional groups within and across scales, demonstrating the importance of strategic alignment. Ecosystems are not to be viewed as static objects, but as dynamic self-organized entities that have their own processes and structures, and are constantly interacting across varying scales, echoing the dynamic nature of strategic renewal, and the notion of technologies or supply chains being living organisms.

Adger (2000) continues this seemingly parallel relationship between ecology and supply chain management by suggesting that resilience is strengthened by integrating features such as networks, inclusivity and trust norms (collaboration), dependency on a narrow range of natural resources decreases stability (multi-sourcing) and that the complexity of resource systems significantly reduces vulnerability to sudden disruptions (industry clusters). One of the cases explored was that of coastal seas in the face of oil spills and the fact that both speed of recovery and buffer capacity are characteristics that confound ecologists, akin to successful supply chain networks using redundancy and velocity as disruption strategies, such as Dell and Zara equally confounding practitioners who cannot replicate their value chains (Holweg and Helo, 2014). Walker *et al* (2004) found that the stability dynamics of all linked systems of humans and nature emerge from three complementary attributes: resilience and adaptability, which are related to the dynamics of a system, and transformability, which means significantly changing the nature of a system in the aftermath of a disturbance. An adaptive cycle is described and suggests, although unpredictable and occurring across multiple scales, that all systems inevitably reach a phase of chaotic collapse, which is followed by a period of re-organization, strengthening the case for senior management attention to disruption preparation. Latitude, resistance, precariousness and panarchy are the four crucial aspects of resilience. Perhaps most applicable to strategic alignment is the latter, which means that 'because of cross-scale interactions, the resilience of a system at a particular focal scale will depend on the influences from states, and dynamics of scales above and below'.

The concept of the new age of the networked company has similarities to *fungal networking* whereby the roots of fungi pass vital resources and communications to trees and plants in return for sugars produced during photosynthesis akin to a *tree*-mail system. Roots and fungi exist in 'subtle symbiosis' and combine to form what is called a mycorrhiza. Individual plants are joined to one another by an underground 'hyphal network': a complex and collaborative structure that has become known as the 'wood wide web' (Macfarlane, 2016). Networks are negotiated with speed and agility without ownership and through mutual benefit and use of all available resources. In a similar fashion to their corporate counterparts, these organisms are adept at managing relationships and understanding their 'markets'.

To begin concluding this chapter, we know that the accelerating forces of globalization, technology and climate change are exponentially causing crises, disasters and breakdowns that result in significant disruption to our supply chains. These are largely interconnected in the sense that the response (both military and business) to misbehaving volcanoes and terrorist acts (closing borders and airspace), typhoons in East Asia damaging or sinking container ships, the juxtaposition of natural and man-made humanitarian disasters seen in places such as Sumatra in Indonesia, a region that was devastated by a tsunami in 2004, and is now destroying the existence of indigenous tribes such as the Orang Rimba through the rapid depletion of rainforests to develop oil palm plantations, or civil war and famine in Sierra Leone, all directly impact supply chain management and consumerism. We know that an agile and phased strategic response is needed to build organizational resilience to disruption. Mitigation includes increased collaboration, multiple supplier sourcing, inventory management such as redundancy and emergency stock, more efficient supply chain re-engineering and network design, product substitution and new technologies.

However, this is where I break from convention. I am not convinced that supply chain disruption is in itself a valid concept per se Perhaps this is simply disruption, and crises, disasters and breakdowns are not the true source of this disruption. For sure, a container ship sinking in the Indian Ocean impacts a production line in Ireland, and such events need mitigation, but these products were in that part of the world, to begin with, for another reason. Policy. Strategy. In my two decades in industry, many company strategies have been observed to be without initial consultation with supply chain divisions. Perhaps the ensuing supply chain strategies to combat disruption are not strategies, but simply tactics. Perhaps there is a two-tier categorization within supply chain management that has not been recognized formally, whereby the response to certain events can be implemented autonomously by the supply chain division, and a tier or tiers that require negotiation across the top management team prior to implementation, and therefore across multiple company divisions and external actors to collaboratively mitigate risk. Perhaps misalignment between business goals and supply chain tactics needs to be explored. Perhaps senior management strategic formulation is a source of supply chain disruption. I have cause for suspecting all of this. Let me explain.

Business to supply chain strategic alignment: consumer electronics

In May 2004 I joined a consumer electronics multinational organization as a supply chain specialist on a four-month contract that lasted 10 years. The supply chain department was within an original equipment manufacturer (OEM) division and operated in a virtual context. All product manufacturing was in Suzhou (China) and the mainland European customer sites that we supported from our Cork base were continuously moving eastwards. The geography of trade in this industry had changed unrecognizably to that of the previous 20 years when, for example, Ireland (IBM, DELL, Apple), Scotland (HP, Compaq) and Holland were the dominant low-cost manufacturers with 80 per cent of personal computers (PCs) being produced in these regions. A downturn in the PC market caused by factors such as a surge of sales in 1999 due to fears of the millennium bug, and a slowdown in technological advances, had resulted in PC OEMs demanding an annual cost reduction of 15–20 per cent from their suppliers.

To achieve this, companies migrated towards locations with cost-saving benefits. In line with standard trade and comparative advantage theory, unskilled labour-intensive activities (such as PC manufacturing) tend to relocate to low-wage countries. Comparative advantage theory states that specialization is determined by the interaction between country characteristics and commodity characteristics. Since labour may be a small share of the costs of production there can be a large multiplier effect. If labour is 10 per cent of gross costs, then a 50 per cent difference in the productivity of all inputs will translate into a 500 per cent wage difference (Venables, 2006).

The main beneficiaries have been Eastern China and Eastern Europe following the expansion of the EU and introduction of the euro currency. The trade map has changed but will continue to do so. The effect of supplying European customers, for instance, through production in China has resulted in transport costs squeezing the producers' value. Trade costs should, of course, be thought of in much more general terms than just freight charges. Time in transit is costly (up to as much as 0.5 per cent of the value of goods shipped per day). This high cost of time in transit comes partly from the costs of carrying stock, and also from the likelihood that long transit times reduce the reliability and predictability of deliveries. It also makes firms slower to respond to changing demand conditions or cost levels, and this by itself can be a force for the clustering of activities. Transport and trade cost savings are a direct benefit of proximity, but its full economic impact comes from economies of scale associated with operating in an area of dense economic activity close to consumers, workers, and other firms (Venables, 2006). This close proximity is not a luxury afforded to organizations that have shifted production operations eastwards and this becomes one of the most substantial challenges in the satisfaction of customer requirements.

Research at the Cranfield School of Management identified demand risk as a source of supply chain risk, and 'this relates to potential or actual disturbances to the flow of product, information and cash emanating from within the network, between the focal firm and its market' (Sweeney *et al*, 2009). This is particularly relevant to organizations who are satisfying regional demand from a manufacturing base in China. In the case of low-margin products, ocean is the only cost-effective mode of transport, and this effectively means matching customer demand up to months in advance of the point of consumption. Adapting to cultural differences and business rules of foreign nations has become the norm. Instructions can become lost in translation and invariably in developing regions there is a high turnover of operational contacts as new opportunities arise, resulting in re-training and re-establishment of relationships. Lead times that on the surface appear excessive are managed well in conjunction with buffer stock positioning but occasionally inhibit the ability to meet customer demands. Therefore, the global model breeds inflexibility.

In this scenario, I managed the European Hewlett Packard (HP) account. On a routine business review in Prague, Czech Republic, our monthly scorecard was being discussed, and as normal we were placed in the 'meeting expectations' category of 70–79 per cent. This already positioned us as a top supplier, but I asked how we could be promoted to the 'exceeding expectations' category of 80 per cent+. HP responded that this was simply not possible. No supplier had ever reached this level. I immediately set about autonomously and seamlessly aligning all of our internal processes, such as demand management, purchase order management (managing Suzhou production and their supplier base), inventory control, customer invoicing, documentation control, logistics, warehouse management, and new product introduction. In addition, I secured general management support through the alignment of business and supply chain goals, and we attended subsequent business reviews together in the Czech Republic in a *partnership* approach. Container utilization increased to 100 per cent, inventory turns reached the company target of five, customer lead times were reduced from 10 weeks to eight weeks, and proactive customer communication mitigated the impact of disruption. One business goal was to protect what was called a just in time (JIT) adder, which was the landed cost (transport, storage and distribution) added to the product cost. HP had continuously demanded a reduction in the JIT adder, and due to the competitive nature of the business the company continuously conceded.

Accordingly, I analysed the supply chain activities of Foxconn in Pardubice, the HP turnkey operation, and found that its process was directly costing us $58,000 annually. Therefore, we should have been *increasing* our JIT adder. We did not, of course, but HP never again requested a reduction. In parallel I made recommendations that saved HP $148,000 annually. Most significantly, I reached the 'exceeding expectations category' and maintained this for 16 consecutive months before being moved to a new position. Our market share increased proportionally. Perfect business to supply chain internal alignment.

Subsequent to this was the most significant supply chain disruption that I have faced: an internal global management strategy to re-organize the OEM supply chain division into silos. Regional OEM management was removed, political positioning, conflict and misalignment arose, as demand and supply planning, customer replenishment, logistics, component planning, inventory management, etc (even the retail and OEM divisions), now competed. Roles and responsibilities became confused, customer service deteriorated, and metrics declined. A number of recommendations were negotiated with the top management team in my capacity as global OEM supply chain program manager, and many were implemented to good effect. The company became the top Dell supplier in the continuity of supply section, for the first time in over a decade of partnership, a new product introduction gate process ensured maximum revenue return for completed projects (previously, 49 per cent of projects yielded revenue return), annual freight cost savings of 75 per cent were identified through supply chain optimization, and the implementation of a key performance indicator (KPI) dashboard spawned multiple initiatives, such as a sales and operations (S&OP) cross-functional consensus process. However, the disruption of the re-organization was too powerful and, at the time of my tenure ending, the chief executive officer had given the OEM division (operational for 30 years and upon which the organization was founded) one more month to return to profitability before being disbanded.

Business to supply chain strategic alignment: aviation

Another organization that faced disruption was a Cork-based commercial jet engine repair and overhaul company that serviced most of the major airlines. American Airlines was one such customer. Whereas the previous case encountered demand risk due to China manufacturing, this company, reliant on continuous throughput of engines, faced supply risk resulting from inadequate demand planning. Engine components would literally arrive for repair at the back door unannounced. A 28-day re-manufacturing lead time was expected regardless. These components consisted of gas turbine nozzle guide blades and vanes from the hot section of the engine.

The repair process began and ended with visual, dimensional and in-process inspection, in addition to non-destructive testing such as x-ray and fluorescent penetrant inspection. Many parts were non-repairable if cracking, foreign object damage (bird-strikes) or blockages from cement sucked up from the runway was excessive. Remaining parts passed through welding, brazing, blending, EDM and laser, blasting, coating cycles, hot-form, milling and grinding. The disruption caused by the drop-in demand resulted in an extremely expensive JIT process, whereby a full engine set would be shipped to American Airlines in Fort Worth, Texas, upon receipt of a set for repair, and the new set for repair would in turn be prepared to ship as the replacement set for the next inbound set, and so on. This worked reasonably unless five engine sets suddenly appeared. Did American Airlines consider any disruption to engine turnarounds reasonable? No.

American Airlines introduced an SE2000 program, to monitor key supplier performance. The goal was to achieve 'map' (a score of 90 per cent across all functions such as production, responsiveness, quality, engineering, marketing, finance) for 12 consecutive months, thereby becoming a platinum supplier. Our company had an average score of 60 per cent. I was sent to Texas. Clearly demand planning was a priority, but I remember our CEO very smartly advising that the most critical objective was to make friends with the guy in shipping and receiving. Easier said than done. Such was his frustration with our performance that my first encounter involved being pinned to the wall of the warehouse. But I persevered, and we became the best of pals. Almost immediately 90 per cent was achieved, and this was sustained throughout my tenure, allowing the company to be considered a platinum supplier.

One lesson is that no news is not good news. American Airlines had given up reporting quality issues, most probably because our arrogance would not accept the extent of the problem. The shipping boxes we used looked pristine leaving our stores but were arriving in very bad shape, and late. FAA documentation (8130-3 certification) with the components were non-compliant and this caused aircraft on ground (AOG) situations. Simple actions taken across all AA functions (once I was taken down from the wall)

> were resolving FAA 8130-3 certification non-compliance, non-conformance of shipping procedures and outstanding engineering and quality issues (parts were placed on hold without our knowledge throughout the facility); design of sustainable re-usable plastic custom-made packaging for transport of engine components to and from Texas; implementation of a new shipping agent with guaranteed next day delivery to Fort Worth; effective coordination of component overhauls to meet engine build requirements; demand forecasting based on engine flight hours; establishment of cross-functional communication channels; recording of American Airlines quality problem alerts and non-conformance reports to ensure that corrective and preventative actions would take place in Cork.
>
> This was very much a case of an autonomous supply chain response to production-stop problems on both sides but supported by the political will of the top management team. The result of this business to supply chain strategic alignment was platinum status. And all of this was achieved despite my chronic fear of flying!

Supply chain management (and logistics) is often called the invisible profession. Goods magically arrive. Execution is our mandate, and as such we operate in a bubble. It is widely accepted in our profession that supply chains compete, not companies. We discuss supply chain disruption that negatively impacts our supply chain networks. But, of course, the entire organization is affected. Therefore, it is simply disruption. Let me begin the development of a process model (see box) that posits a bubble in which, as seen in ecology, chaos and disruption are inevitable, whatever colour the swan may be. Breaking out of this bubble and aligning with the top management team is the aim of the final model in Chapter 8.

> **Response to supply chain disruption**
>
> Black swan crises and disasters; grey swan breakdowns:
> *what we do inside the bubble of our profession*
>
> **Strategic response**
>
> - Maintain efficiency or existence of function
> - Recover former shape or evolve into a new configuration
> - Rebound from adversity strengthened and more resourceful

- Gain competitive advantage by transcending to a state higher than the one prior to the disturbance. This can only be achieved through top management team negotiation
- Promote top management team ownership
- Nurture a risk management culture

Tactical response

- Implement supply chain disruption management systems and a disaster management framework, structured 'war room' command and control systems coupled with appropriate asset capabilities
- Adopt agile supply chain strategies with an emphasis on reducing complexity
- Prepare for an inevitable and disproportionate increase in consumer demand (panic)
- Introduce supply chain design-thinking, including 'designed-in' resilience
- Specify the sources of risks and vulnerabilities
- Assess probable risk using fault and event trees
- Increase shared information with government agencies (public-private partnership)
- Establish appropriate incentives including non-performance penalties, and risk sharing, among what should be multi-sourced suppliers
- Adapt to evolving economic progress, political shifts, demographic trends and technological advances
- Use offshore suppliers for the bulk of procurement volume, and local suppliers to offset disruption (incremental costs of 'strategic' redundant inventories are the premium for reduced risk), the cost depends on probability of risk, and a form of hedging and deployment of supplies to strategic locations could also be adopted
- Develop information systems and knowledge back-up processes
- Implement improved aggregate forecasting
- Reduce product variability and increase product postponement (build-to-order)
- Invest in shipment visibility tools (Bar Coding, RFID, LEOS) to minimize the transportation system 'black-hole'. This is particularly relevant to the last-mile of logistics

- Increase supplier socio-technical collaboration and techno-process integration
- Interactions produce resilient ecosystems, and therefore, supply chain network design should consider migration to industry clusters
- Understanding how the top management team interacts across scales within a company, and bridging any gaps, can help supply chain managers reduce strategic mis-alignment
- Functional overlap: Foster a culture of cross-training and shared understanding across organizational functions and levels as a form of redundancy
- Ensure that all tactical responses do not breach the boundaries of the core competencies of the organization and do not conflict with the strategic goals of the top management team

Please indulge me while I now take two centuries in the proceeding chapter to establish the concept that policy is the source of supply chain disruption. This is later supported by empirical evidence derived from discussions with supply chain managers across multiple organizations.

References

Adger, WN (2000) Social and ecological resilience: Are they related? *Progress in Human Geography*, 24(3), pp 347–64

Aggarwal, R and Bohinc, J (2012) Black swans and supply chain strategic necessity, *Journal of Transportation Security*, 5(1), pp 39–49

Annarelli, A and Nonino, F (2016) Strategic and operational management of organizational resilience: Current state of research and future directions, *Omega*, 62, pp 1–18

Brady, L M (2015) *Nature as Friction: Integrating Clausewitz into environmental histories of the Civil War*

Center, ADP (2009) The International Federation of Red Cross and Red Crescent Societies Disaster Management Center

Chaina (2009) Parking space in short supply for world's containers, *Chaina: The magazine for global supply chain leaders*, March–April, pp 8–9

Chopra, S, Reinhardt, G and Mohan, U (2007) The importance of decoupling recurrent and disruption risks in a supply chain, *Naval Research Logistics (NRL)*, 54(5), pp 544–55

Christopher, M and Peck, H (2004) Building the resilient supply chain, *The International Journal of Logistics Management*, 15(2), pp 1–14

Christopher, M and Towill, DR (2002) Developing market specific supply chain strategies, *The International Journal of Logistics Management*, 13(1), pp 1–14

Clausewitz, C von (1832/1940) *On War*, Jazzybee Verlag

Copeland, EJ, Sami, M and Tsujikawa, S (2006) Dynamics of dark energy, *International Journal of Modern Physics D*, 15(11), pp 1753–935

Craighead, CW, Blackhurst, J, Rungtusanatham, MJ and Handfield, RB (2007) The severity of supply chain disruptions: Design characteristics and mitigation capabilities, *Decision Sciences*, 38(1), pp 131–56

Drucker, P (1992) New priorities. [Online] https://www.context.org/iclib/ic32/drucker/

Economist, The (2006) Financial services Australia, June

Friedman, TL (2016) *Thank You for Being Late: An optimist's guide to thriving in the age of accelerations*, Farrar, Straus and Giroux

Gattorna, J (2009) *Dynamic Supply Chains: Delivering value through people*, FT Prentice Hall

Gattorna, J (2015) *Dynamic supply chains*, Pearson Education Limited

Gattorna, J (2018) Designing contemporary supply chains for faster clock-speeds to cope with the increasingly volatile operating environment, Gattorna Alignment, January

Grandin, G (2010) *Fordlândia: ascensão e queda da cidade esquecida de Henry Ford na selva*, Rocco, pp 35–46

Hamner, MP, Stovall, SS, Taha, DM and Brahimi, SC (2015) Emergency management and disaster response utilizing public–private partnerships. [Online] http://search.ebscohost.com/login.aspx?direct=true&scope=site&db=nlebk&db=nlabk&AN=961640

Handy, C (2020) *The Age of Unreason*, Harvard Business School Press

Harland, CM (1996) Supply chain management: Relationships, chains and networks, *British Journal of Management*, 7(1)

Heaslip, G and Barber, E (2014) Using the military in disaster relief: Systemising challenges and opportunities, *Journal of Humanitarian Logistics and Supply Chain Management*, 4(1), pp 60–81

Hendricks, KB, and Singhal, VR (2005) An empirical analysis of the effect of supply chain disruptions on long-run stock price performance and equity risk of the firm, *Production and Operations Management*, 14(1), pp 35–52

Holweg, M and Helo, P (2014) Defining value chain architectures: Linking strategic value creation to operational supply chain design, *International Journal of Production Economics*, 147, pp 230–38

Ismail, S (2014) *Exponential Organizations: Why new organizations are ten times better, faster, and cheaper than yours (and what to do about it)*, Diversion Books

Kleindorfer, PR and Saad, GH (2005) Managing disruption risks in supply chains, *Production and Operations Management*, 14(1), pp 53–68

Kovács, G and Spens, KM (2007) Humanitarian logistics in disaster relief operations, *International Journal of Physical Distribution and Logistics Management*, 37(2), pp 99–114

Lee, HL (2004) The triple-A supply chain, *Harvard Business Review*, 82(10), pp 102–113

Lia, B and Hegghammer, T (2004) Jihadi strategic studies: The alleged Al Qaida policy study preceding the Madrid bombings, *Studies in Conflict and Terrorism*, 27(5), pp 355–75

Macfarlane, R (2016) The secrets of the wood wide web. [Online] https://www.newyorker.com/tech/annals-of-technology/the-secrets-of-the-wood-wide-web

May, RC, Stewart, WH and Sweo, R (2000) Environmental scanning behavior in a transitional economy: Evidence from Russia, *Academy of Management Journal*, 43(3), pp 403–27

O'Riordan, J, Karlsen, E, Sandford, B and Newman, L (2013) *Climate Change Adaptation and Canada's Crops and Food Supply: Summary for decision-makers.* [Online] http://act-adapt.org/wp-content/uploads/2013/07/07-13-CFS-Summary-WEB.pdf

Peterson, G, Allen, CR and Holling, CS (1998) Ecological resilience, biodiversity, and scale, *Ecosystems*, 1(1), pp 6–18

Pettit, S and Beresford, A (2009) Critical success factors in the context of humanitarian aid supply chains, *International Journal of Physical Distribution and Logistics Management*, 39(6), pp 450–68

Rajesh, R, Ravi, V and Venkata Rao, R (2015) Selection of risk mitigation strategy in electronic supply chains using grey theory and digraph-matrix approaches, *International Journal of Production Research*, 53(1), pp 238–57

Rogan, D (2011) *Marketing: An introduction for students in Ireland*, Gill & Macmillan

Roh, J, Hong, P and Min, H (2014) Implementation of a responsive supply chain strategy in global complexity: The case of manufacturing firms, *International Journal of Production Economics*, 147, pp 198–210

Rose, DS (2014) *Angel Investing: The gust guide to making money and having fun investing in start-ups*, John Wiley & Sons

Schlegel, GL and Trent, RJ (2014) *Supply Chain Risk Management: An emerging discipline*, CRC Press

Sheffi, Y (2001) Supply chain management under the threat of international terrorism, *The International Journal of Logistics Management*, 12(2), pp 1–11

Simchi-Levi, D, Wang, H and Wei, Y (2013) Increasing supply chain robustness through process flexibility and strategic inventory, *Operations Research*

Smith, D (2016) The future of companies, *Global Futures and Foresight*. [Online] http://www.thegff.com/Groups/72275/Global_Futures_and/Reports/The_Future_of/The_Future_of.aspx

Sodhi, MS, Son, BG and Tang, CS (2012) Researchers' perspectives on supply chain risk management, *Production and Operations Management*, **21**(1), pp 1–13

Soneye, A (2014) An overview of humanitarian relief supply chains for victims of perennial flood disasters in Lagos, Nigeria (2010–2012), *Journal of Humanitarian Logistics and Supply Chain Management*, **4**(2), pp 179–97

Sweeney, E (2009) *Supply Chain Management and Logistics in a Volatile Global Environment*, Blackhall Publishing

Sylla, C (2014) Managing perceived operational risk factors for effective supply-chain management, *AIP Conference Proceedings*, December, **1635**(1), pp 19–26

Tang, CS (2006) Robust strategies for mitigating supply chain disruptions, *International Journal of Logistics Research and Applications*, **9**(1), pp 33–45

Venables, AJ (2006) Shifts in economic geography and their causes, CEP Discussion Paper No 767, December

Wagner, SM and Bode, C (2008) An empirical examination of supply chain performance along several dimensions of risk, *Journal of Business Logistics*, **29**(1), pp 307–25

Walker, B, Holling, CS, Carpenter, S and Kinzig, A (2004) Resilience, adaptability and transformability in social–ecological systems, *Ecology and Society*, **9**(2), p 5

Watts, B D (2004) *Clausewitzian Friction and Future War*, Revised Edition, National Defense Univ Washington DC Institute for National Strategic Studies

Wu, T, Wu, YCJ, Chen, YJ and Goh, M (2014) Aligning supply chain strategy with corporate environmental strategy: A contingency approach, *International Journal of Production Economics*, **147**, pp 220–29

Yang, Y and Xu, X (2015) Post-disaster grain supply chain resilience with government aid, *Transportation Research Part E: Logistics and Transportation Review*, **76**, pp 139–59

Supply chain strategic friction   02

Broadening the taxonomy of supply chain disruption to include policy is a new concept. To counter any controversy, it is important to note that my thesis is by no means a criticism of the top management team. As a supply chain professional, I have not been directly exposed to the many (economic, political and social) factors and pressures facing policy makers at the highest levels. The objective here is raising awareness that friction is a real phenomenon, acknowledged as far back as the Napoleonic Wars, but not explored, and that policy can have a negative impact on supply chain networks in terms of increased complexities. Responding to any disruptive event takes time, which I will describe as a *gap of pain*. Greater inclusion of supply chain managers in the strategic renewal process can reduce this *gap of pain*.

Academia is taking notice. Roh *et al* (2014) suggest that disruption risks belong to the low-probability, high-consequence domain of outcomes, but this area of management is starting to receive boardroom attention, and that being responsive to supply chain disruptions requires strategies that are closely aligned to corporate strategy. It has long been argued that strategic priorities at the functional level should be aligned with business-level strategies (Rebolledo and Jobin, 2013) and therefore the strategic response to disruptions should not be uni-dimensional and dichotomous, thereby broadening supply chain management to a wider perspective (Wu *et al*, 2014). There is an inevitability to disruption and the mitigation strategies adopted by supply chain risk management remain critical. However, greater alignment between business goals and supply chain strategies (tactics) can support disruption counter-measures that organizations have in place, all for the purpose of reducing that *gap of pain*. In the most simplistic terms, a container ship going aground in the Indian Ocean is disruptive to your organization's supply chain. Let's take a step back through history to see that it was policy that put your products on that ship.

Some historians, military or otherwise, and economists may object, and others still may turn in their graves at my analysis of how the past two centuries have evolved. That's fine. The only objective is to demonstrate that policy is a source of supply chain disruption, and my text has *sufficient* accuracy and academic support in that regard. This needs signposting:

- First a brief historical context to demonstrate the true cause of supply chain disruption from my personal perspective, which begins with the Napoleonic Wars: Policy.
- This is broadened to focus on the concept of *friction*, which was identified by one of Napoleon's adversaries and observers, General Carl von Clausewitz.
- Next is an overview of the evolution of strategy and how two distinct categories of supply chain management's response to disruption emerged.
- Business strategy has been described as a process since the early 1970s, but Clausewitz described it thus in 1832. The processual nature of strategy is explored.
- The top management team lends power to strategy and therefore I discuss their role within the strategic renewal process, and discover that policy implementation can come from a position of managerial uncertainty.
- Strategic alignment between business and supply chain goals is the aim of this book, and in the next section I borrow from business to information systems strategic alignment literature given that supply chain management literature is silent in this regard.
- A final section then to validate what I am proposing through Clausewitz, by analysing the cyclical evolution of globalization, and how policy has shaped certain major events.

Historical context

The terms globalization and supply chain management may only have been coined in recent times, but their concepts are ancient and interconnected, dating back to the barter system of ancient times or to 300 BC when Caesar established trading posts in East Asia. Little consideration, though, is given to the fact that the birth of logistics and indeed supply chain management can be traced back to ancient war times of Greek and Roman empires when military officers titled as *logistikas* were assigned the duties of providing services related to the supply and distribution of resources, a crucial factor in determining the outcome of battles. Genghis Khan had *yurtchis* for the same purpose. His warriors only had the bow, the horse and an iron discipline born from a land of ice, hunger and death (Iggulden, 2008). Genghis Khan united the most warlike tribes on earth in order to forge a new nation from the wild plains and mountains of Mongolia in circa 1206 AD. To achieve this, he broke the ancient enemy of the Chin Empire of northern China, who had kept his people divided, by attacking them in their fortresses and walled cities. He found a new way of warfare, while at the same time coping with his restless generals, ambitious brothers and growing sons. Having proved himself as a warrior and leader, the birth of the new nation brought immense challenges of civilization. Although speed of movement across the plains was a major factor in the success of Genghis, progress was hampered by daily consultations with his generals, until the great Khan realized that he could not take sole responsibility for the crucial management of supplies such as cattle herds, weapons, iron and spoils of war. Consider also the movement of goats, camels, oxen, yaks, tents, carts, lumber, salt and ponies. When he appointed his Shaman brother Temuge as, in effect, the leader of supply chain management, and delegated control of warrior groups to his generals, a positive impact was immediate, which allowed even further expansion to include destruction in present day Russia, Iran and Iraq, and the edges of India.

Later in history, another empire-builder, Napoleon Bonaparte, strategically used logistics to great effect to conquer allies through superior strength in troop numbers and deadly speed. Ironically, logistics was also his downfall. Under the tentative leadership of Tsar Alexander, the Battle of Borodino in September 1812 saw Napoleon's Grande Armée lured deeper into Russian territory, further from supply lines, with fatal consequences for the French. It seems in fact, that Napoleon's initial key success factors of no theory, no tactics, just speed (later described by General Charles de Gaulle as a war of movement, for which he vehemently lectured France to adopt during the Second World War, replacing horse-power with tanks), enthusiasm, surprise and risking death, not impeded by formal strategy (albeit this was a strategy in itself), were also the cause of his demise. He was the first modern general, affectionately called little corporal because of his hands-on approach (ironically, de Gaulle was nicknamed Colonel Motors for similar reasons). He lacked or most probably ignored the political support mechanism of senior management to balance his strategic approach. Also ignored by French leaders were Charles de Gaulle's lectures and four publications between 1924 and 1938 in which he pleaded for a mobile and professional army guided by political leadership. A terrible irony is that the notorious Adolf Hitler did not ignore de Gaulle and was an avid reader of his theories, which he used to devastating effect to overwhelm France. When de Gaulle was finally given the opportunity to prove himself in battle, which he did, it was already too late. De Gaulle advocated Napoleon's tactics but realized that top management must guide. Alignment works both ways.

Conversely, Napoleon's failure was a demonstration by Russian commanders to use logistics to overcome seemingly hopeless situations through *attrition* rather than direct engagement. This was the strategy of exhaustion, described by Hans Delbruck as *Ermattungsstrategie*, as opposed to Napoleon's *Niederwerfungsstrategie*, the strategy of annihilation (Freedman, 2015). The rapid development of road infrastructures and modes of transportation during that period, and indeed cartography, enabled this shift in military strategy. Another example was that in 1780 the fortunes of the war of independence swayed from Lieutenant General Charles Cornwallis and the British, when the Americans unconventionally introduced guerrilla tactics to tease their superior enemy away from their supply base in Yorktown. Of course, the Russians again employed such tactics in the Second World War, aided by a horrendous winter, when Hitler's Wehrmacht attempted Operation Barbarossa in vain in June 1941, while in the same war Colonel Harold Harris was initially accused of cowardice in the South Pacific, when instead of a frontal attack on a strong Japanese elevated position he favoured attrition to great effect, and admirably declared that he was lavish with ammunition and stingy with men's lives.

Back to Napoleon and two prominent and competing observers of his art of war. Antoine-Henri Jomini (1779–1869) is credited with being the founder of modern strategy. Strategy of course existed before 1800, in fact as far back as the Battle of Heaven. However, at this time, logistical support changed strategy due to a rise in republicanism and nationalism, which altered battles from a 'chance of arms' to total annihilation, and the need to mobilize, motivate, move and direct mass armies (Freedman, 2015). Transport and supplies now heavily influenced what could be achieved. Jomini, Swiss by birth, was a general in the French army serving directly under Napoleon but resigned in 1813 because of harsh treatment by the Chief of Staff. He then served with the Russian Army and was instrumental in establishing the War College and General Staff. He was a prolific 27-volume writer on military history, mainly studies of Frederick the Great, the French Revolution and Napoleon, and produced the greatest military textbook of the 19th century, *Art of War*. His ideas continue to be prominent in military institutions such as Westpoint, the United States Military Academy, and in particular influenced in real-time General Winfield Scott in the Mexican War (1846–48) and senior officers in the American Civil War (1861–65). Scott never lost a battle in which he commanded, but the great General Ulysses Grant was critical of Jomini because his approach produced conservatism, indecisiveness and bloodletting, favouring instead Carl von Clausewitz (1780–1832) whose publication *On War* eventually guided him to civil war success (Pohl, 1973; Bassford, 1993). I too am departing from Jomini because his teachings did not consider politics, tactics, logistics or historical contexts.

Carl Von Clausewitz

Clausewitz began professional soldiering in the Prussian army at the age of 12 until his death from cholera at 51. He experienced, first-hand, disastrous military humiliation at the hands of Napoleon in 1806 and was captured before returning to Prussia where he wrote the *Principles of War* in 1812. That year he joined the Russian Army in order to get revenge on Napoleon during the 1812 campaign and the Wars of Liberation of 1813 and 1814. As Chief of Staff, his Corps played a decisive role in defeating Napoleon at Waterloo in 1815. His work *On War*, published posthumously by his wife in 1832, guides my concept of supply chain strategic friction, and that policy is a source of disruption. Clausewitz had his critics such as Jomini, who said, 'pity the soldier who must crawl among these scraps of rules', claiming that genius instead had more value in battle, and others referred to Clausewitz as Napoleon's high priest, suggesting that he was an extension of the Emperor. In fact, his ideas were more aligned to the Prussian military reformer Gerhard von Scharnhorst (Bassford, 1993; Freedman, 2015). Both Clausewitz and Jomini are mentioned here because both have equal status, but you are either in one camp or the other. Clausewitz shapes this book. To put one perspective on it, and it is just that, the American Civil War was won by a force with greater mass and finances. It was the Confederacy who displayed greater military genius with Clausewitz-influenced *Ermattungsstrategie*, whereas, against Lincoln's wishes, the North was predominantly commanded by single-minded Jominians who adopted *Niederwerfungsstrategie*, which resulted in a horrendous death toll. It was sheer exhaustion that ended the war. Policy matters.

Carl Von Clausewitz: friction

Clausewitz developed several principals, such as: war is a continuation of policy by other means; politicians have an authority over the military; policy is shaped by a trinity of primordial violence, hatred and enmity; strategic plans are based on a series of connected steps; flexibility must be maintained, opportunities seized as they arise; a calculated culminating point of victory must be kept in mind. All this, however, is restrained by friction, minor unforeseen incidents causing delays and confusion, resulting in generals being doomed to disappointment. Here I synopsize the concept of friction, shaped to my own cause, whereby policy makers become the top management team, war becomes supply chain management:

- For a top management team (TMT) without personal knowledge or experience, supply chain management (SCM) seems simple, 'all the requisite branches of knowledge appear so plain, all the combinations so unimportant'. But within SCM, all 'becomes intelligible and it is extremely difficult to describe what it is that brings about this change, to specify this invisible and completely efficient factor' (Clausewitz, 1832).
- Everything in SCM is simple, but the simplest thing is difficult. Here, Clausewitz describes a traveller (and I imagine the long journey of an ocean container from Hong Kong to the Netherlands) who expects to very simply accomplish a journey on a high road, four or five leagues, using post-houses. But he arrives at the second last station, and 'finds no horses, or bad ones, then a hilly country, bad roads, it is a dark night', and eventually he reaches the final station and 'finds there some miserable accommodation'. SCM is similar in that, 'through the influence of an infinity of petty circumstances, which cannot be properly described on paper, things disappoint us, and we fall short of the mark'. 'A powerful iron-will crushes this friction' and therefore SCM is more about people than process. It is also apt to repeat the fact that the complexity of supply chain management has been compounded by the force of globalization along the dimensions of replenishment, time and distance' (Christopher and Towill, 2002).
- Friction is the only conception that distinguishes real SCM to SCM on paper. The SCM machine is simple and easy to manage in theory. But the supply chain network is comprised entirely of individuals, each of whom is faced with their own friction in all directions. Again, it is about people,

and in the context of war, individual fatigue or fear can be the greatest source of friction (despite standard operating procedures being there for individuals to follow). It is people. Not process.

- 'This enormous friction, which is not concentrated, as in mechanics, at a few points, is therefore everywhere brought into contact with chance, and thus incidents take place upon which it is impossible to calculate, their chief origin being chance. As an instance of one such chance, take the weather. Here the fog prevents the enemy from being discovered in time, a battery from firing at the right moment, a report from reaching the general; there the rain prevents a battalion from arriving at the right time, because instead of for three it had to march perhaps eight hours; and the cavalry are prevented from charging effectively because it is stuck fast in heavy ground'.

- SCM 'is movement in a resistant medium. Just as a man immersed in water is unable to perform with ease and regularity the most natural and simplest movement, that of walking, so in SCM, with ordinary powers one cannot keep even the line of mediocrity'. Here I use Clausewitz to liken the top management team to swimming masters who teach dry land movements but have never 'plunged in themselves'.

- 'It is this friction, which makes that which appears easy in SCM difficult in reality. The top management team must be aware of this friction so that, where possible, it can be overcome, and must learn not to expect a precision in results because of this friction. Know friction and triumph over it. Friction cannot be learned theoretically, but experience and tact will enable the supply chain manager to make decisions based on situational needs, whereby they 'decide and determine suitably to the occasion'.

- This warns 'against excessive strategic ambition, and in fact Clausewitz acknowledged the impact of policy as a particular form of friction. The 'strategists' chessmen do not have the kind of mobility that is essential for stratagem. Accurate and penetrating understanding is a more useful tool and essential asset for the top management team than any gift of cunning (Freedman, 2015).

On War endures today as a business reference. Clausewitz describes the challenge of a 'positive theory' on strategy given that the 'fog of war puts a veil of uncertainty over all information'. Clausewitz also sees strategy as 'a socio-political mechanism that can be used to educate the mind of the future leader but cannot accompany him on the battlefield' (Kornberger, 2013).

Strategy: an evolution

This brings me to a different take on strategy in terms of definition and application of that definition, and to the essential features of strategy. Although strategic management is one of the 'most taught subjects, it is paradoxically also the most misunderstood' (Ronda-Pupo and Guerras-Martin, 2012) due to its diverse nature and lack of consensus on how it is defined. As an academic field its consensual meaning is fragile (Nag *et al*, 2007). Strategy has nevertheless become so ingrained in the language of business organizations that it is now perceived to be a determinant of success or failure (Greckhamer, 2010). The word strategy is Greek in origin and means *strategos*, general in command of an army. Long before Antoine-Henri Jomini, Heraclitus and Pericles are generally regarded as the founding fathers of strategy (Carter *et al*, 2010) but this link to contemporary organizations is unfounded. Edward Luttwak (2001) noted that Clausewitz expanded on the word *strategos* to include *strategike episteme* (generals' knowledge), *strategon sophia* (generals' wisdom) *taktike techne* (tactics plus rhetoric and diplomacy).

Luttwak suggests that tactics ascend to the operational level and this allows me to make a distinction here between strategy and tactics, in order to make a case for a categorization of supply chain disruption. Interestingly, for me at least, is that tactics preceded strategy as a term, when it was used to describe the science of military movements, before strategy was adopted to align with the means by which a commander may defend his own lands and defeat his enemies. This terminology has gone through many iterations, including Jacques Antoine Hippolyte, Comte de Guibert, in his 1770 *Essai General de Tactique*, or Paul Gedeon Joly de Maizeroy in 1771, who wrote that strategy is the province of dialectics or reasoning, the highest faculty of the mind (top management team) and separate to the subordinate spheres of tactics (supply chain management). I am comfortable to posit that strategy is the commander-in-chief projecting and directing the larger military movements and operations of a campaign, and tactics relate to the art of handling forces in battle or in the immediate presence of the enemy (Freedman, 2015).

In the supply chain management domain, we talk about supply chain strategy, but I propose that the response to supply chain disruption, where in many cases the ultimate source is the strategic renewal process of the top management team, a micro-autonomous categorization of supply chain friction deploys tactics, and not strategies. I further propose a second, macro categorization, in which mitigation strategies involve supply chain network redesign.

> **Policy: the source of supply chain disruption**
> **External policy: political, economic, social, technological, climatic**
> **Internal policy: supply chain industry policy and top management team strategic renewal process**
>
> ## Supply Chain Disruption
> **Macro: impacting supply chain network design**   **Micro: supply chain friction**
>
> **Supply Chain Disruption:**
> Black Swan Crises and Disasters
> Grey Swan Breakdowns
> *what we do inside the bubble of our profession*
>
> **Supply Chain Strategies:**
> both TMT negotiation and autonomous
>
> **Supply Chain Friction:**
> Petty circumstances
> Blind natural forces
> *know what we do inside the bubble of our profession and triumph over it*
>
> **Supply Chain Strategies:**
> autonomous

The latter requires negotiation with the top management team to approve elements such as capital investment and customer alignment, whereas tactics are autonomous in nature. The academic literature is robust in its treatment of supply chain disruption and the taxonomy of crises, disasters and breakdowns, but this is a sticking plaster approach, accepting an inevitability of disruption, and needs to be packaged within the strategic renewal process, in order to cut off the head of the snake, as illustrated in the policy schema above. Perhaps this is why misalignment and disruption persist.

Strategy is the central political art, the art of creating power, and only comes into play when there is actual or potential conflict, when interests collide, and forms of resolution are required (Freedman, 2015). Since the beginning of time, either through God or a top management team chief executive officer (to some CEOs, the distinction is not clear), the people making decisions are more important than those tasked with implementation, such as supply chain professionals, and within all strategies three elemental features are a constant, albeit to varying degrees: deception, coalition formation and violence. Aligned to these elements, Clausewitz identified that each strategy has its own trinity, which I now use interchangeably with the top management team and supply chain management:

- **Politics (policy):** This imposes strategy but competes with the probability of chance since it is created in analogical conditions such as fog, dusk or moonlight. This makes it a particular source of friction and is entrusted to military commanders and top management teams. It is critical that policy acknowledges this friction and triumphs over it. Throughout history there have been two main approaches to policy implementation, Cunning, which the Greeks, in particular Homer, called *Mêtis* (such as the Trojan Horse), and the Chinese referred to as *Zhi*, and Strength, or *Bīe* (such as Achilles killing Hector before being shot through his heel with an arrow by Patroclus, Hector's friend). *Mêtis*, of course, was the wife of Zeus, who turned her into a fly and ate her because it was prophesized that she would give birth to two children, including a boy set to become much more powerful than Zeus. Our cunning fly had other ideas, however, and created a protective shield over her first child, and so Athena was 'born' through the head of Zeus, wearing full armour. As you do. To repeat a previous line to show that Clausewitz favoured *Bīe* in battle: the 'strategists' chessmen do not have the kind of mobility that is essential for stratagem. Accurate and penetrating understanding is a more useful tool and essential asset for the TCM than any gift of cunning (Freedman, 2015). My own view is that we need a blend of both. A top management team with *Mêtis* but also a deep understanding of *Bīe*, a marriage of both. *Bīe* in isolation has the danger of moving outside the boundaries of an organization's core competencies. Napoleon displayed tremendous *Bīe* but could have benefited from a touch of *Mêtis* in Borodino, as could the First Lord of the British Admiralty, Winston Churchill, who in February 1915 boldly but disastrously ordered an attack on the Gallipoli Peninsula on the northern side of the Dardanelles. Around 65,000 Turkish (Ottoman Empire) and 46,000 British and French troops died over the next nine months. Policy matters. In defence of Churchill, and I do defend whom I consider to be the greatest Briton in history, naval strategy was non-existent from the Battle of Trafalgar (1805) to 1914, simply because Britain had complete dominance at sea and any attempts at strategizing were just ineffective borrowings from Jomini and Clausewitz. In all strategic approaches, rhetoric, deception and coalition formation are key characteristics.

- **Military (chance):** This is the implementation stage of policy, the front line where violence is enacted. Violence was in fact avoided at all costs in earlier military history, until the rise of nationalism in Napoleon's era changed the game to complete annihilation. In this arena, blind natural forces, and effects that cannot be measured, as they are largely due to chance, cause delay and confusion. This is supply chain disruption. We use strategies aligned to business goals to mitigate macro disruption, and tactics to respond to micro friction. Strategic success has as much to do with circumstances as the military commander or the top management team (Freedman, 2015).

- **People (hatred):** Enmity can also spill over to the citizens of nations at war. There may have been strategic success on the battlefield but there can be a potential escalation or disproportionate explosion of discontent if citizens do not agree with the manner in which this success was achieved. Tony Blair was a victim of this phenomenon when the public later perceived him to have waged war in Iraq under false pretences. In the previous chapter I mentioned that costs and other consequences such as damage to a brand can be even more challenging than terrorist acts because they have a greater cumulative effect over time and have a disproportionate effect on demand (Sylla, 2014; Sheffi, 2001). Just as consumer sophistication has evolved, the rise in nationalism around 1800 also led to increased enmity from the public.

Of course, we are not concerned only with military strategy. Business policy (later becoming strategy), was taught first at Harvard Business School in 1912 (Bower, 2008) but as a business concept, strategy was first associated academically with management studies in 1947 when Von Neumann and Morgenstern published their book *Theory of Games and Economic Behavior*. This led to the recommended addition of 'business policy' as a business school curriculum course by the Gordon-Howell Report in 1959. Prior to this, Ian Hamilton (1853–1947), among others, and through his experiences as a military leader during the Great War, realized 'the need to balance formal structure and the policies that give soul to an organization' (Drucker, 1986). Peter Drucker first defined strategic management in 1954, suggesting that structure follows strategy, which determines what the key activities are in a given business and the idea of 'distinctive competence' was later introduced by Selznick in 1957 (Ronda-Pupo and Guerras-Martin, 2012).

This first period of theoretical development has been described as the precursor due to a greater emphasis on economic ideas. In the 1960s, during the second period when the field of strategic management was formed (Furrer *et al*, 2008), the concept of strategy was used to enable managers to 'translate the chaos of events and decisions they faced on a daily basis in an orderly way to evaluate the position of the firm within its environment' (Porter, 1983). The defining seminal texts of this period included Alfred

Chandler's *Strategy and Structure* in 1962, Igor Ansoff's *Corporate Strategy* in 1965 and Learned *et al*'s Harvard textbook *Business Policy: Text and cases* in 1965, all of which had a managerial orientation and a new approach of adapting and aligning to external environmental forces (Furrer *et al*, 2008). These texts included single firm in-depth case studies and therefore lacked generalizability. This was addressed in the third period of evolution in the 1970s, described as the 'transition to a research orientation' (Furrer *et al*, 2008), when a dichotomy of ontological and epistemological perspectives developed. The first was the process approach, whereby strategies were arrived at indirectly such as 'logical incrementalism' coined by Quinn in 1980 and 'emergent strategies' observed by Mintzberg in 1978 and Waters in 1985 (Furrer *et al*, 2008).

Process research has two ontological distinctions traced to Democritus, whereby the world comprises stable components, known as the variant method, and Heraclitus, who determined that the world is comprised of dynamic processes and activities that are in a constant state of interaction, fluctuation and evolution that result in 'changing outcomes', known as the process method (Caffrey and McDonagh, 2015). Heraclitus is seen as the founding father of process philosophy, famously saying that a river is not an object but an ever-changing flow, akin to the assessment that strategy may be understood as events, values, and actions through which a context flows (Pettigrew, 1977), and that the sun is not a thing, but a flaming fire. Heraclitus used the term *panta rhei* (everything flows) to teach that all elements within nature are subject to process, activity and change (Rescher, 1996). A man cannot step into the same river twice. Especially me. I cannot swim.

The alternative approach to process was to use deductive large-scale statistical studies to test the relationship between strategy and performance. This new phase of empirical tradition and rigor led to the renaming of business policy to strategic management by Schendel and Hofer in 1979 resulting from a meeting of minds at a 1977 Pittsburgh conference (Herrman, 2005; Nag *et al*, 2007). The 1980s were synonymous with a change in focus from analysing an organization in terms of industry structure to the study of internal structure, resources and capabilities. A new focus was on the firm and Michael Porter provided the first dominant design in strategic management with his five forces model, which claimed that industry attractiveness determines organizational success (Herrman, 2005). Other streams of research emerged such as transaction costs economics (TCE) and the resource based view (RBV), which analysed the relationships between the multifunctional nature of large organizations and the firms' resources, respectively, and performance (Furrer *et al*, 2008).

Burn (1993) and Elshamly *et al* (2014) offered another phased evolutionary perspective. The 1970s were shaped by functionally based long-term planning, which was highly prescriptive and top-down, and business planning and corporate planning which had top-down guidance and bottom-up plans at divisional and functional levels. Kenneth Andrews, Igor Ansoff and Alfred Chandler were again recognized as the founding fathers of strategic management and this period introduced not only measurable identifiable factors of strategy but also the non-tangible aspects of political agenda, conflict, intuition and emotion. The 1980s introduced a mixed approach: in a portfolio approach, the organization was seen as a series of separate strategic business units having largely independent products, markets and missions. We were also introduced to competitive strategies and during this phase, approaches such as cost leadership, differentiation and focus, and value chain analysis were used to identify how value is added to products and services. In parallel, a power-behaviour approach focused on a social-political context. The 1990s were defined by an incremental and steady convergence of ideas. Strategy formulation developed in the context of a broader holistic analysis, emphasized by Mintzberg describing strategy as 'a plan, ploy, patter, position and perspective which captures both the component parts of strategy as well as the context' (Burn, 1993). This latest period adopted an activities-based view and introduced conceptual frameworks such as strategy as a process and strategy as practice.

Having analysed over 90 definitions since the pioneering days of Drucker and closing the loop on the opening concern of this section, Ronda-Pupo and Guerras-Martin (2012) offered a consolidated view of strategy as the 'dynamics of the firms' relationship with its environment for which the necessary actions are taken to achieve its goals and to increase performance by means of the rational use of resources'. Strategy is a master concept that has performative qualities and to be meaningful must be underpinned by the relations of power (Carter *et al*, 2010) such as a top management team. Production and reception of strategy knowledge are articulations of power (Ezzamel and Willmott, 2004) and I now turn my attention to this power source.

Strategic management as a process

Strategy has been described as a process that is both continuous (Pyburn, 1983) and dynamic, operating in an open system (Mintzberg *et al*, 1976) and this view has remained a constant to the present day. Miles *et al* (1978) defined an organization as 'both an articulated purpose and an established mechanism for achieving it', a reflection of the central importance of strategy. The strategic renewal process was said to be dynamic and complex, maintaining a balance between environmental and internal interdependencies. This could be penetrated by searching for patterns that could predict the future, although limited by a strategic-choice perspective in that the choices that the top management team made were the critical determinants of organizational structure and process in what was called the adaptive cycle (Miles *et al*, 1978).

A strategic typology was devised to describe how organizations move through the adaptive cycle. A defender enacts and maintains a stable environment, similar to exploitation as previously described. A prospector seeks new opportunities in a more dynamic environment, similar to exploration. An analyser combines both approaches and a reactor is both inconsistent and unstable (Miles *et al*, 1978). Strategic exploration, an adaptive perspective, is necessary when forces such as globalization, new technologies and new competition threaten the organization, whilst exploitation, a selective perspective, brings stability to short-term competitive challenges (Volberda *et al*, 2001). Strategy not only consists of formulation and implementation that requires top management team functional alignment, but also the simultaneous sub-processes of competence definition, modification and deployment, each having a different perspective for the top management team, middle management and operations management (Floyd and Lane, 2000). Within the definition sub-process, top management team members perform the role of ratification, articulating strategic intent, monitoring progress and endorsing and supporting decisions. During the modification stage, they recognize strategic potential, set strategic direction and empower and enable decisions. Finally, they perform a director's role during the deployment sub-process, planning, deploying resources and commanding middle management. Conversely, through the sub-process stages, middle management champion, synthesize, facilitate and implement strategy, while operations management experiment, adjust and conform. This complexity is heightened considering a recent trend of increased involvement by boards of directors in the strategic decision-making process, due to the liberalization of financial markets and the resulting need for transparency and accountability, and this poses an additional challenge to the top management team (Pugliese *et al*, 2009).

Volberda identified four journeys within the strategic renewal process – emergent, directed, facilitated and transformational – and went beyond the parameters of exploitation and exploration to include co-evolution across multiple business units that aligns competencies with the environment. Within the emergent journey of renewal, top management take an entrepreneurial approach and 'amplify market forces' in order to support business unit managers. Targets are set based on profitability as opposed to internal processes. There are elements of strategic selection and adaptation, also stated as expansion and contraction, and retention, which empower the business units to search for new ideas and business models, but variation from the core competencies of the organization is discouraged by the top management team. Maintaining the boundaries of competencies requires active but non-disruptive top management team involvement.

The directed journey assumes full top management team control over purposeful and adaptive strategic formulation and implementation with little to no autonomy enjoyed by middle management. This requires in-depth top management team industry knowledge but can be restrictive in a dynamic and disruptive business environment because exhaustive analysis is needed before action is taken. In the facilitated journey the top management team creates a nurturing context for business unit managers to search for new opportunities to enhance performance within highly complex and dynamic markets and acts as a 'retrospective legitimizer' in support of initiatives. Metrics other than profitability alone, such as speed of new product and service introductions, are used to measure performance and these organizations tend to be in a permanent state of adaptation. This perspective facilitates continuous learning but prohibits the development of synergies across units due to a lack of direct top management team control. Front-line managers are involved in the more holistic transformational renewal process, in which they collectively develop strategic schemas or frames of reference (Volberda et al, 2001). Shared schemas are difficult to implement and can lead to reduced performance, or failure, if changes are piecemeal and not systematic across all units.

Organizations may adapt a hybrid of two or more of the four perspectives depending on the period or context of the renewal journey. For each perspective the organization must 'define the appropriate managerial roles, specify the knowledge design and elaborate on the pacing of renewal in terms of risk, speed and competitive positioning' (Volberda et al, 2001). Agarwal and Helfat (2009) suggested two types of strategic renewal, continuous incremental strategic renewal and discontinuous strategic transformations. The latter are caused by major environmental changes such as in technology and customer demand, largely magnified by globalization, which cannot be confidently predicted by any firm. Such changes can at times be catastrophic and competence-destroying, resulting in entire industries exiting the market. Organizations can prepare by introducing routines, incentives and altering structure to deal with change management that do not conflict with current tasks.

A more recent perspective that is influenced by the process method redirects the focus of study away from the organization to the managerial strategist, as an individual practitioner (Whittington, 1996). In one sense it returns to the traditional view of the manager as a strategy maker, but there is an added dimension of how the manager acts and interacts in the sequence of strategic renewal. How they 'do strategy'. This can be anything from setting up and attending meetings, making presentations, identification of opportunities, budgeting and writing documents. It blends knowledge that is tacit and formal, local and general. Each organization has its own distinct and regular patterns that are intertwined with the various roles of arbitrating, advocating, analysing and advising performed by the company executives.

A practice definition of strategy has emerged 'as a situated, socially accomplished activity, while strategizing comprises those actions, interactions and negotiations of multiple actors and the situated practices that they draw upon in accomplishing that activity' (Jarzabkowski *et al*, 2007). The actors are the practitioners who do the work of strategy, practices are 'the social, symbolic and material tools through which strategy work is done' and praxis is the flow of activity in which strategy is accomplished (Jarzabkowski and Spee, 2009). There is also increasing interest in the discursive nature of strategy as a supplementary element that brings a socio-material and psychological dimension to the sense-making of policies. 'Strategy is up there. Right up there. At the top. The language that it mobilizes is what puts it there' (Lilley, 2001). This can include water-cooler discussions, the distribution of Post-its, rumours and gossip or informal meetings. Research on this stream has largely focused on language and communication that perhaps provides the grouting for the processual and/or practice approaches to strategic management. Simply to avoid the need to discuss the tongue-twister of practice, praxis and practitioner, my preference is to focus on the process method.

Strategic management and the top management team

In traditional organizations, a top management team member is a 'senior executive responsible for one or more functions in their organization' and a key participant in the strategic renewal process (Floyd and Lane, 2000; Menz, 2012). Strategic renewal includes the 'perennially unfinished' and 'ongoing journey of activities a firm undertakes to alter its path dependence' (Iszatt-White, 2010; Volberda *et al*, 2001) or alternatively the 'process, content, and outcome of refreshment or replacement of attributes of an organization that have the potential to substantially affect its long-term prospects' (Agarwal and Helfat, 2009). The top management team composition can include a chief executive officer (CEO), chief financial officer (CFO), chief operating officer (COO), chief marketing officer (CMO), chief strategy manager (CSO) and a chief information officer (CIO).

Michael Cohen described firms as a series of emergent ideas rather than 'coherent structures', and 'organized anarchies characterized by problematic preferences, unclear technology, and fluid participation'. Preferences arise and are discovered from actions taken, rather than acting on preferences. A second characteristic is that despite their survival, its members are not completely knowledgeable about the technology and processes of the firm and adapt through learning from past accidents. In addition, participation is fluid, which could be in terms of staff turnover or the degree of effort and motivation applied at any one time. Cohen proceeded to describe decision opportunities as 'ambiguous stimuli' and organizations as 'vehicles for solving problems, structures or processual procedures, within which, conflict is resolved through bargaining'. A further, more cynical, observation was that organizations are institutions in which strategic timing is quite opportunistic and depends on the availability of the appropriate energy for a corresponding task, in the sense that members are looking for problems to apply the choices they have already made, decision situations are sought to provide a platform for articulating certain issues or feelings, searching for disruptions for which pre-conceived solutions may be the political right response, and in fact decision-makers looking for work (Cohen *et al*, 1972).

Henri Fayols' 1916 assertion that managers plan, organize, coordinate and control was a dominant view held until Mintzberg observed that there is no science in managerial work and that many roles are held within the groupings of interpersonal, information processing and strategic decision-making. The manager was an information generalist and the nerve centre of the organization's information systems (Mintzberg, 1971). This reflects a general evolution of management theory from the traditional model of the late 19th to the early 20th centuries that was dominated by top management team control of the strategic decision-making process, whereby individual roles were prescribed and commanded by stable hierarchies and evaluation of employees was principally through the discernment of their superiors (Ismail, 2014), to the human relations model of the late 1940s to the early 1950s that emphasized the social needs of employees for belonging and recognition, whilst maintaining top management team control, to the human resources model from the mid-1950s that conceded that most organizational members represent a resource for performance improvement (Miles *et al*, 1978).

The embracing of member involvement in the decision-making process across the organization, although a positive development, has led to significant strategic role conflict, or polarized dissensus as Biddle described it in 1979, for the present-day top management team member, who has to balance the need to exploit existing competencies and the need to explore new options for strategic renewal, across multiple levels of management. The top management team must also contend with a political dimension (Floyd and Lane, 2000; Smith, 2014). Operations managers are positioned to gather new information from both internal and external sources, and the manner in which this information is communicated to the top management team is subject to middle management interpretation, often manipulated due to personal agendas. In fact, strategy formulation has been described as a process of political decision-making whereby strategic demands are 'politically feasible only if sufficient power can be mobilized and committed to it' (Pettigrew, 1977). How the top management team responds to the tensions of competing demands through their actions, rhetoric and decisions can create organizational context and they must also simultaneously balance strategic exploitation and exploration, profit maximization and social welfare, integrating locally and adapting globally (Smith, 2014).

Angwin *et al* (2009) observed that strategy is now the domain of all senior functional managers, with many including strategy in their titles, who achieve their aims through both direct authority and reflected CEO authority. This demonstrates a pressure to respond rapidly to environmental change but there are very few studies on how they connect up strategy. This can assist in confirming a categorization of supply chain strategy, a tier consisting of strategies that can be implemented autonomously by the supply chain division (direct authority), and a tier or tiers that require negotiation across the top management team prior to implementation (reflected authority). This is a departure from the traditional view of environmental 'scanning' in which top managers played a significant role in gathering intelligence 'about events and relationships to assist in the task of charting the company's future course of action' (Boyd and Fulk, 1996). Earlier research did suggest, however, that scanning was ad hoc and was carried out by 'boundary spanners' from both senior and middle-management, including 'shared concern' cross-functional scanning that is often 'unassigned' (Hambrick, 1981).

The environment in this context is the 'relevant physical and social factors outside the boundary of an organization that are taken into consideration during organizational decision making' (Duncan, 1972). It comprises a layer close to the organization, such as suppliers, competitors and customers (task environment), and a second layer (general environment) that has an indirect impact, such as political and social sectors (Elenkov, 1997). Information can consist of objective measures that provide industry-level data, and perceptual measures through surveying key informants. The process of scanning is a concept that has been researched since the 1960s and is driven by perceived uncertainty in support of strategic planning. It is the first link in the chain of perceptions and actions that lead to organizational adaptation to its environment (Elenkov, 1997). It was observed that the greater the perceived complexity or uncertainty in the environment the more intensified the scanning, and before making any decision to monitor a particular issue, executives first considered factors such as 'scope and urgency, relationship to long-term plans, potential significance as a 'problem area', and whether the information is readily definable' (Boyd and Fulk, 1996).

This is a challenging task for the top management team because the environment is complex and managers experience 'bounded rationality' in that they 'cannot comprehensively understand the environment' (Elenkov, 1997). The process can include 'environmental interpretation, problem formulation, problem sensing, issue management and strategic issue diagnosis'. Scanning for actual or potential changes is the first of three tasks that the manager performs. State uncertainty may occur if the manager is not confident that they understand the major environmental events or trends. This data is then analysed and interpreted to identify critical threats and weaknesses. Effect uncertainty exists when the manager does not know whether or not the findings of this analysis poses a significant threat or opportunity to the organization. The manager must then take action based on the findings but may encounter response uncertainty if they are unsure about the best approach to take and subsequently a degree of learning takes place during this stage. 'There are tremendous differences in how managers respond to the same environmental conditions' (Milliken, 1990). Surely, then, certain strategic choices must lead to disruption.

Strategic uncertainty is heightened in transitioning sectors and this has a direct impact on the frequency of scanning activities. This is particularly relevant for Brexit. Preceeding the collapse of the Soviet Union in December 1991, which resulted in the creation of 15 separate countries, managers in the Russian Federation faced 'unparalleled environmental discontinuity, instability, complexity and concomitant uncertainty'. This was caused by the introduction of economic policies and significant market reforms by Boris Yeltsin, such as abolishing controls over prices, resource allocation, wages and employment (May *et al*, 2000). This period was characterized by continuous dynamic and volatile, high-velocity environments coupled with discontinuous change. An initial steady growth in unemployment and inflation to a height of 30 per cent paralleled a decline in industrial output by 40 per cent. The underground economy flourished and accounted for 40 per cent of Russia's gross domestic product (GDP) amidst deteriorating social conditions. Political uncertainty abounded, and the Communist Party gained a majority in the Lower House of the State Duma (Parliament). Yeltsin's health was unpredictable, ensuring that his succession was uncertain, and organized crime reached such a high level that Russia became a security threat to other nations.

It is noteworthy that managers were observed to have limited knowledge of strategic management processes, additionally displaying inertia, and were therefore not prepared for the turbulence ahead. Responding to this deficiency, in such an incipient free market system, involved environmental scanning. The task environment was targeted through the use of personal contacts in order to secure scarce resources and supplies. In the general environment it was also essential to build direct relationships within the Communist Party for career and company advancement. This supports earlier research that found that top managers tend to gather information increasingly from personal sources in changing environments and have a preference for verbal communication.

General theory developed in the West suggests that there can be a sense of panic amongst managers whenever they face disruptive and uncertain conditions. They exhibit 'threat rigidity', which curtails their ability to objectively gather information. Their control of the situation becomes tight and this impacts the generation of solutions, the flow of information becomes less fluid and the burden of decisions is spread across other actors (as it should be, although seen as a negative in this context). This can cloud judgement and warning signs can be missed. They freeze, as such, and focus instead on the most 'dominant cues' (May *et al*, 2000). When policy in general comes from this position of strategic uncertainty, the result is supply chain disruption. Mitigation must include greater alignment between the top management and supply chain management teams, and to understand this I have explored business to information systems strategic alignment literature due to the apparent absence of similar research in the supply chain management academic domain.

Strategic alignment

Strategy is a continuous process of power mobilization within the senior leadership team in relation to dilemmas facing the organization (Pettigrew,

1977). Strategic alignment is contextual, situational, evolutionary and dynamic, in that existing internal and external firm-specific competences need to be explored and exploited at several organizational levels to address changing environments (Burn, 1993; Henderson and Venkatraman, 1993; Teece *et al*, 1997; Luftman, 2000; Balhareth *et al*, 2012). However complex this may be, analysis of patterns in organizational behaviour can enable firms to articulate and forecast the 'process of organizational adaptation' (Miles *et al*, 1978).

Within the field of strategy there is mutual acceptance as to the critical importance of strategic alignment (Rebolledo and Jobin, 2013). The vertical fit between business strategy and functions such as manufacturing and information systems has been explored extensively in academic literature. For example, the alignment of business and information system strategies is the primary concern of CIOs and has been repeatedly ranked as the most critical and chronic unsolved problem facing corporations since the mid-1980s (Benbya and McKelvey, 2006; Walentowitz *et al*, 2010; Baker *et al*, 2011). However, research on dynamic supply chain alignment is more recent (Rebolledo and Jobin, 2013) and generally silent. Borrowing from business to information systems strategic alignment literature to set the scene for a new strand of *business to supply chain alignment* research, I note that functional alignment of strategy and enterprise systems operates within the dynamic and complex internal and external confines of a physical, social and political process.

A key participant is the CIO, a top management team position that has increased in number since the late 1980s, reflecting an increasing importance of information technology (IT) as a functional area (Menz, 2012). The CIO holds the greatest organizational power to influence the exploitation of IT but there are many factors that determine how successfully he can enact this influence (Li and Tan, 2013). A close relationship between the CIO and CEO is crucial and this extends to solidarity between the CIO and all functional top management team members (Li and Ye, 1999; Walentowitz *et al*, 2010; Peppard *et al*, 2011). The CIO is first and foremost a business leader and must participate as a real general management peer, displaying such characteristics as a diplomat, visionary, leader, strategic thinker, relationship builder, and reader of markets, and have the acumen to appreciate the tactics used for influencing top management team members (Pyburn, 1983; Peppard *et al*, 2011; Enns and McDonagh, 2012).

Organizations are a reflection of their senior managers (Menz, 2012) and this echoes upper echelons theory that states that 'organizational outcomes, strategic choices and performance levels are partially predicted by managerial background characteristics' (Hambrick and Mason, 1984). One of the CIO's multiple and ambiguous roles is that of an IT evangelist, selling the value of IT within the organization (Peppard *et al*, 2011) but it has been found that strategic alignment is also influenced by shared understanding between IT and the business, and indeed the IT savviness of all functional top management team members (Peppard, 2010; Jentsch and Beimborn, 2014). The capability of the IT leadership team reporting to the CIO is also an important element. Without their expertise and high performance, the CIO lacks credibility (Peppard *et al*, 2011). Strategic alignment, 'applying information technology in an appropriate and timely way, in harmony with business strategies, goals and needs' (Luftman, 2000) has been the primary concern of top management team members for the past number of decades and many scholars have given due focus to finding a resolution.

The fact that strategy is a 'perennially unfinished project' (Iszatt-White, 2010) makes this quite the challenge. Predating alignment literature, strategy has been described as a process that is both continuous (Pyburn, 1983) and dynamic, operating in an open system (Mintzberg *et al*, 1976) and this view has remained a constant to the present day, although perhaps not a consistent reflection in the output of alignment frameworks. Whilst Nolan developed a stages of growth model in 1973 for information systems that involved initiation, contagion, control, integration, later updated to include data administration and maturity in 1979 (Burn, 1993), it was King (1978) that began the alignment journey with his strategy set transformation model. This was a one-way sequential integration of the organization set (mission, objectives, strategy, and other strategic organizational attributes) to the management information systems (MIS) strategy set (system objectives, constraints and design strategies).

There was a subsequent recognition that IS strategic planning can be used to influence business strategies (King and Zmud, 1981) and a resource-based view found that there was a need for organizations to grow their technology capabilities to improve their market position (Wernerfelt, 1984). It was concluded that IS strategy should emanate directly from business strategy (Henderson and West, 1979; Pyburn, 1983), and coordination of these plans was thought necessary to meet organizational goals (Lederer and Mendelow, 1989). However, there was no guidance in the literature on *how* this was to be achieved (Pyburn, 1983), and the value of IS strategic planning was not empirically validated until Henderson and Sifonis (1988) found that the strategic process must provide internal consistency between business and IS, a link confirmed by further empirical studies during that period (Tavakolian, 1989; Zviran, 1990). McFarlane (1984) devised a strategic grid model that explained how IS related both to strategy and business operations within an organization using four quadrants: support; factory; transition; strategy, each representing a situation for the company.

At the start of the 1990s it was recognized that IS strategies need to be developed in the same process, simultaneously with business strategies (Goldsmith, 1991), just as the largest and most authoritative research program yet conducted into the impact of IT on organizations was published, MIT-90s (Brown, 1993). This study (1984–91) established beyond debate that IT investment decisions and their implementation were crucial to the future of organizations and that the responsibility for these decisions rests with the top management team and not the CIO alone. A five-level model of IT organizational maturity was developed from localized applications with little potential for competitive advantage (level one) to business scope redefinition enabled by IT (level five). Venkatraman, a major contributor to MIT-90s, then partnered with Henderson to produce the seminal strategic alignment model (SAM). According to SAM, strategic alignment is based on two fundamental assumptions, economic performance, which directly relates to the strategic fit of external positioning, and internal arrangements, and that strategic fit is inherently dynamic, and reaching dynamic capability depends on the organization's ability to continuously exploit IT functionality. It is therefore not one event but a process of adaptation and change.

SAM consists of four dominant alignment perspectives (Henderson and Venkatraman, 1993). The first two arise when business strategy is the driver, *strategy execution* whereby the top management team have responsibility for strategy formulation and the CIO has an implementation role, and *technology transformation* where the CIO has the role of architect to the top management team's technology vision. The last two perspectives have IT strategy as the *enabler*, and include competitive potential, in which the top management team is the business visionary to the CIO's catalyst role of developing emerging IT capabilities, and finally *service level*, which is concerned with building a world-class IS service organization with the CIO enacting an executive leadership role, and the top management team prioritizing the allocation of resources accordingly. Other notable frameworks during the 1990s were the dynamic capabilities approach of 'exploiting existing internal and external firm-specific competences to address changing environments' (Teece *et al*, 1997) and the management by maxim model that described how an organization should consider its strategic context and articulate both business and IT maxims on how IT resources should be deployed (Broadbent and Weill, 1997). Interestingly, this study introduced the concept of business units having unique needs and that political weight was a determinant of how demands are met.

Luftman then developed the strategic alignment maturity model (SAMM) which suggested that strategic alignment is evolutionary and dynamic, and achieving this demands maximizing alignment enablers, top management team support for IT being the top ranked one, and minimizing the inhibitors, lack of close business–IS relationships correspondingly heading that list. The model outlines five levels of maturity from an initial or ad hoc process (level one) to an optimized process (level five), and attaining mature alignment is dependent on IT and other business functions adopting their strategies together. Luftman described alignment as a six-step process of setting goals, understanding the IT–business linkage, analysing and prioritizing gaps, specifying actions, choosing and evaluating success criteria, and sustaining alignment by developing and cultivating an alignment behaviour (Luftman, 2000).

The punctuated equilibrium model argued that 'periods of gradual evolution are punctuated by sudden, revolutionary periods of rapid change' (Sabherwal et al, 2001). This was coined by Elderidge and Gould in 1972 to explain the disconnect between Darwin's theory of gradualism despite the existence of geological gaps in the recording of fossils, but this concept had its critics who questioned the notion of stable periods and it was instead argued that strategic alignment is a continuous co-evolutionary process that reconciles top management team 'rational designs' and operational 'emergent processes' (Benbya and McKelvey, 2006). Chen et al (2010) proposed IS innovation and IS conservatism as a new typology of IS strategy, and organizations should seek to be ambidextrous to derive higher levels of performance, not dissimilar to Miles and Snow's analyser. Al-Hatmi and Hales (2010) agreed that alignment is a dynamic process and suggested five main components: IT strategy; corporate activity framework; IT governance framework; IT project management framework; value assessment model, and that this mechanism can be generalized across organizations.

Other scholars suggested that, while how to achieve alignment remains unclear, success depends on the development of a mechanism of knowledge integration across the top management team (Wagner and Weitzel, 2006; Balhareth et al, 2012), a view held by Jentsch and Beimborn (2014) who argued that shared understanding was crucial to achieving high performance. Reynolds and Yetton (2015) said that there is little guidance on *how* to build and sustain alignment and called for research into the dynamic nature of cross-functional relationships within firms and the time-sensitive nature of strategic decision making, whilst Pelletier and Raymond (2014) suggest that a reconciliation between strategic formulation and implementation is still needed. This is concerning given that it was suggested by Miles and Snow as early as 1984 that the process of achieving a company's strategic fit begins with the alignment to its marketplace (Wu *et al*, 2014).

Within this strategic context it is important to acknowledge that supply chains are not uncontrollable, inanimate beasts, but 'living systems propelled by humans and their behaviour' and that 'people may be getting in the way' of attaining dynamic alignment (Gattorna, 2009). The absence of this thinking is not uncommon in strategic alignment literature. One significant challenge in business–IS strategic alignment, for example, is that an information system is 'not an external object, but a product of ongoing human action, design, and appropriation, which, over time, becomes imbricated, embedded, entangled and intertwined' (Wilson *et al*, 2013) subject to social negotiation and sensemaking, 'materializing through anchoring and objectification'. There is a process of user improvisation and adjustment, due to perception and understanding of technology features that demonstrates that strategic plans are 'resources for situated action that do not in any strong sense determine their course' (Iszatt-White, 2010; Dulipovici and Robey, 2013).

A first stage of adjustment is decoupling, whereby organizational members form personal views and interpretations of enterprise system strategies based on their own local context. According to their situational needs, users then reframe the technology, and when the adjusted practices become repackaged and stable, these are then recognized as strategic in relation to the formal strategy (Wilson *et al*, 2013). The nature of information systems within the process of strategic alignment is therefore unpredictable. However, the dominant assumption within strategic alignment literature is that the IS 'artefact' is a stable and unproblematic entity, but in practice is an 'organism', 'an idea that drastically changes the traditional notion of IS alignment' (Benbya and McKelvey, 2006).

A resource-based view found that there was a need for organizations to grow their internal capabilities to improve their market position (Wernerfelt, 1984), and Gattorna suggests delivering value through people, describing dynamic supply chain alignment as the 'alignment of supply chain strategies to customer segments using customer buying behaviour as a direct reference point' (Gattorna, 2009). Despite rigorous research on business to information systems' strategic alignment, summarized in the following box, it is evident that this phenomenon remains a challenge, but as supply chain professionals we must make a start, and the final chapter provides a descriptive model in that regard. Next is a section on globalization to validate what I am proposing through Clausewitz: that policy is *the* source of disruption.

Dynamic business to information systems strategic alignment – *interchangeable with supply chain management*

- Strategic alignment is based on two fundamental assumptions, economic performance which directly relates to the strategic fit of external positioning and internal arrangements, and that strategic fit is inherently dynamic, and reaching dynamic capability depends on the organizations' ability to exploit supply chain functionality on a continuous basis
- Success depends on the development of a mechanism of shared knowledge integration across the top management team
- Consider the cross-sectional linkages within an organization and the temporal nature of strategic decision making. Alignment is a continuous co-evolutionary process that reconciles top management team 'rational designs' and operational 'emergent processes'
- There is a process of user improvisation and adjustment, due to perception and understanding of information systems features. Strategic plans are therefore resources for situated action that do not in any strong sense determine their course
- An information system is not an external object, but a product of ongoing human action, design, and appropriation, which, over time, becomes imbricated, embedded, entangled and intertwined', subject to social negotiation and sensemaking, materializing through anchoring and objectification
- Alignment must include setting goals, understanding the business to information systems linkage, analysing and prioritizing gaps, specifying actions, choosing and evaluating success criteria, and sustaining alignment by developing and cultivating an alignment behaviour
- Alignment can occur through information systems transformation where the CIO has the role of architect to the top management teams' IT vision
- IT strategy can be the enabler, and has competitive potential, whereby the top management team is the business visionary to the CIO's catalyst role of developing and exploiting emerging IT capabilities to impact new products
- A world-class IT organization can be developed if the CIO enacts an executive leadership role, and the top management team accordingly prioritizes the allocation of resources

- Business to information systems strategic alignment enablers: top management team support for CIO; CIO involved in strategy development; CIO understands the business; business-IT partnership; well-prioritized IT projects; CIO demonstrates leadership
- The CIO must first and foremost be a business leader and must participate as a real general management peer, displaying such characteristics as a diplomat, visionary, leader, strategic thinker, relationship builder, and reader of markets and the tactics used for influencing top management team members. A close relationship between the CIO and CEO is crucial and this extends to solidarity between the CIO and all functional top management team members

Alignment inhibitors and challenges:

- Top management team threat rigidity impedes judgement and information gathering. This impacts strategy itself but also alignment in the sense that often the safest or most dominant cues within their inner circles are settled on
- The environment is complex, and managers can experience 'bounded rationality' in that they 'cannot comprehensively understand the environment'. Strategy is formed in these situations
- Strategic formulation and implementation: the simultaneous sub-processes of competence definition, modification and deployment, each have a different perspective for the top management team, middle management and operations management
- Operations managers are positioned to gather new information from both internal and external sources, and the way this information is communicated to the top management team is subject to middle management interpretation, often manipulated due to personal agendas
- Strategy formulation is a process of political decision-making whereby strategic demands are 'politically feasible only if sufficient power can be mobilized and committed to it'
- The top management team responds to the tensions of competing demands through their actions, rhetoric and decisions and they must also simultaneously balance strategic exploitation and exploration, profit maximization and social welfare, integrating locally and adapting globally

Globalization

The last chapter described the fact that the forces of globalization, technology, climate change and, indeed, terrorism are all accelerating beyond our ability to adapt. However, as leading economists point out, technology is not exogenous, determined by the gods. Rather, it is endogenous, determined from within the economic and social system. Technological advances have reflected a global race between the demand for educated workers and the expansion of an educated population (Atkinson, 2016), and it is all determined by policy. Consider the fact that technology development is localized to production techniques and this is within our power to control. Consider also this notion of acceleration beyond our ability to adapt, which is very true in the sense of the planet's resources being finite, but all development is relative. Were we ever able to adapt without the risk of dramatic disruption?

The global financial crisis in 2008 was not new. Friedman (2016) asked, 'what the hell happened in 2007?', but what the hell happened in 1800? Of course, 1800 is used in the interest of simplicity. Many might assume that globalization and supply chain management rose to prominence in the early 1990s, as they were defining terms of that decade, but this would preclude an ability to learn from the lessons of the past. Migration in search of food has been a feature since the birth of mankind. From 1250 to 1350 a *Pax Mongolica* enabled an international trade economy between China and north-western Europe; in 1492 Christopher Columbus discovered America and its spices, resulting also in a transfer of technologies, plants, animals and indeed diseases considered by some to be the Big Bang of globalization; in 1498 Vasco da Gama stole African monopoly rents from Arab and Venetian spice traders; and in the 16th century Shakespeare wrote about a merchant from Venice (O'Rourke and Williamson, 2002).

However, true globalization was established in the 1800 period. I have mentioned that Jomini and Clausewitz founded modern strategy at this time, influenced by developments in physical infrastructures, logistics and cartography. Also founded was the discipline of economics, or political economy as it was known then, when Adam Smith published the seminal *Wealth of Nations* in 1776, later supported by David Ricardo (1772–1823) with the introduction of comparative advantage theory, producing and exporting the goods that you are much better at to a country you are engaged in trade with, and importing other goods from this country, further enhanced by Marx (1818–83), who advocated accelerating global expansion to increase value, the development of multinational companies, and the promotion of imperialism so that governments could protect indigenous organizations. The policy of capitalism and free trade was consequently established and replaced feudalism in Great Britain, and the dynamism of this policy led to pressure to expand beyond borders (Michie, 2017).

What enabled this expansion? As part of the Industrial Revolution, a transportation revolution emerged in the early 1800s when American Robert Fulton (1765–1815) launched the first steamboat for commercial use, almost simultaneously as the British engineer Richard Trevithick (1771–1833) constructed the first railway steam locomotive. Long-distance international integration was now possible, and further policy changes to break down monopolies were implemented. Steamboats and railroads made it so much easier to trade and move bulk goods across continents cheaper than domestic prices. This brought other nations such as Russia, India, West Africa and the Ottoman Empire into the global economy, and of course the importance of economic forces led to the Opium Wars between Britain and China, not just for the opium trade but for trade rights in general. This gave Hong Kong to Britain. How did the policy of free trade work out for Britain? Britain was the dominant power and the international monetary system was based on the gold standard linked to the British pound. A huge increase in global trade and a scramble for Africa ensued. A great war was the result.

Policy and war

The aforementioned policies were the true cause of the horrific events of the First World War (1914–18), overshadowed by the assassination in Sarajevo of Austro-Hungarian Archduke Franz Ferdinand and his wife Sophie, Duchess of Hohenberg, on 28 June 1914. In the intervening years up to the Second World War (1939–45) we had further major disruptive events, such as the 1929 Wall Street Crash and the 1930s global depression, the rise of fascism in Italy, Spain and Portugal, militarism in Japan (the latter leading to a prolonged war between China and Japan due to the Marco Polo Bridge incident on 8 July 1937), against a backdrop of Winston Churchill's policy of re-establishing the gold standard linked to the British pound, against the strong advice of one of the great economists, John Maynard Keynes (1883–1946). There was also Nazism in Germany. Again, policy fuelled this, and ultimately the German invasion of Poland on 1 September 1939, causing the tragic death of 55 million, including the mechanized extermination of a people through unprecedented global destruction over the next six years. Another policy choice could have prevented this death toll. While the German forces were occupied in Poland, the French launched an offensive through western Germany, and when no resistance was met after three days, General Maurice Gustave Gamelin ordered a retreat. One can only wonder what the outcome would have been if the Allies had pushed forward their advantage. Choices matter.

Take a step back. Democracy was restored in Germany at the end of the First World War. However, Armistice Day on 11 November 1918 was met with bewilderment by German troops on the front line, who did not feel defeated. This abrupt end was blamed on Marxism and Judaism, with the Jews accused of calling for an end to the war back home, bitterness grew, and Nazism was born in Bavaria. This coincided with the Treaty of Versailles on 28 June 1919, and policies contained within that were again against the advice of John Maynard Keynes. These included Allied blockades on Germany, leading to hunger, tuberculosis and influenza, and polarized politics with conservatives and socialists becoming radicalized, reparation payments to the allied nations, and loss of territories. Policies matter.

The German Workers Party was formed in 1919, and just as many other small parties did, repeatedly claimed that Versailles was a crime and the Jews were behind it (not helped by the fact that a communist revolution between 1919–23 by the Friekorps mercenaries had a predominantly Jewish leadership, and the feeling around Germany was that Bolshevism and Judaism were one and the same). The 55th member of this party, Adolf Hitler (officially Number 555 to give the illusion of a larger membership) became its leader in 1921, and the name was changed to the Nationalist Socialist German Workers Party (Nazi). Hitler called for a national revolution in 1923, when the French policy to send in troops to the Ruhr to enforce reparation payments humiliated German citizens. This French occupation crisis was a revenge strategy, but ordinary citizens were brutalized. Policies matter.

The Americans stepped in and lent monies to Germany to make payments to France and Britain. A period of decadence came, and the economy soared again. Interestingly, the only sign of global trade at this time was American investment in Germany with the establishment of Ford and General Motors manufacturing plants there (Michie, 2017). Youth groups sprung up around Germany in protest against this newfound decadence, such as the *Wandervogel* movement, whose slogan was 'Germany awake', calling for order and a simple way of life (which was later capitalized on by the Nazis and the Hitler Youth). Unfortunately, they got their wish when plunging global agricultural prices created poverty in Germany and the subsequent Wall Street Crash led to the Americans calling in their loans. Economically, Germany was the worst-hit nation in the world, unemployment reached 5.5 million, 20,000 businesses folded and five major banks collapsed in 1931. The middle class was impacted. Germans were finally ready to listen to Nazi policy, and the party went from 2.8 per cent in the 1928 general election vote to 37 per cent in 1932. Out of desperation, citizens who had never heard or seen Hitler were now voting for him. President Paul von Hindenburg named Hitler as Chancellor of Germany in 1933, making the mistake of thinking that Hitler could be tamed within parliament.

In parallel, on the other side of the globe, a sequence of economic and political policies ultimately led to the end of the Second World War, not before another wave of tragic disruption. Franklin Roosevelt became President of the United States of America and inherited a poverty-stricken country with a 70,000-strong military, ranked 17th in the world. His first policy act was a 'New Deal' that regulated the financial system and implemented a major works project that brought 4 million back to employment. So successful was this policy that he was unconventionally elected for a third consecutive term in 1940 without much resistance. He declared that America was a champion of peace and that he hated war. The Great War had cost the country tens of billions of dollars and 100,000 troops, which was still felt by the population. Meanwhile, Japan and its growing ideology that matched that of Hitler needed a vital space in which to be all-dominant. This they called the Greater East-Asia Co-Prosperity Sphere, spanning from Mongolia to Northern India. The United States had Pacific bases in the Mariana Islands, Philippines and Hawaii, and Japan viewed this as aggression towards them. Japan invaded Manchuria in 1932 and their puppet government was not recognized by the United States. Anti-Japanese sentiment grew in the US when Japan invaded, gassed and bombed the Republic of China in 1937 where they subsequently inflicted terrible horrors on the Chinese up to 1941.

Roosevelt was forced to prepare for war, while maintaining his peace stance. His policy was to focus this preparation on Japan, whilst supporting the allies in their defence against Germany. He stepped outside the neutrality act and sold arms to the allies, becoming the arsenal of democracy. He stopped commercial agreements with Japan, including the supply of 90 per cent of their oil, and moved the bulk of his war fleet to Pearl Harbor, later described by the Japanese as a dagger in their heart. Japan then expanded their space to the entire Asia-Pacific region and signed a tripartite agreement with Hitler and Mussolini. This Tokyo–Rome–Berlin axis was discovered by the United States through Enigma decoding and prompted Roosevelt to implement an embargo on Japan that included aviation equipment, kerosene, engine oil, steel and iron materials, paralyzing their war machine. Simultaneously, Japan sent envoys to Roosevelt in Washington to negotiate a modus vivendi, in which they requested free reign in Asia in return for a pact of non-aggression. Of course, the United States were aware that this free reign also meant attacking British interests in Hong Kong, Burma, Malaysia and Singapore. Roosevelt rejected the request and countered with a demand for Japan to break their pact with Germany.

On 14 August 1941 Roosevelt met with his good friend Winston Churchill on a warship off Newfoundland. They signed the Atlantic Charter, a precursor to the United Nations in 1945, which called for the destruction of Nazism and disarmament of Nazi-supporting countries. This further provoked Japan. Roosevelt introduced new policies. Japanese assets on US soil were frozen, 7,000 US Marines were sent to Iceland to guard British supply ships, and to deter German invasion, a policy to sink any ships of the Axis found in US waters was implemented, and the US sent additional arms to Britain and China without recompense. The effects of these policies on Tokyo were known through wire-tapping. Further provocation. Japan requested a new modus vivendi in Washington, but simultaneously naval warships were deployed from Tokyo bound for Pearl Harbor, should they fail. The envoys requested the US to stop supplying China with arms, to supply Japan with oil again, and in turn they would not attack British interests in Asia-Pacific. The response was to banish the 'scoundrels' from Washington. 7 December 1941... Pearl Harbor. 8 December... global war.

Americans say that but for them the British would be German-speakers, and it is true that the decisive atomic bombing of Nagasaki and Hiroshima by the Enola Gay Boeing B-29 had a big impact on the end of the war. However, it was the brilliance of General Gueorgui Konstantinovitch Joukov of the Russian forces, coupled with Hitler's over-ambitious policy decisions, that had more significance. Supply chain management and economics had a huge bearing on these decisions. Despite a non-aggression pact signed by Hitler and Joseph Stalin on 23 August 1939, Hitler expanded his *blitzkrieg* policy, in his quest for his own vital space, by launching the largest ground offensive in history, opening fire on Russian lines. Stalin had ignored 80 direct warnings of this attack, including a letter from Churchill and a

German defector crossing the border on the eve of the attack to warn Russian officers. The German machine included 210 divisions, 3 million armed soldiers, 3,000 aircraft and 3,500 tanks. Leading up to the attack, roads in Poland were widened, railway tracks doubled, and airfields built along the border to logistically support the campaign.

In January 1941 Joukov simulated a German attack and the result was the decimation of Russian forces. This enraged Stalin, who showed his fear by sending oil, wheat and iron to Germany, to delay an invasion, but contradicted himself by promoting Joukov to Chief of Staff. After the initial destruction, Joukov implemented a war of attrition that tied up nine-tenths of the German Army for two years. Hitler underestimated the resolve of the Russians and his campaign lacked long-term logistical planning, given that he expected to take the country within four weeks before winter arrived. In the period from 22 June 1941 to Victory Day on 9 May 1945 a total of 607 Nazi divisions were destroyed or captured on the Russian front (four times more than they lost on the other fronts of North Africa, Italy and Western Europe) as a result of nine campaigns and 210 operations mounted by the Soviet armed forces. Interestingly, having strategically lured the Nazis in, seven of the campaigns and 160 of the operations were Russian offensives.

However, there was another battle going on simultaneously, a second policy failure. Hitler's global ambitions were running out of fuel, but actually not to the extent that his economists were advising him. Already, his beloved Luftwaffe, for instance, could not do what he envisioned for it due to low fuel reserves. He believed that he needed the oilfields of the Caucasus region, declaring 'If I do not get the oil of Maikop and Grozny then I must end this war' (Hayward, 1995). He over-committed troops to Caucasus and this was a step too far, but even if he had succeeded in securing the oil stocks, which were reached, but had been destroyed by the Russians, he had no means of transporting the oil back to Germany. These two policies did not immediately dissolve the German war machine, but when the Allies landed on Normandy, Germany's strength had been too greatly diminished by that point. Policy matters. Tragically, the Russian strategic choices that won the Second World War for the Allies (including the liberation of 113 million people in lands to the west of the Soviet Union) came at a horrendous price. When you think of the pure evil of the Holocaust and the loss of up to 6 million Jews, consider that these prolonged campaigns led to the death of a staggering 20 million Russian citizens. A less tragic loss was the material damage to the value of US$485 million. Sadly, the subsequent Cold War and current Russian–Western tensions erased this from our thoughts.

The Second World War prompted new policy. John Maynard Keynes was finally listened to. Keynes led the British contingent in the establishment of the International Monetary Fund (IMF) at Bretton Woods in 1944, when (most of) his policies finally gained deserved approval. The Great Depression had led to nations putting up barriers that devalued currencies and restricted global trade. New cooperation was agreed, and this created a golden economic age. However, Keynes warned that austerity measures were not good policy, as with the German reparation payments, and he seems to have lacked the persuasive skills to bring this particular idea over the line within the IMF. He favoured strong nations rebalancing funds to struggling nations in times of need, but this was rejected. Certain nations suffered accordingly when the economic utopia ended in 1975.

One cause was that Keynes' policy intent of full employment conflicted with the institutional arrangements dictated by the Americans, who did not wish to give workers too much control. Good IMF policies in general did result in stability, but of course the IMF did not prevent wars during the same period, not limited by any sense to the Korean and Vietnam conflicts. Neither did the establishment of other institutions, which really need to re-evaluate themselves and enforce their founding intentions, such as the World Bank tackling climate change, the IMF controlling global financial flows, the Organisation for Economic Co-operation and Development (OECD) policing tax evasion and avoidance, and the United Nations focusing on the peaceful resolution of conflicts (Michie, 2017). I digress. What happened next was another shift in policy, leading to the 2008 global financial crisis, known also in Ireland as the St Patrick's Day massacre.

New economic policy arose in the form of Milton Friedman, the guru of anti-Keynesian monetarism, and advisor to Margaret Thatcher and Ronald Reagan. In 1979, Thatcher introduced the policy of deregulation and the abolishment of exchange controls, which preceded privatization and competition in public services, tax cuts for the rich, and outsourcing. Globalization accelerated once more. Private producers and investors rose to prominence, as did multinationals, which became wealthier than nations. Government control and policy became secondary. It was capitalism unleashed. Tax avoidance and evasion increased, facilitated in part by Deutsche Bank, the financers of the Nazi regime and purchasers of stolen Jewish gold, leading to the 'German miracle' of rapid growth up to the 1970s, and whose many other *recent* malpractices have attracted fines of $23 billion (Michie, 2017). Global financial speculation rose (gambling, in other words), and a system was formed to respond to short-term financial greed, magnified by incentive structures for banks and financial traders. This was an era of neo-liberal laissez-faire economics that relied on linear mathematical models to predict the future (which proved to be inadequate) and did not account for a dynamic and chaotic global environment, returning to pre-First World War patterns.

Economics was not to blame, though. It was the policy choices of 'de-regulation, privatization, demutualization and financialization, combined with the free movement of capital across the globe' (Michie, 2017). Policy matters. Through concerted political will, the balance of capitalist power changed with the industrialization of Japan and China, and India exploited the acceleration in technological advancements. We now had several large economies, none of which were strong enough to hold up the international monetary system in isolation. Global inequality reduced but domestic inequality increased. Technology encouraged high-skilled employment (skill-biased technical change hypothesis), nations such as India created an elite class of professionals, but this strangled low-skilled workers globally and the trade unions that supported them. The policy of certain economies such as China was to maintain export surpluses, which pushed global interest rates down, dangerously raising the costs of assets (housing). An older generation had increased financial assets through the sale of homes to a younger generation with mounting debt. A portion of the older generation, however, needed to part with their financial assets to pay for the education of a younger generation who needed qualifications to meet the skill-biased technical change hypothesis (Atkinson, 2016). Consequently, a highly leveraged global banking system buoyed by intense consumer greed and sub-prime mortgages collapsed, and once again a recession.

It seems quite cyclical. So cyclical that the current tensions among the power nations is quite concerning. However, there is a third Thomas Friedman accelerating force leading to supply chain disruption. Climate change. Globalization has resulted in significant increases in CO_2 emissions arising from industrial production, transportation and deforestation. These emissions contribute to global warming through the greenhouse effect, which is the excessive retention of solar energy in the atmosphere. This is a serious phenomenon that needs to be addressed through a concerted global policy effort. The very existence of our planet is at stake, much more critical than localized supply chain disruption such as a 22 per cent reduction in ski-lift orders from French manufacturers in 2006, when the hottest temperature in 500 years was recorded. Road transportation is largely contained within borders and therefore these emissions are not attributed to globalization, which I would disagree with, because nations who benefit from globalization will see increased domestic consumerism.

However, transnational road transport *is* recognized as an important source of global emissions, as is sea transport, which accounts for up to 4 per cent of our planet's fossil fuel consumption. This consumption is to support 70 per cent of all international goods moved towards the European Union and 95 per cent of goods to the United States. The biggest culprit is aviation, which accounts for up to 9 per cent of greenhouse gases. In the period from 1990 to 2004, aligned to the acceleration period of globalization, emissions from aviation increased by 86 per cent. Again, it is argued that the growth in domestic aviation is not a globalization effect. However, we have seen that political will enabled India to enter the global game, buoyed by the capitalization of technological advances, which in turn created an elite class of workers. Between 2005 and 2007, Airbus and Boeing received orders for 500 aircraft from Indian airline companies to support increased demand for domestic routes (Huwart and Verdier, 2013). We cannot say that this new elite class of workers, and globalization, has not driven this demand.

Postponement strategy

It would be too simplistic to suggest that organizations should increase their sea versus air freight ratio, as this is determined by manufacturing strategies and business models. Continuous flow manufacturing enables better forecasting, and this can support six-week ocean transit times rather than the much costlier one-week transit times of air freight, whereas opportunistic demand, or products with many variations, are less predictable and therefore more prone to air freight. Take the manufacturing of computer keyboards as just one example. A keyboard may have a total supply chain lead-time of 26 weeks, including the procurement of the longest lead-time component, manufacturing lead time, and transit time to Europe. In a long-term project with continuous forecasting, this lead-time becomes a rolling one and can effectively be managed within 13-week demand windows.

However, knowing your actual customer demand in 13 weeks' time is a challenge in itself, but consider that most keyboard projects have up to 27 languages and therefore 27 different keyboard layouts. In such a scenario, air freight is inevitable without strategizing. You know that the majority of customer demand will be for English, French and German layouts. These

> can be sea freighted. For the remaining 24 languages, a postponement strategy can be implemented whereby blank keyboards can be locally printed within a European facility, with a five day lead-time (laser or tampo printing). I implemented this strategy in Limerick, Ireland and Lodz, Poland for Dell. A small portion of blank keyboards can be air freighted as a form of redundancy, and the balance can be sea freighted. Demand is managed better, there is less excess inventory (what can you do with 300 unsold Hebrew keyboards?), less transport costs, and while a reduction in climate-related supply chain disruption will not be noticed by the individual organization, adoption of this approach universally could help the environment and contribute to the mitigation of disruption.

Industrialization is a substantial enabler of globalization, and this has been predominant in the developed nations, with the United States emitting 20 per cent of global greenhouse gases. Policy, however, has encouraged a reduction in economic inequality and this brought Japan, China and India into the arena, thereby increasing industrialization within those nations, in support of which, China opens one coal-fired plant every week. Coal is the cheapest and most abundant fossil fuel. But it is also the most polluting, and China is now the greatest global emitter of CO_2. Policy also encourages the development of emerging markets, and of course the more development, the more industrialization, and the more emissions, but certain emerging nations are already indirectly contributing to the greenhouse effect through deforestation. The cyclical interconnectedness is such that, as China benefits from free trade and improved conditions for its citizens, another country, Brazil, is destroying its rainforests to feed China's increasing consumer demand. Between 1996 and 2003 Brazil's export of soy to China escalated from 15 thousand, to 6 million tonnes.

According to the United Nations, this deforestation will lead to a poverty boom and desertification (by 2060 around 90 million sub-Saharan African hectares will be sterile), causing water shortages (in the next 70 years 1.8 billion people will be without water). Global warming has caused supply chain disruption through ever-increasing hurricanes and storms. Within a decade we will be consuming twice what the planet can produce. National policy makers must continue to come together to take bilateral and regional pro-environmental measures. Government policy can use globalization as a positive force to implement green technologies and to align industrial development with environmental conservation (Huwart and Verdier, 2013). We need sustainable globalization.

Sustainable globalization in the context of climate change is a challenge for all of us and is easy to say. For many reasons, it is not so easy to implement. Sure, there has been progress. In 2015, there was a global investment of $286 billion in clean energy against $130 billion for fossil fuels, and there has been a 70 per cent increase among the 20 major economies in sourcing energy from the sun and wind. However, this is not having a significant impact because economies are too dynamic and unpredictable. They are not cooperating with the equilibrium of policy. One policy proposal is to change the business model of built-in obsolescence, by incentivizing repair and reuse through VAT reductions and income tax reclaims (Michie, 2017). Unified policy on a global scale is much more challenging. One issue is that negotiating a climate change agreement is not a stand-alone exercise, but rather it 'sits alongside trade negotiations, nuclear weapons negotiations, migration and human rights negotiations' (Helm and Hepburn, 2009).

Another challenge is that climate change affects individual states in vastly varying ways, and some nations, and the political elite of others, are even benefiting from global warming, such as gas and oil sources being much easier to exploit now in the northern regions of Canada and Russia, there is now an abundance of tar sands in Canada, and coal is expanding its share in energy alternatives. From a logistics perspective, the Northeast and Northwest Passages of the Arctic Ocean are now opening up for shipping. It is also very difficult to allocate the responsibility of carbon emissions across nations. This is largely due to climate being so complex that the direct relationship between gases and temperature changes is almost impossible to predict, and while China and India, as examples, are known to account for an 85 per cent increase in coal consumption, they have the lowest emissions per head (Helm and Hepburn, 2009).

To mitigate further disruption, including the threat of a global war, what we need now is to have 'decisions made, not by default, but consciously, and by a broad set of stakeholders' (Atkinson, 2016). History has shown that policy is the snake's head of disruption. It is no different at firm level and the top management team. Choices matter. Atkinson (2016) agrees with me: 'Globalization is the result of decisions taken by international organizations, by national governments, and by corporations. The form it has taken, and the regulation of the industry, have been subject to economic and political choices'. The process of alignment of business strategy and supply chain tactics must be developed as a model and become part of organizational culture. James Carville, the 1992 Bill Clinton presidential campaign strategist, said, 'It's the economy, stupid.' In relation to supply chain disruption, I say: 'It's policy, stupid.'

Borrowing from Lord King, the British economist, Governor of the Bank of England from 2003 to 2013 and author of *The End of Alchemy* (2016), I liken economics to supply chain management in that it is a social science that has 'no natural constants, no laws shaping a future that is inherently unknowable, and there is no rational basis on which to form expectations'. Policies continue. Supply chain disruption will therefore continue. It is critical that we minimize this disruption through greater alignment of top management policy decisions with the troops on the front line... the supply chain professionals. Let us now see if my approach reflects reality. I begin with an examination of the Irish Defence Forces through both their rotation within the 2014 Nordic Battle Group and their 2017–18 deployment to Lebanon.

Policy as the source of (supply chain) disruption

Sample policies that led to disruption

- The Napoleon Bonaparte strategy of war of movement in numbers amassed an empire in Continental Europe. This same strategy led to the disruption of the empire because it was applied to the vast land of Russia, too far from supply chain support
- In what could be described as a tsunami, building momentum, the policy of capitalism and free trade with the gold standard linked to the British pound replaced feudalism in Great Britain. This led to conflicts such as the Britain-China Opium wars for trade rights. A huge increase in global trade and a scramble for Africa ultimately led to the great disruption, the First World War
- The First Lord of the British Admiralty, Winston Churchill, used Clausewitz land-based strategy that caused disruption in the Dardanelles in February 1915 and the death of 110,000 lives
- Policies in the 1919 treaty of Versailles such as German reparation payments, loss of German territories, allied blockades on Germany, Churchills' policy to re-establish the gold standard linked to the British pound led to another tsunami of events such as the 1929 wall street crash and the 1930s global depression, the rise of fascism in Italy, Spain and Portugal, militarism in Japan, and the Japan-China war, ultimately leading to the next great disruption, WWII
- French policies to ignore Charles de Gaulle's lectures and four publications between 1924 and 1938, to construct (and have unreasonable reliance on) the Maginot Line along the French-German border, and to enable the lame German invasion (and more significantly, the return) of General Maurice Gustave Gamelin, resulted in severe disruption for France
- The deranged policy of Hitler to invade Russia failed for the same reasons as Napoleon's bid. This was acerbated by a strategy to source oil in Maikop and Grozny. From the outset this lacked the logistical capacity to transport the oil back to Germany
- The Franklin Roosevelt policy to become the arsenal of democracy and to implement an embargo on Japan that included aviation equipment, fuel, steel and iron materials, led to disruption in Pearl Harbor and the USA entering WWII, and the use of atomic bombs

- The Margaret Thatcher (and Ronald Reagan) policies of deregulation, privatization, outsourcing, demutualization and financialization, combined with the free movement of capital across the globe, ultimately resulted in the 2008 global financial crisis, further great disruption
- Without the authorization of a United Nations mandate, the United States and British policy to invade Iraq in March 2003 instead of a diplomatic solution, due to Saddam Hussein's alleged development of nuclear and biological weapons, led to the death of up to 7,500 civilians, and later proved to be controversially based on manipulated evidence
- The prioritization by the leading nations of trade negotiations, nuclear weapons negotiations, migration and human rights negotiations over climate-change agreements, is causing accelerating disruption in our environment, and by extension our supply chain networks
- A global policy deficiency to contain the accelerating force of technology and the skill-biased technical change hypothesis has led to increased domestic inequality through disruption in the low-skilled sector and a corresponding decline in the supporting trade unions. Technology is not exogenous, determined by the Gods, but endogenous, determined from within the economic and social system
- The policy failure of the International Monetary Fund to support developing nations due to their inability to contain multinational organizations (and private producers and investors), has led to disruption in nations whose leadership does not have the political will to raise the standards of its citizens. Global inequality has decreased but domestic inequality has increased. The IMF in 2016 admitted to damaging developing nations through strategic choices.

References

Agarwal, R and Helfat, CE (2009) Strategic renewal of organizations, *Organization Science*, 20(2), pp 281–93

Al-Hatmi, A and Hales, K (2010) *Strategic Alignment and IT Projects in Public Sector Organization: Challenges and solutions*

Angwin, D, Paroutis, S and Mitson, S (2009) Connecting up strategy: Are senior strategy directors a missing link? *California Management Review*, 51(3), pp 74–94

Atkinson, AB (2016) Inequality: What can be done? *Panoeconomicus*, 63(3), pp 385–94

Baker, J, Jones, DR, Cao, Q and Song, J (2011) Conceptualizing the dynamic strategic alignment competency, *Journal of the Association for Information Systems*, 12(4), p 299

Balhareth, H, Liu, K and Manwani, S (2012) Aligning business and IT from multi-level learning perspectives, UKAIS, March, p 36

Bassford, C (1993) Jomini and Clausewitz: Their interaction. [Online] http://www.Clausewitz.com/CWZHOME/Jomini/JOMINIX. htm, an edited version of a paper presented to the 23rd Meeting of the Consortium on Revolutionary Europe at Georgia State University

Benbya, H and McKelvey, B (2006) Using coevolutionary and complexity theories to improve IS alignment: A multi-level approach, *Journal of Information Technology*, 21(4), pp 284–98

Bower, JL (2008) The teaching of strategy: From general manager to analyst and back again? *Journal of Management Inquiry*, 17(4), pp 269–75

Boyd, BK and Fulk, J (1996) Executive scanning and perceived uncertainty: A multidimensional model, *Journal of Management*, 22(1), pp 1–21

Broadbent, M and Weill, P (1997) Management by maxim: How business and IT managers can create IT infrastructures, *MIT Sloan Management Review*, 38(3), p 77

Brown, A (1993) New management patterns: Key findings from the MIT90s research study, *Journal of Information Technology*, 8(1), pp 58–61

Burn, JM (1993) Information systems strategies and the management of organizational change: A strategic alignment model, *Journal of Information Technology*, 8(4), pp 205–16

Caffrey, E and McDonagh, J (2015) *The Theory and Application of Process Research to the Study of IT Strategy-Making: Enhancing qualitative and mixed methods research with technology*, IG Global, pp 392–427

Carter, C, Clegg, S and Kornberger, M (2010) Re-framing strategy: Power, politics and accounting, *Accounting, Auditing and Accountability*, 23(5), pp 573–94

Chen, DQ, Mocker, M, Preston, DS and Teubner, A (2010) Information systems strategy: Reconceptualization, measurement, and implications, *MIS Quarterly*, 34(2), pp 233–59

Christopher, M and Towill, DR (2002) Developing market specific supply chain strategies, *The International Journal of Logistics Management*, 13(1), pp 1–14

Clausewitz, C von (1832/1940) *On War*, Jazzybee Verlag

Cohen, MD, March, JG and Olsen, JP (1972) A garbage can model of organizational choice, *Administrative Science Quarterly*, 17(1), pp 1–25

Drucker, PF (1986) *Management: Tasks, responsibilities, practices*, Truman Talley Books

Duncan, RB (1972) Characteristics of organizational environments and perceived environmental uncertainty, *Administrative Science Quarterly*, **17**(3), pp 313–27

Dulipovici, A and Robey, D (2013) Strategic alignment and misalignment of knowledge management systems: A social representation perspective, *Journal of Management Information Systems*, **29**(4), pp 103–26

Elenkov, DS (1997) Strategic uncertainty and environmental scanning: The case for institutional influences on scanning behavior, *Strategic Management Journal*, **18**(4), pp 287–302

Elshamly, ABM, Gear, T, Davies, B and Verschueren, RB (2014) The anatomy of strategy process stages: Post-processual and strategy as practices, BAM2014 Conference

Enns, H and McDonagh, JJ (2012) Irish CIOs' influence on technology innovation and IT–business alignment, *Communications of the Association for Information Systems*, **30**(1)

Ezzamel, M and Willmott, H (2004) Rethinking strategy: Contemporary perspectives and debates, *European Management Review*, **1**(1), pp 43–48

Floyd, SW and Lane, PJ (2000) Strategizing throughout the organization: Managing role conflict in strategic renewal, *Academy of Management Review*, **25**(1), pp 154–77

Freedman, L (2015) *Strategy: A history*, Oxford University Press

Friedman, TL (2016) *Thank You For Being Late: An optimist's guide to thriving in the age of accelerations*, Farrar, Straus and Giroux

Furrer, O, Thomas, H and Goussevskaia, A (2008) The structure and evolution of the strategic management field: A content analysis of 26 years of strategic management research, *International Journal of Management Reviews*, **10**(1), pp 1–23

Gattorna, J (2009) *Dynamic Supply Chains: Delivering value through people*, FT Prentice Hall

Goldsmith, N (1991) Linking IT planning to business strategy, *Long Range Planning*, **24**(6), pp 67–77

Greckhamer, T (2010) The stretch of strategic management discourse: A critical analysis, *Organization Studies*, **31**(7), pp 841–71

Hayward, J (1995) Hitler's quest for oil: The impact of economic considerations on military strategy, 1941–42, *The Journal of Strategic Studies*, **18**(4), pp 94–135

Hambrick, DC (1981) Specialization of environmental scanning activities among upper level executives, *Journal of Management Studies*, **18**(3), pp 299–320

Hambrick, DC and Mason, PA (1984) Upper echelons: The organization as a reflection of its top managers, *Academy of Management Review*, **9**(2), pp 193–206

Helm, D and Hepburn, C (eds) (2009) *The Economics and Politics of Climate Change*, Oxford University Press

Henderson, JC and Sifonis, JG (1988) The value of strategic IS planning: Understanding consistency, validity, and IS markets, *MIS Quarterly*, **12**(2), pp 187–200

Henderson, JC and Venkatraman, H (1993) Strategic alignment: Leveraging information technology for transforming organizations, *IBM Systems Journal*, **32**(1), pp 472–84

Henderson, JC and West Jr, JM (1979) Planning for MIS: A decision-oriented approach, *MIS Quarterly*, 3(2), pp 45–58

Herrmann, P (2005) Evolution of strategic management: The need for new dominant designs, *International Journal of Management Reviews*, **7**(2), pp 111–30

Huwart, J-Y and Verdier, L (2013) What is the impact of globalisation on the environment?, *Economic Globalisation: Origins and consequences*, OECD Publishing

Iggulden, C (2008) *Wolf of the Plains, Lords of the Bow, Bones of the Hills, The Epic Story of the Great Conqueror*, The Conqueror Series, Harper Collins Publishers

Ismail, S (2014) *Exponential Organizations: Why new organizations are ten times better, faster, and cheaper than yours (and what to do about it)*, Diversion Books

Iszatt-White, M (2010) Strategic leadership: The accomplishment of strategy as a 'perennially unfinished project', *Leadership*, 6(4), pp 409–24

Jarzabkowski, P and Paul Spee, A (2009) Strategy-as-practice: A review and future directions for the field, *International Journal of Management Reviews*, **11**(1), pp 69–95

Jarzabkowski, P, Balogun, J and Seidl, D (2007) Strategizing: The challenges of a practice perspective, *Human Relations*, **60**(1), pp 5–27

Jentsch, C and Beimborn, D (2014) Shared understanding among business and IT: A literature review and research agenda, *ECIS 2014 Proceedings*

King, MA (2016) The end of alchemy, Audible Studios on Brilliance Audio

King, WR (1978) Strategic planning for management information systems, *MIS Quarterly*, **24**(15), pp 27–37

King, WR and Zmud, RW (1981) Managing information systems: Policy planning, strategic planning and operational planning, *ICIS*, December, p 16

Kornberger, M (2013) Clausewitz: On strategy, *Business History*, **55**(7), pp 1058–73

Lederer, AL and Mendelow, AL (1989) Coordination of information systems plans with business plans, *Journal of Management Information Systems*, 6(2), pp 5–19

Li, Y and Tan, CH (2013) Matching business strategy and CIO characteristics: The impact on organizational performance, *Journal of Business Research*, **66**(2), pp 248–59

Li, M and Ye, LR (1999) Information technology and firm performance: Linking with environmental, strategic and managerial contexts, *Information and Management*, 35(1), pp 43–51

Lilley, S (2001) The language of strategy, *The Language of Organization*, 1, pp 66–87

Luftman, J (2000) Assessing business–IT alignment maturity, *Strategies for Information Technology Governance*, 4, p 99

Luttwak, E (2001) *Strategy: The logic of war and peace*, Harvard University Press

McFarlane, FW (1984) Information technology changes the way you compete, *Harvard Business Review* [Online] https://hbr.org/1984/05/information-technology-changes-the-way-you-compete

May, RC, Stewart, WH and Sweo, R (2000) Environmental scanning behavior in a transitional economy: Evidence from Russia, *Academy of Management Journal*, 43(3), pp 403–27

Menz, M (2012) Functional top management team members: A review, synthesis, and research agenda, *Journal of Management*, 38(1), pp 45–80

Michie, J (2017) *Advanced Introduction to Globalisation*, Edward Elgar Publishing

Miles, RE, Snow, CC, Meyer, AD and Coleman, HJ (1978) Organizational strategy, structure, and process, *Academy of Management Review*, 3(3), pp 546–62

Milliken, FJ (1990) Perceiving and interpreting environmental change: An examination of college administrators' interpretation of changing demographics, *Academy of Management Journal*, 33(1), pp 42–63

Mintzberg, H (1971) Managerial work: Analysis from observation, *Management Science*, 18(2), pp B–97

Mintzberg, H, Raisinghani, D and Theoret, A (1976) The structure of 'unstructured' decision processes, *Administrative Science Quarterly*, 21(2), pp 246–275

Nag, R, Hambrick, DC and Chen, MJ (2007) What is strategic management, really? Inductive derivation of a consensus definition of the field, *Strategic Management Journal*, 28(9), pp 935–55

O'Rourke, KH and Williamson, JG (2002) When did globalisation begin? *European Review of Economic History*, 6(1), pp 23–50

Pelletier, C and Raymond, L (2014) The IT strategic alignment process: A dynamic capabilities conceptualization. [Online] https://aisel.aisnet.org/cgi/viewcontent.cgi?article=1645&context=amcis2014

Peppard, J (2010) Unlocking the performance of the chief information officer (CIO), *California Management Review*, 52(4), pp 73–99

Peppard, J, Edwards, C and Lambert, R (2011) Clarifying the ambiguous role of the CIO, *MIS Quarterly Executive*, 10(1), pp 197–210

Pettigrew, AM (1977) Strategy formulation as a political process, *International Studies of Management and Organization*, 7(2), pp 78–87

Pohl, JW (1973) The influence of Antoine Henri de Jomini on Winfield Scott's campaign in the Mexican War, *The Southwestern Historical Quarterly*, 77(1), pp 85–110

Porter, ME (1983) *Cases in Competitive Strategy*, Simon and Schuster

Pugliese, A, Bezemer, PJ, Zattoni, A, Huse, M, Van den Bosch, FA and Volberda, HW (2009) Boards of directors' contribution to strategy: A literature review and research agenda, *Corporate Governance: An International Review*, 17(3), pp 292–306

Pyburn, PJ (1983) Linking the MIS plan with corporate strategy: An exploratory study, *MIS Quarterly*, 7(2), pp 1–14

Rebolledo, C and Jobin, M-H (2013) Manufacturing and supply alignment: Are different manufacturing strategies linked to different purchasing practices? *International Journal of Production Economics*, 146(1), pp 219–26

Rescher, N (1996) *Process Metaphysics: An introduction to process philosophy*, Suny Press

Reynolds, P and Yetton, P (2015) Aligning business and IT strategies in multi-business organizations, *Journal of Information Technology*, 30(2), pp 101–18

Roh, J, Hong, P and Min, H (2014) Implementation of a responsive supply chain strategy in global complexity: The case of manufacturing firms, *International Journal of Production Economics*, 147, pp 198–210

Ronda-Pupo, GA and Guerras-Martin, LÁ (2012) Dynamics of the evolution of the strategy concept 1962–2008: A co-word analysis, *Strategic Management Journal*, 33(2), pp 162–88

Sabherwal, R, Hirschheim, R and Goles, T (2001) The dynamics of alignment: Insights from a punctuated equilibrium model, *Organization Science*, 12(2), pp 179–97

Sheffi, Y (2001) Supply chain management under the threat of international terrorism, *The International Journal of Logistics Management*, 12(2), pp 1–11

Smith, WK (2014) Dynamic decision making: A model of senior leaders managing strategic paradoxes, *Academy of Management Journal*, 57(6), pp 1592–623

Sylla, C (2014) Managing perceived operational risk factors for effective supply-chain management, *AIP Conference Proceedings*, 1635(1), pp 19–26

Tavakolian, H (1989) Linking the information technology structure with organizational competitive strategy: A survey, *MIS Quarterly*, 13(3), pp 309–17

Teece, DJ, Pisano, G and Shuen, A (1997) Dynamic capabilities and strategic management, *Strategic Management Journal*, 18(7), pp 509–33

Volberda, HW, Baden-Fuller, C and Van Den Bosch, FA (2001) Mastering strategic renewal: Mobilising renewal journeys in multi-unit firms, *Long Range Planning*, 34(2), pp 159–78

Wagner, HT and Weitzel, T (2006) Operational IT business alignment as the missing link from IT strategy to firm success, *AMCIS 2006 Proceedings*, p 74

Walentowitz, K, Beimborn, D and Weitzel, T (2010) The influence of social structures on business/IT alignment, conference paper, JAIS Theory Development Workshop (Pre-ICIS Workshop), St Louis, MO

Wernerfelt, B (1984) A resource-based view of the firm, *Strategic Management Journal*, 5(2), pp 171–80

Whittington, R (1996) Strategy as practice, *Long Range Planning*, 29(5), pp 731–35

Wilson, A, Baptista, JJ and Galliers, R (2013) Performing strategy: Aligning processes in strategic IT. [Online] https://pdfs.semanticscholar.org/e769/c0aae0eb958b03c5a2c5312b7b483999244d.pdf

Wu, T, Wu, YCJ, Chen, YJ and Goh, M (2014) Aligning supply chain strategy with corporate environmental strategy: A contingency approach, *International Journal of Production Economics*, 147, pp 220–29

Zviran, M (1990) Relationships between organizational and information systems objectives: Some empirical evidence, *Journal of Management Information Systems*, 7(1), pp 65–84

Ad omnia paratus – prepared for anything

03

Under the current stewardship of Chief of Staff Vice Admiral Mark Mellett DSM, international renown surrounds the Irish Defence Forces (DF), regarded as one of the finest in the world in areas such as special forces (army rangers), bomb disposal, peace-keeping, humanitarian missions and shooting. In 2015, the army ranger wing placed first among 36 teams in the international and overall categories of the 15th international United States sniper competition in Fort Benning, Georgia. Other participants included US Rangers, Airborne, Marine Corps and Mountain Divisions, FBI SWAT, and teams from Britain, Canada, Germany and Denmark. The Irish Naval Service recently acquired three new state-of-the-art offshore patrol vessels, LÉ Samuel Beckett P61 (named after the 1969 Nobel laureate for literature), LÉ James Joyce P62 (after one of the most influential novelists of the last century) and LÉ William Butler Yeats P63 (after Ireland's greatest poet, who influenced the Irish revolution and ultimately the 1916 Easter Rising). These ships are presently deployed in rotation to assist the Italian authorities in humanitarian search and rescue operations in the Mediterranean, saving hundreds of lives to date.

Since 1958, Ireland (DF) has had a continuous presence on United Nations peace support operations in Central America, Russia, the former Yugoslavia, Cambodia, Lebanon, Iran, Iraq, Afghanistan, Kuwait, Namibia, Western Sahara, Liberia and East Timor, having become a UN member in 1955. Article 29.1 of the constitution states: 'Ireland affirms its devotion to the ideal of peace and friendly co-operation amongst nations founded on international justice and morality'. All operations must be mandated by the United Nations, approved by the Irish government, and, if the mission involves more than twelve personnel, further authorized by the Irish parliament (Dáil Éireann). This is triple-lock authorization. Such is their proud tradition of international conflict prevention and crisis management, that the DF have held the prestigious positions of Force Commander in Cyprus (UNFICYP), the Syria–Israel border (UNDOF) and Lebanon (UNIFIL), Chief of Staff of the United Nations Troops Supervision Organization in the Middle East (UNTSO) and the United Nations Mission in Liberia (UNMIL), and Chief Military Observer India-Pakistani Border (UNMOGIP). An Irish Major General was EU Operational Commander of the EUFOR Mission to TCHAD/CAR 2008-2009, an Irish General commanded the Multi National Task Force Centre in Kosovo (KFOR) in 2007, and DF Officers have served in key positions at the UN headquarters in New York (military.ie). The DF has also been prominent in the rapid-response EU Battlegroup concept. Quite impressive for such a small, neutral nation.

This chapter begins my empirical research to demonstrate that supply chain disruption is not confined to the external taxonomy of crises, disasters and breakdowns, but is sourced from internal strategic forces, the mitigation of which *must be* alignment of business and supply chain goals. Two cases are explored. In the first section, Ireland's role in the Nordic Battle Group is contextualized through historical reference, prior to an examination of how the logistics branch operationalized a service level agreement, both a governmental and senior management directive, to overcome significant challenges leading up to and during deployment. The success of this mission and the accolades received from their Swedish counterparts for the manner in which they overcame many situational challenges suggests that the proficiency and resolve of the Logistics Branch is indistinguishable from that of their peer divisions mentioned above. Commandant (Major) Robert Moriarty, then of Collins Barracks (Cork), the origins of which ironically reside in the threat of Napoleon and the French Revolution, articulated, over a series of interviews, the supply chain friction that he encountered and resolved, as officer in charge of logistics.

Chartered Institute of Logistics and Transport and the Irish Defence Forces

The opportunity to research the Irish Defence Forces came to fruition as a result of Commandant Laurence Egar generously hosting a very insightful Chartered Institute of Logistics and Transport (CILT) Southern Section event at Collins Barracks on 16 June 2016. A guided tour of the military museum and an impressive display of military logistical equipment captivated the attendees. However, this preceded what was to be the main highlight of the evening, certainly for me, which was an impactful Nordic Battle Group presentation by then Captain Moriarty. Impactful in the sense that, despite my 20 years' experience, logistics was profoundly brought to life for me that evening.

Grainne Lynch, Chairperson, CILT Southern Section, kindly asked me to write an article on this topic, published in August 2017 in the CILT journal, LinkLine. Extending from this, the second section summarizes the historical United Nations peace support operations of the Irish Defence Forces, before focusing on the present deployment of troops in Lebanon. Once again, the recently promoted Commandant Moriarty, this time in the capacity of Irish–Finnish Battalion logistics officer, generously facilitated this research by taking time out of his schedule to make a number of video calls.

Nordic Battle Group: historical context

The Nordic location of Finlandia Hall in Helsinki during the summer of 1975 appropriately sets the scene for Ireland's contribution to the pursuit of global security. Attended by then Taoiseach (prime minister), Liam Cosgrave, the Conference on Security and Co-operation in Europe (CSCE) resulted in the signing of the non-binding Helsinki Accords aimed at reducing tensions between the Communist bloc and the West. European Union members subsequently signed the Helsinki Headline Goal 1999 in accordance with the Common Security and Defence Policy (CSDP), which created a Helsinki Force Catalogue to enable the completion of so-called Petersburg Tasks (Petersburg Declaration 1992). These included humanitarian and rescue, peacekeeping and crisis management tasks. Primarily, it was considered that it took too long to raise a United Nations reactionary force to deal with global disruptions and crises, and from this, an EU Battlegroup was established, now comprising 18 sub-groups of small, independent, self-sufficient, rapid-response units capable of deployment in a theatre of operation (the market-place of the military).

One such unit is the Nordic Battle Group (NBG), which has been active since 2008 and has a force of 2,500 troops (soldiers). NBG members include Sweden, Finland, Norway (despite non-EU membership), Republic of Ireland, Estonia, Latvia and Lithuania. This is not a permanent unit, rather it is mobilized on a rotational basis and was headquartered in Enköping, Sweden, for NBG 2015-1, the focus of this study. A modular organization

> with a mechanized infantry battalion is at the core of the unit, but since 2011 a framework exists for the integration of additional resources ranging from artillery, air defence, and intelligence, to additional logistical support. The Republic of Ireland, with the second largest troop count behind Sweden, is the eyes and ears of the Battlegroup, providing an ISTAR component: intelligence, surveillance, target acquisition and reconnaissance. However, another vital Irish element has been the aforementioned logistical support, the execution of which has met with and overcome many challenges, both strategic and tactical.

Nordic Battle Group: Irish Defence Forces rotation

The Irish Defence Forces operational rotation of the Nordic Battle Group (NBG 2015-1) spanned 18 months, with training taking place between January and December 2014, before a six-month 72-hour on-call period from January to June 2015, proceeded by the German Battlegroup who stood to for the next six months, succeeded by the British Battlegroup in 2016, and so forth. From an Irish perspective, the mission statement, a memorandum of understanding (MOU) signed by the Deputy Chief of Staff (D-COS) of the Irish Defence Forces, mandated the Director of Logistics of the Irish Defence Forces HQ in McKee Barracks, Dublin, to have the capability to set up a theatre of operation anywhere in the world within a 72-hour notice period from its base in Collins Barracks, Cork.

To develop this capability, an expeditionary logistics concept was initiated to integrate with the Swedish armed forces and set up within a green field site in Skillingaryd on a one-month deployment. This concept derived from the commanding officer for this operation, Lieutenant Colonel Paul Carey, who issued a commander's intent of operation to Commandant Robert Moriarty to lead tactical deployment, supported by Commandant James Hourigan at strategic procurement level. This outlined the purpose, method and end state of the mission. Finalizing the method was subject to constant, and at times innovative, group training and integration, known also as training, tactical and procedures (TTPs). The memorandum of understanding adopted a non-traditional all-arms approach that facilitated cross-organizational support to the battle group, such as knowledge and equipment sharing.

Commandant Moriarty was issued with Armaments and Equipment (AAE) and CS-41 documents that outlined the available resources to meet the mission objectives, together with the empowerment, through D-COS support, to internally 're-distribute' equipment as needed. This was effectively what we would know as a service level agreement. Supply, sustain and maintain were the tenets applied to developing a self-sufficient unit of excellence, food and hygiene being at the forefront of considerations, using a front load policy that meant positioning all personnel and equipment in Sweden at the start of the operation. By contrast, militaries such as Sweden used a push policy, whereby strategic air support was used to sustain units as needed. Future deployment would necessitate integration with the Swedish push policy, as there are limitations to front loading. The AAE and CS-41 made certain provisions from which certain challenges arose within a broad categorization of 'constraints, restrictions, freedoms':

- 51 personnel included four officers, medical and signals (communication) detachments, three engineers, three ordnances to maintain equipment such as weapons (valued at €1.6m) and catering systems, transportation which included two DAF 6x6 trucks, each with two drivers.
- 19 containers (660 CBM and 164,400kg, with a combined value of €3.8m), carried tents on two units, 3,000 pack rations within a 20' reefer, capable of sustaining the brigade for 20 days in a remote environment as a form of redundancy, dry goods that complemented the Irish policy of purchasing fresh produce from the local community, fuel pod, ammunition, pyrotechnics, which needed to be in a separate container and thereby not completely utilized, weapons systems, together with dangerous goods certificates, and generators.
- Due to the front load policy, and for security reasons, the Irish moved ammunition, baggage, a fuel pod, generators, weapons and communications to the brigade assembly point in Skillingaryd, Sweden, in advance of the exercise. This included a C2 container housing the Tactical Operations Centre (TOC) which became the epicentre of the site from which all other elements developed.

The main strategy, or NBG logistical concept, was to conduct operations, regardless of environment, from 30 to 120 days, characterized by a high level of flexibility, modularity and endurance. A statement of requirement (SOR) provisioned the use of host nation support (HNS), contractor support to operations (CSO), third party logistic support (TPLS) and other multinational (including unconventional) solutions to minimize challenges. Supply chain disruptions are contextual and environment-specific, and despite the availability of an After-Action Review (AAR) from a previous exercise (NBG 2011), which was certainly beneficial, a number of challenges arose at various stages of operational preparations.

For example, in advance of the exercise in August 2014, Commandant Moriarty attended a SOR coordination conference in Sweden and discovered that an MOU signed between the Irish and Swedish Governments did not legislate for electricity maintenance, which was assumed (as with standard deployment policy) would be provided by the Swedish forces. The DF cannot have more than 850 troops overseas at any one time, and a subset of the SOR, a Raise and Concentration Order (RCO), did not permit additional electricians, etc. The Irish needed a solution. One option was to secure site generators for the exercise, but the challenge was that these were all deployed on other missions, and had to be transported in pairs, each one in a 20-foot container, necessitating an unplanned additional sealift with an engineering detachment. Instead, an improvisation was made to transport smaller generators and lighting systems within the allocated 19 containers on the manifest.

The mission readiness exercise (MRE), which commenced in June 2014, giving clearance to build all systems, identified further challenges. An example in the corporate world would be a pilot product launch. An initial problem concerned the newly purchased HP 508 tents, which were not fit for purpose, due to the fact that they were not previously integrated into the defence forces, and this resulted in damage (note: visualize substantial marquees housing a large contingent of troops, kitchen, dining hall, sleeping quarters, etc, hence their criticality). Whilst the tents were erected through power from vehicles, there were three topside struts that needed to be secured manually and the troops simply could not reach these without potential injury. Therefore, A-frame ladders were added to the manifest and these were placed neatly to the rear of the tent racking systems during transportation to Sweden.

These systems were themselves not without challenges, in particular with regard to optimization of container space, for which an outsourced solution was sought. Standard state procurement legislates the tendering of three requests for quotations to vendors (RFQs). Timeframe was a key component to NBG tenders, coupled with the vendor listening to very specific needs. Certain suppliers offered generic storage units for the transport of tents, whereas the successful company (TDH Design Engineering) invested time and resources into designing a bespoke racking system with significantly improved utilization. This was an example of the Irish Defence Forces investing in the local community and supporting a start-up SME in East Cork. The additional engineering cost of this was offset by:

- additional space to take an armoured vehicle, thereby increasing troop safety;
- one less (soft-skin) truck meaning one less driver, enabling one additional specialist to support the maintenance of the site. In addition, one less 'soft-skin' means less protection needed from a security perspective;
- one less container on a ship or aircraft, meaning less weight, resulting in greater fuel efficiency, and by default incremental cost savings on subsequent DF missions;
- maximum return for the tax payer by coordinating procurement, engineering and operations. Commandant Moriarty was particularly proud of this triangular alignment.

Other adjustments to the manifest were the inclusion of tent repair kits and clip flooring to prevent floor damage. The tents simply were not soldier-proof and needed specialist assembly. Generators for the mission were also found to be temperamental but this was resolved through specialist training and maintenance. The DF were burning 60 litres of fuel per day per heating system (VAM), a problem for both cold and hot climates, twice as much as the Swedes, who used built-in thermostats and lagging systems, which not only reduced fuel usage, but also evenly distributed heat throughout the tents. This was identified as a need after the mission but did not materialize during MRE. Food portion sizes and storage of plates was resolved by securing stackable and sectioned prison service plates.

The Raise and Concentration Order (RCO) also did not provide for cooks and it was recognized that the field kitchen should be part of exercise/certification training in Ireland. Both the provision of a pot wash facility (hygiene being so critical), since procured as part of the capability development of the NBG, and the leasing of local sanitation equipment (dropped on site) were also identified. In addition, ordnance technicians needed to be co-located with the field kitchen in order to maintain the VAMs. In terms of information systems, the TOC enabled increased situational awareness, range of operation and capabilities when delivering orders, a significant increase in data transfer rate, and the provision of live streaming. However, the satellite communications link was intermittent, and additional equipment was needed, such as, batteries, laptops and phones. Constant training in all computer information systems was essential.

Movement of vehicles also presented challenges and it was immediately evident that a low-loader would be extremely beneficial for future rotations. Bulk collection was arranged for all Mowags (armoured) and six Nissans, which resulted in significant time and labour savings. By contrast, the collection of five infantry light tactical vehicles (LTAVs) was not as coordinated, due to other mission needs, and this caused minor delays. This strategy was later adopted for the transfer of vehicles to the German Battlegroup. Another consideration was the training of drivers and fitters to enable licences and qualifications in fuel pod operation, and LTAV/Mowag maintenance. In the absence of military aircraft, a third party logistics (3PL) ocean freight solution was needed.

Equipment was loaded at Ringaskiddy Port using LIFO (last in/first out) bound for Halmstad Port in Sweden. The loading concept of choice was RO-RO (roll on/roll off, eight-hour operation) but LO-LO (lift on/lift off, 20-hour operation) was the procured system due to 3PL availability and sailing schedules. This presented another immediate challenge in that it would have required two drivers moving four containers at a time from Halmstad to the brigade assembly point 141km away in Skillingaryd. Commandant James Hourigan expertly negotiated with the Swedish forces and secured their assistance to move 13 of the Irish containers using seven of their trucks. Another challenge was that these movements necessitated weapons declarations and thereby the availability of specialist weapons inspectors at specific points along the route to Sweden. This needed to be factored into the transit time. Finally, there were planning considerations such as parking space for 20 containers, stores requirement for 660 cubic metres, and storage bays for the Mowag and LTAV fleet including a provision for trickle charging.

Ireland was again involved from July to December 2016, as part of the German–Czech–Austrian Battlegroup. The North Atlantic Treaty Organization (NATO) established in August 1949 remains the most important defence organization for most European Union countries, Ireland not being one of them, but the Battlegroup concept gave EU members a 'soft power' to act autonomously if needed (Elshout, 2016). However, since its inception, no group has been actively deployed, for several reasons such as political inertia, divergences in strategic cultures, a varying range of capabilities, financial restrictions, and Atlanticism versus Europeanism (willingness or not to deploy outside of Europe), emphasized through the case of Germany and

Poland (Chappell, 2009). In addition, there is a high cost to train groups, troops may be needed in their home countries, and the limited operational rotation period may be a significant restriction. Former Swedish Foreign Minister Carl Bildt warned that if a group does not see military action soon, the concept would fade away (Andersson, 2015). Brexit is also a threat to the concept, given that Britain is one of the largest EU military powers. Focus is now turning from Battlegroup to United Nations operations.

Irish Defence Forces: United Nations peace support operations

The Irish Defence Forces are presently involved in many global missions. 'There are very deep emotional ties between the United Nations and Ireland' (Burke and Marley, 2015). In Africa, there are 17 personnel deployed between MINURSO on the north-west African coast (since September 1991), a dispute over the former Spanish Sahara, MONUC, an observer mission in the Democratic Republic of Congo (since June 2001), and EUTM, training of the Mali security forces (since February 2013), while in Asia seven personnel are assisting with ISAF, established to secure peace and stability in Afghanistan (since December 2001). There are 19 personnel across missions in Europe, EUFOR/SFOR in Bosnia Herzegovina (since May 1997) and KFOR in Kosovo (since August 1999). In the Middle East 12 personnel are operating in Syria, Jordan, Lebanon and Israel as part of UNTSO (since December 1958), established in 1948 to monitor truce agreements following conflict in Palestine.

More substantial is a battalion of 138 personnel in the Golan Heights to manage the disengagement of Israeli and Syrian forces following the end of the Yom Kippur War, as part of UNDOF (since September 2013). UNDOF (the UN Disengagement Observer Force) is the only military presence permitted in this 80km separation area, and the DF provide reinforcement, reaction, escort and other operations as the Force Mobile Reserve. This is a quick response force (QRF) and mechanized capability is critical. Ireland is aiming to gain a seat on the UN Security Council, and UNDOF provides a good political platform to achieve this. As we speak (23 March 2018), 130 personnel of the 57th Infantry Group are marching towards Kilkenny Castle to be reviewed by the Minister with Responsibility for Defence, Mr Paul Kehoe, TD, accompanied by the Deputy Chief of Staff (Operations), Major

General Kieran Brennan, prior to their six-month deployment to Syria, becoming the 10th contingent to do so. 'Unfortunately, this service has not been without cost. To date 85 members of the Defence Forces have given their lives in the cause of world peace' (military.ie).

I am reminded of the Siege of Jadotville in September 1961, when a UN contingent of 155 Irish soldiers, with limited ammunition and no access to resupply or reinforcement, under the command of Commandant Pat Quinlan, held their ground for six days against attacking waves of Katanga Gendarmerie troops in Congo-Léopoldville, Central Africa. Eventually the Irish soldiers were captured and imprisoned for one month, incredibly with no loss of life. However, 300 Katanga Gendarmerie troops were killed and up to 1,000 wounded in the conflict. The DF have done just as well in Syria. On 30 August 2014, Al-Qaeda's affiliate Jabhat al-Nusra attacked DF troops, having taken 45 Fijian soldiers hostage, seized UNDOF bases, weapons and equipment, and surrounded two further bases manned by Filipino troops, demanding their surrender. Despite being under substantial firepower, the Irish troops successfully relieved and evacuated 93 of their encircled comrades while maintaining their own security (Burke and Marley, 2015). It is worth repeating... Quite impressive for such a small, neutral nation. Now to Lebanon, and Commandant Robert Moriarty.

United Nations Interim Force in Lebanon

An Israeli–Palestinian conflict from 1968 to 1977, in which the Palestine Liberation Organization (PLO), strengthened by 3,000 returning militants from the Jordanian Civil War, established a quasi-state in southern Lebanon, a Lebanese Civil War (1975–90) between the Maronite Christians and Druze, and Muslims, and an Israeli bombing in November 1977, killing 70 mainly Lebanese, provide a simplistic background to the tensions that led to the Irish Defence Forces' presence in this region. In March 1978, Khalil Ibrahim al-Wazir, founder of the nationalist party Fatah, and an aide of PLO Chairman Yasser Arafat, planned to take control of a hotel in Tel Aviv and hold hostages in exchange for Palestinian prisoners in Israel, and also to disrupt Israeli–Egyptian peace talks between Menachem Begin (Israeli Prime Minister) and Anwar Sadat (Egyptian President). Fatah did not reach the hotel because of a navigation issue, and instead hijacked a bus, having first murdered an American tourist on a nearby beach, and 38 Israeli civilians were subsequently killed in what was named the Coastal Road Massacre. The response was Operation Litani, an invasion of south Lebanon by the Israeli Defence Forces, and the death of 2,000 Lebanese and Palestinians.

The United Nations Interim Force in Lebanon (UNIFIL) was immediately established to supervise the withdrawal of Israeli forces and restore peace and security to the area. Ireland has been a part of UNIFIL since May 1978. Conflict did not end in 1978. In May 1982, the Reagan administration in the United States was formulating policy under Secretary of State Alexander Haig to end the Persian Gulf War between Iran and Iraq that had been raging since September 1980, and to also end the internal strife in Lebanon. This all fell apart two weeks later. An attempted assassination of the Israeli ambassador to Great Britain was blamed on the PLO. In fact, it was carried out by Abu Nidal of the Fatah Revolutionary Council, who was expelled from the PLO in 1974. Despite a 10-month cease-fire of peace and tranquillity, Israel bombed PLO positions in Beirut. There was no political cause for the strike. It was a military action. This was in complete contrast with the teachings of Carl von Clausewitz: 'The subordination of the political point of view to the military would be unreasonable, for policy has created the war; policy is the intelligent factor, war only the instrument, and not the reverse' (Davis, 1995). The conflict persists to this day.

For instance, an Iran-funded political and military organization comprising pro-Syrian Shia Muslims, Hizbullah (Party of God), emerged in 1982 as the Lebanese resistance to Israel. They were instrumental in the departure of the last Israeli troops from Lebanon in 2000 and they have remained in place, despite being a terrorist organization, due to a weak Lebanese state (Makdisi, 2011). The US invasion of Iraq in 2003 changed the situation again, when the US and France sponsored UN Resolution 1559 to withdraw Syria from Lebanon, and to disband all remaining militias. This 'challenged both Hizbullah's armed presence, as well as its status as the prime national resistance movement' (Makdisi *et al*, 2009). Subsequently, Hizbullah captured two Israeli soldiers, killing three others, in a 2006 cross-border attack, and a huge, destructive war between the nations ensued. UN Resolution 1701 halted the war. This was coined UNIFIL II due to a more robust mandate.

The Irish Defence Forces had a continuous infantry battalion in Tibnin on a six-month rotation from May 1978 to November 2001, patrolling an area of approximately 100 square kilometres. A mobile mechanized infantry company returned on 31 October 2006 for 12 months alongside a Finnish engineering company as part of a joint Irish–Finnish Battalion. A mechanized infantry battalion of 440 personnel again deployed in June 2011, manning two posts along the Blue Line, a border demarcation between Lebanon and Israel established by the United Nations on 7 June 2000. The unit was equipped with Mowag Piranha III APCs, Light Tactical Armoured Vehicles (GR32), heavy machine guns, anti-tank guns and Javelin missiles, heavy and medium mortars, and reconnaissance surveillance equipment. In November 2013, the DF changed operations to a 336-personnel 'high visibility, low profile' infantry group.

Together with a contingent from Finland and a platoon of 38 Estonian soldiers, they form(ed) IRISHFINBATT based at UNP 2-45 in UNIFIL Sector West (military.ie). This sector is also supported by Ghanaian, Italian, Korean and Malaysian battalions. The east sector consists of Indian, Indonesian, Nepalese and Spanish battalions. Seven Brazilian naval vessels provide a maritime task force, and the total mission strength is 10,490 uniformed troops. Ireland is the largest per capita troop contributor (Lawrence et al, 2016).

On 1 November 2017, Commandant Robert Moriarty deployed for six months, in time to see the December visit of Taoiseach (Prime Minister) Leo Varadkar to a memorial erected to commemorate the 47 Irish peacekeepers who have lost their lives serving in Lebanon. With four decades of peace support operations, you would assume a degree of internal stability to this current mission, and that the only supply chain disruption would come from the external forces of Hamas, Hizbullah, Fatah, Israel or Syria. Not so in this case. In December, the Finland mandate expired (this was renewed annually) and they withdrew from the mission. This came as a complete surprise. A sudden unplannable change.

Both forces have a history of strong collaboration since the establishment of UNIFIL and developed joint operating capability through regular overseas pre-deployment training, alternating between Irish and Finnish installations, and of course through active duty together. Each quarter they formally held joint meetings at national headquarters (J-level) in the format of a Bilateral Military Coordination Group. In these meetings, issues reported by battalion staff (S-level) from the area of operation (AO) were resolved. It could never have been envisaged at an operations level that such a harmonized partnership would not continue. This significant disruption presented two major challenges to the mission:

1 Loss of serious operating capability:

- A mechanized company of 130 Finnish personnel including an integrated Estonian platoon of 38 soldiers. This provided a manoeuvring element that conveyed presence in the area of operation (AO).
- A 15-tonne armoured personnel carrier (APC) fleet of 11 vehicles, a critical capability in the event of threat levels increasing, weapons systems (including ammunition and storage) and ancillary equipment.
- Infrastructure, barrack services, welfare facilities to keep up morale, and a SEPURA communications system with 99 per cent coverage of the area of operation.

2 Force protection had to be maintained:

- Security could not be compromised and in the immediate aftermath of the Finland withdrawal, the DF troops had to work twice as hard to fill the void within significant budgetary restrictions. Such restrictions had already been tested, with troop clothing requirements and other critical supplies, supplies that were (not ideally) being pushed from Ireland as opposed to being positioned in advance. Therefore, this posed a serious challenge of having to potentially increase troop presence by 33 per cent without a corresponding 33 per cent increase in finances (this remains under government departmental consideration, as a secondary priority to APC replacement). This situation was heightened when considering that 25 per cent of the troops did not have overseas experience. Despite the reduced resources and capability shortfall, outputs simply could not fall. An alternative resolution is to secure a new partner nation (also under consideration at government level).
- A further impediment was that a major refurbishment program was in progress to send the DF fleet of Mowags (APCs) from the previous six-month rotation to Switzerland. Such a task was of course important, but one can only imagine the sense of exasperation within the area of operation, watching these vehicles being loaded on to ocean vessels while Finland were simultaneously removing their fleet (and combat support capability).
- The Finnish fleet of APCs needed to be replaced with utility vehicles (SUVs) that now became mission critical but did not have the same capability. These are end of production, high-end vehicles, for which the DF had no doctrine or training. Maintenance is a learning curve, and during our first discussion, already two were off the road. This of course put significant strain on mechanical fitters to keep these vehicles

90 Supply Chain Disruption

operational and there was a much greater demand on spare parts. Further challenges included fuel and water. These particular Scania and Ford SUVs take diesel in line with NATO standard operating procedures, a fuel that is restricted in Lebanon, and diesel engine parts are consequently difficult to source. Around 60,000 litres of water are used daily, and SUVs that cannot have water access will not function. Two water trucks are used, each draws 10,000 litres and so the DF lifts 20,000 litres three times per day.

- An ironic twist of circumstance is that there is no financial DF incentive to maintain equipment and this points to extreme professionalism and discipline. Fleets are positioned as contingent owned equipment (COE) under a United Nations wet-lease. The United Nations in turn performs quarterly checks of all vehicles and reimburse annually. However, this is not into the DF account, but into a general government fund. Operationally, of course, maintenance is critical, and it is the right thing to do for the wider organization.

'Outputs simply could not fall' and fall they did not. In particular, the Finland withdrawal of the mechanized company (Mech Coy), APC fleet, weapons systems and other ancillary equipment potentially had the most direct impact on operations, and therefore, to assess the gravity of the situation, this initiated an analysis system taught in the DF military college known as the military decision making process (MDMP), involving the operations officer (S3) and the logistics officer (S4). According to Comdt Moriarty (S4), 'this is a thought process that we apply when presented with planning issues and can take several hours, it can be laborious and time consuming, but it ensures that no areas are missed'. In terms of strategic alignment and response to supply chain disruption, this process is a lesson for all domains in our profession. This analysis (including here, Comdt Moriarty comments and some MDMP actuals) considers:

- What is your higher commanders' intent? In this context, the intent (also called the Factor) stated that Finland would not renew its current memorandum of understanding, indicating that it would withdraw significant quantities of assets to Finland and UNP 9-1 (another deployment) but was prepared to leave some infrastructure in UNP 2-45 (DF post in Lebanon) for sale or lease to the DF. Comdt Moriarty (S4) was requested to conduct analysis of FINCON (Finland contingent) equipment, implications of its withdrawal and to provide costing to national headquarters (J4). The deduced disruption was that the withdrawal of FINCON would mean a reduction of one-third of IRISHFINBATT operating capability. Mitigation against this reduction was an examination of the specific shortfall in equipment and the means by which Ireland needed to increase its contribution, or alternatively if it required a new strategic partner. The logistics (4) function was the main effort in this task, a task and purpose that needed to be achieved. Success was dependent on obtaining a costed inventory of FINCON equipment to be withdrawn and analyses of the impact of its withdrawal to IRCON (Irish contingent). All information obtained at the tactical level was to be forwarded to the strategic (J4) level in order to inform the strategic decision-making process.

- What are your specific tasks to achieve? The main (superior officer-issued) task was for S4 to conduct analyses of the impact on IRCON of the FINCON withdrawal. This required clarification from higher headquarters (but in other contexts and cases could also be directed at subordinate staff) on whether Ireland's intent was to move to full battalion strength or whether a new strategic level partner was to be sought. Planning guidance (PG) tasked the operations officer (S3) to advise the S4 on the operational imperatives of such a withdrawal with emphasis on combat support requirements (namely APCs) to ensure credibility in DF posture. PG tasked the S4 to liaise with FINCON logistics to obtain a complete inventory and cost of the contingent owned equipment (COE) to be withdrawn in order to provide a cost estimate to J4 and subhead managers. This was anticipatory combat service support. S4 was also tasked under planning guidance to identify critical infrastructure required by IRCON if it increased its battalion strength, such as vehicle servicing and logistics storage tents. A final task was to liaise with UNIFIL HQ on developments. The main purpose of these tasks was to prevent a reduction in Ireland's capability to provide a safe and secure environment in its area of operation and to provide efficient combat service support planning on the FINCON withdrawal. The planning guidance is a set of constraints, restrictions and freedoms (or, in military language, 'left and right of arc') and was the battalion commander instrument to communicate all needs to the S4.

- What are your constraints (must do), restrictions (cannot do) and freedoms (can do)? Assets available (personnel/equipment), acceptable risk (on UN operations, the DF must accept some level of risk but mitigate against it), TEST (time, opposing capabilities, size of AO, terrain), actual (Finns are pulling out) or likely changes (new partner nation) in planning, are there any 'implied' tasks not specifically mentioned by higher HQ but required? For example, a specific task is to 'repatriate vehicles' but implied tasks arising from that are liaison with customs and shipping agents, and the movement of the vehicles, essential tasks (specified tasks with possible vital implied tasks added in).

One can observe that this approach ensures that the supply chain division does not breach the boundaries of the organizations' core competencies and suggests that the role of our profession is execution. Perhaps this should be applied to all 'stable' situations to reduce potential disruption and thereby the *gap of pain* in strategic implementations. For the DF, this process of analysis resulted in a 'restated mission for the unit', from which a number of papers were constructed at a tactical (ground) level, to inform the strategic (decision-making) level. One very positive outcome of the planning guidance was a capability development in the form of a DF investment in a communications system similar to SEPURA, for which a budget allocation was secured, and a tender was initiated. This is categorized as contingent owned equipment (COE) and therefore the Irish government would be reimbursed by the UN under a wet-lease agreement. In addition to this, Comdt Moriarty forwarded a new list of equipment to be added to a new memorandum of understanding (MOU) to be signed by Ireland and the United Nations.

The remaining Finnish loss of infrastructure, barrack services and welfare facilities are under negotiation for purchase but again the DF have re-shaped this to their benefit. For example, when factoring in the cost of disassembly, transport to Finland, and depreciation of maintenance vehicle servicing tents (MVSTs), Comdt Moriarty secured this equipment for less than the standard purchase price. Another big win. Other items of infrastructure were identified as non-essential, such as container units for accommodation or offices, for which an offer at a fraction of their value was made. In the words of Comdt Moriarty, 'Divorces are not cheap!' Nevertheless, the DF have secured additional combat support capability at an absolute cost to the Irish tax payer of less than 18 per cent of market value. This is supply chain resilience in action, a demonstration of an organization with the ability to 'evolve to a new and more desirable state after being severely disturbed' (Yang and Xu, 2015) ... by policy.

Supply chain disruption: Irish Defence Forces

The source of the supply chain disruption described here is *policy*. For the combined Nordic Battle Group and UNIFIL missions I am going to dispense with a preparatory phase so as not to absorb into the discussion the purpose of the one-month joint exercise in Skillingaryd Sweden, or indeed the mission readiness exercise prior to deployment to Sweden, as this was a clearance to build all systems, or the coordinated Irish and Finnish pre-deployment training. Whilst Skillingaryd unearthed further supply chain friction, this was not caused by the mission itself, but by the AAE and CS41 strategic documents. I say this because the literature informs of a phased response to disruption. In equal measure, I found recovery to be consequential to the response. One could argue that an after-action review forms part of the recovery. However, it seems that this instrument is based on conditions that are too contextual and conditional, and do not influence improved business to supply chain strategic alignment. This viewpoint is strengthened by a 2016 joint report from the International Centre for Defence and Security, and the Irish Department of Foreign Affairs and Trade, in relation to Ireland, Finland and Estonia in UNIFIL, which concluded that: 'there does not appear to be a high-level process for identifying the strengths, weaknesses, successes and failures of each rotation. There is certainly no such exercise involving all three states, nor has the United Nations undertaken a substantive and critical appraisal of the UNIFIL mission' (Lawrence *et al*, 2016). This indicates that supply chain challenges and successes (operational and financial) are not factored into the strategic renewal process. This is what we need to change as a profession.

So, what exactly do we want to change as a result of these and further case studies? Firstly, we must increase our understanding of supply chain managers' engagement in the process of dynamic business to supply chain strategic alignment, within the context of supply chain disruption, and secondly, as suggested by Wu *et al* (2014), contribute to the broadening of supply chain management to an integrated perspective across the top management team rather than a uni-dimensional and dichotomous view. Extending from these aims are specific objectives:

- *Determine how supply chain managers operationally identify, predict, cope and recover from supply chain disruptions:* The Nordic Battle Group and UNIFIL disruptions could not have been identified or predicted in the absence of business to supply chain strategic alignment. Therefore, Comdt Moriarty had to respond to AAE and CS-41 strategic documents that needed to be reshaped to situational needs, whilst staying inside the core competencies of the DF, and the sudden change of the UNIFIL withdrawal of Finland after a partnership that dated back to May 2012. The logistics branch needed to cope with the non-provision of electricity, HP 508 tent equipment that was not fit for purpose, a troop profile that did not sufficiently resource the mission, an inadequate heating system, the absence of the most efficient ocean vessel loading concept, and the loss of a mechanized company, APC fleet, weapons and communications systems, infrastructure, barrack services and welfare facilities. The coping mechanism applied in each case by Comdt Moriarty resulted in recovery that was an evolution to a new and more desirable state. On a general note, it is important to acknowledge that the DF pre-positions (prepares) redundant supplies based on average consumption to mitigate supply chain risk. According to United Nations standard operating procedures at least 14 days of supply (DOS) must be held in reserve. For instance, the average daily consumption of diesel is 2,000 litres and therefore 28,000 litres are maintained. This can only be consumed with the authority of Comdt Moriarty in the event of an emergency, or for stock rotation. The commanding officer must be informed any time stock levels go below the required DOS.

- *Identify which phases in the supply chain disruption process require engagement with top management to implement strategic solutions aligned to business goals:* This objective will develop throughout the case investigations. In the case of the DF, engagement came during the response phases of the sudden disruptive events, the nature of which were impossible to predict and identify (prepare for) in advance. This response demonstrated a supply chain that was both agile and fully flexible.

- *Consequently, determine whether a categorization of supply chain strategy exists, such as a tier consisting of strategies that can be implemented autonomously by the supply chain division, and a tier or tiers that requires negotiation across the top management team prior to implementation, to collaboratively mitigate risk:* Yes, it was found that negotiation across the top management team was needed to re-shape the troop profile for Skillingaryd, such as the provision of cooks and ordnance technicians, or to secure a gross investment to the value of €820,000 for combat capability developments in Lebanon. The absolute cost of this investment was €150,000 and this value creation was largely due to the expertise at S-level, comprising price negotiation and wet-leasing. Fully flexible. A sub-tier of autonomous tactical response was found in the context of supply chain friction such as solutions to electricity provision, robust tent infrastructure, improved container utilization, vehicle movement in Skillingaryd, provision of SUVs, the efficient use of mechanical fitters, and provision of petrol and water. Agility. This autonomous tactical sub-category also demonstrated value creation that transcended the contextual and situational elements of the mission at hand.

- *Determine how supply chain managers engage with the top management team in the process of aligning business and supply chain strategies, thereby identifying key enablers and inhibitors:* Reynolds and Yetton (2015) said that there is little guidance on how to build and sustain alignment. Therefore, the military decision-making process (MDMP) is a valuable tool. This analyses supply chain capabilities and tasks whilst simultaneously aligning with top management team strategy (the foremost consideration) and respecting the boundaries of core competencies (restrictions and TEST). Even in such a directed environment as the military, I suggest that this is a tool that should be applied to all formal strategic situations at the formulation stage, to reduce the *gap of pain* in responding to disruption. This is especially true of an organization that repeatedly demonstrates sustainable value creation (when coping with, and triumphing over sudden change events), compounded by the fact that policy itself is a source of disruption. Strategic alignment does not diminish TMT authority.

- *Develop a process model that establishes the phases of supply chain managers' engagement in dynamic business to supply chain strategic alignment*: This will be finalized once all organizational cases have been examined. The contributions of the DF case studies alone validate the concepts of policy as a source of disruption (disruption that contributed to an extended *gap of pain*, in the absence of enemy engagement), the existence of strategic friction, and the recognition of both an autonomous tactical tier and a strategic negotiation tier within supply chain management. As the model progresses and evolves, we can consider an MDMP-type process at both the strategic formulation stage and during the disruption response phase. We also need to include value creation as a proactive force rather than exclusively a reactive force.

As I now conclude this chapter, I wish the Irish Defence Forces a safe journey in all its endeavours. It has been my privilege to be given a small glimpse into such a highly professional organization and am reassured that the concepts introduced in Chapter 2 are validated thus far. The origins of these concepts lie within the military and now I turn my attention to the humanitarian, freight and logistics, and corporate worlds in search of further validation. I also take a break from historical references, but their critical importance must be maintained in the battle against supply chain disruption.

'Those who cannot remember the past are condemned to repeat it.'
George Santayana

References

Andersson, JJ (2015) If not now, when? The Nordic EU battlegroup, *EUISS Alert*, 11, p 2015

Burke, E and Marley, J (2015) *Walking Point for Peace: An Irish view on the state of UN peacekeeping*, Center on International Cooperation

Chappell, L (2009). Differing member state approaches to the development of the EU Battlegroup Concept: Implications for CSDP, *European Security*, **18**(4), pp 417–39

Davis, HT (1995) *40km into Lebanon: Israel's 1982 invasion*, Diane Publishing

Elshout, A (2016) Plan voor militaire macht Europa komt op pikant moment, de Volkskrant, 29 June

Lawrence, T, Jermalavičius, T and Bulakh, A (2016) *Soldiers of Peace: Estonia, Finland and Ireland in UNIFIL*. [Online] https://icds.ee/wp-content/uploads/2016/ICDS_Report_Soldiers_of_Peace_December_2016.pdf

Makdisi, K (2011) Constructing Security Council Resolution 1701 for Lebanon in the shadow of the 'War on Terror', *International Peacekeeping*, **18**(1), pp 4–20

Makdisi, K, Göksel, T, Hauck, HB and Reigeluth, S (2009) UNIFIL II: Emerging and evolving European engagement in Lebanon and the Middle Eas, EUROMESCO paper, (76)

Military.ie (2018) Home: Defence forces. [Online] http://www.military.ie/home/

Reynolds, P and Yetton, P (2015) Aligning business and IT strategies in multi-business organizations, *Journal of Information Technology*, **30**(2), pp 101–18

Wu, T, Wu, YCJ, Chen, YJ and Goh, M (2014) Aligning supply chain strategy with corporate environmental strategy: A contingency approach, *International Journal of Production Economics*, **147**, pp 220–29

Yang, Y and Xu, X (2015) Post-disaster grain supply chain resilience with government aid, *Transportation Research Part E: Logistics and transportation review*, **76**, pp 139–59

The art of responding to disruption through the physical supply chain

04

On 27 March 2018 my commute home from the office took the usual route through Cork City. But on this day? Mayhem. Chaos. Traffic was at a complete standstill. Cars were entering bus lanes, buses were crossing over and blocking the main flow. Emergency services had no way of getting through to the hospital or scenes of accidents, and freight trucks were missing ETA commitments. Between flashing lights, sirens and car horns, Armageddon had finally reached the 'real capital' of Ireland. I imagined (because I had time) plant warehouses across the north side of the city such as Yves Rocher and the European Headquarters of Apple Inc, or Stryker NeuroVascular and Boston Scientific just to the west from where my journey began. This situation would cause late deliveries and supply chain disruption to each of these sites within the classification of breakdowns.

Management would want answers and the planning teams would cite 'transportation delays' as the reason for production interruption. This would satisfy the taxonomy found in academic literature. What really caused this? As we Corkonians say, it must have been a guy in a suit in an office somewhere (as if this makes him some cynical character, detached from reality). This poor guy gets a lot of abuse, whoever he is. True enough, on that day, Cork City Council implemented a new movement strategy that banned private cars from entering the main (Saint Patrick) street between the hours of 3pm and 6.30pm. The real Saint Patrick had fewer difficulties in banishing snakes from Ireland. New bus lanes and road markings sprung up overnight, causing great confusion, requiring our police force to take a break from policing to direct our hapless commuters. The point is that strategy caused supply chain disruption in this case. Greater alignment with a wide range of stakeholders could have minimized the impact, but in reality, Cork is too small a network for such a design, and the strategy continued to wreak havoc for a number of weeks, until business leaders revolted and forced the council to reverse its decision. Policy matters.

This brings me to transportation and distribution, and the real logisticians who physically resolve supply chain disruption on a continuous basis. This is the hidden side of supply chain management, because very few members of an organization can comprehend the stages and challenges of an air or ocean shipment. Many assume that pallets for ocean freight are moved from a manufacturing plant in China and loaded directly on to the vessel at the port, or think nothing of asking for a carton to be removed from an ocean container just prior to sailing and shipped via air freight instead due to a sudden demand change. Alignment needs education.

Morrison Express Corporation

Morrison Express Corporation (MEC) was founded in 1972, so-named as it was guarded by the highest mountain in Taiwan, Morrison Peak of the Jade Mountain Range. The company has remained true to its original aspirations of reaching the top of the global transportation and logistics mountain, with many milestones marking its ongoing ascent. In 1979 (ironically) a facility was opened in El Paso, Texas to support cross-border movements from Mexico. Their ocean freight division was opened in 1986, before establishing a United States HQ in El Segundo, California, and a Los Angeles branch office in 1990. In 1992, a European HQ was formed in Luxemburg, and expansion into China began with a Shanghai warehouse in 1999. All global logistics, air and ocean freight segments were unified on their 30th anniversary. Development continued with multiple logistics warehouses in Latin America, United States and Netherlands (2003) and expansion in the greater China region with the launching of operations in Guangzhou (2005). Hamburg became its 70th international branch office in 2011. On its 40th anniversary, Cathay Pacific Cargo presented the Taipei office with an 'outstanding strategic partnership' award, followed in 2013 by a Hong Kong

Airlines Cargo 'outstanding partner' award, and AOE certification in Rotterdam and Amsterdam. Further partnership awards were received from China Airlines and Eva Air in 2014. New offices were established in Los Angeles, Cleveland, Ohio and Dusseldorf, Germany, in 2015, and again in 2018 in Eindhoven, Netherlands, where this next section will conclude.

Lean inventory strategies and organizational failure to prepare for annual events

What strikes me most about Morrison Express is their investment in fantastic people, and their culture of outstanding customer service. Eduardo Vargas, Regional Director Los Angeles, United States Southwest and Mexico, and Jeroen van Beek, District Manager, Netherlands, epitomize these traits. The Acropolis of Athens, Greece, was an imposing backdrop to my initial discussion with Eduardo, perhaps symbolic of Morrison Peak. According to Eduardo, logistics is measured on time, cost and service. Supply chain disruption occurs when there is a negative change to any one of these factors. Throughout his 20 years in the business, he has seen disruption within the taxonomy of terrorist attacks, political instability, natural disasters, labour force disputes, equipment failures, supplier defaults, product recalls, poor communication and financial issues, aligned to John Gattorna's crises, disasters and breakdowns.

Morrison Express manages disruption on a regular basis – this after all is their value-add to clients, and Eduardo agrees with my suggested two-tier strategic response. Disruptions can be light (a misunderstanding on fees) or mild, that can be responded to autonomously, or severe, which require teamwork to solve (vessel accidents, or a previous company US$5 million case with customs authorities in South America due to wrong documentation). The threshold for TMT involvement is based on the investment value. Morrison Express mitigation is in the form of financial investment (insurance, labour and equipment) and service (customer terms and conditions). Eduardo sees a phased approach of avoidance and containment within a resistance category, whereby investments prepare for known risks, such as those in the chemical industry, and stabilization and return within a second category of recovery, whereby we must plan for uncertainties, such as in the fashion industry. Within each phased sub-category, Eduardo suggests various key strategies subject to contextual and situational considerations:

- **Avoidance:** Discovery (this can be declining bookings for personal goods that require complex documentation and thereby open to customs events, or high value cargo that is not covered under client insurance as the risk is too great), information (it is critical for freight forwarders to gather all information on cargo, such as in the case of client non-disclosure of dangerous goods, which could lead to additional charges, customs events, and losing control of the cargo entirely), security, preparedness (safeguarding the cargo prior to shipment to minimize risk).
- **Containment:** Indirect investments (Morrison insurance covers up to $0.5/lb liability, and insurance certificates can also be created for each shipment to cover the full value), supply chain design, redundancy, operating flexibility, security, preparedness.
- **Stabilization:** Supply chain design (optimizing routes for clients, offering hub solutions and advising on air and ocean combinations), redundancy, operating flexibility, preparedness.
- **Return:** Operating flexibility, preparedness.

One case of excellent Morrison Express preparedness was an equipment installation at a tier one automotive plant in Alabama, where it was in operation for three months before being transported again to Mexico. This machine was big, initially arriving at a US port in different containers as break-bulk cargo and transported on nine vehicles to the end destination in Cottondale: three low-bed over-dimensioned, one wide legal flat, and three legal flat trucks, in addition to two 53' box vans. For the transfer to Zitlaltepec, Mexico, the same vehicle portfolio was used. A timeline schedule for the client was regularly updated as the transfer progressed, showing the position and routing of each vehicle on a US–Mexico map. Transit time was an estimated two to three days to the border in Laredo, Texas, factoring in a legal driving time of eight hours daily, excluding weekends. The plan had all vehicles being inspected in unison as the machine was expected to be imported into Mexico as one entity. This inspection was an estimated three days depending on availability of inspectors on either side of the border (this was adjusted in transit, enabling separate truck inspections). Transit time from Nuevo Laredo to Zitlaltepec was a further three days. Unloading, rigging and sitting, including assembly, required 10–12 working days to be completed. There was no ramp or dock door at the Zitlaltepec Plant, and therefore unloading required lifting equipment. Plug in, testing, calibration and programming were all handled in-house but were included in the schedule.

It was agreed in advance of shipment that Eduardo would implement remedial action and move to deploy contingency plans determined and agreed by program management and approved by a project steering committee upon identification of delays, potential delays or other issues that may have negatively affected the project. Exceptions would be measured as part of the project KPIs so that trends could be identified, and alternate solutions implemented in a timely manner. Notifications to the customer would include any revision to the shipping schedule, such as the case of missing or discrepant shipping documents for the pre-clearance of goods, an inland haulier failing to uplift or unload at the appointed time, or any delays in despatch and arrival. An impressive 15-page document contained all details of the movement. Preparation was even more considered in terms of packing. Protection was applied to acrylic doors, arm structures were supported with wooden columns, and metallic rings were robustly secured using wooden crates and containers. Hoses, modules, cables, bars, structures and plates were cleaned and restrained. Tie bars were affixed to wooden supports and flatbeds to avoid spinning. Reinforced pallets were then lashed and restrained to the vehicles to further avoid movement and damages. This was risk avoidance in action. Perfect alignment.

Planning for resilience is based on the highest risk probabilities but Eduardo has a very refreshing perspective on this. Risk should not be measured solely in terms of cubic metres or value in dollars such as the billions described in Chapter 1. Morrison Express air freights 300–400 tonnes of consumer electronics on a weekly basis for a global brand leader, and any disruptions most probably will cause loss of month-end sales (but no impact on absolute sales due to customer loyalty) and some heated communications with the clients' planners. This scenario must of course be avoided but on the other end of the scale, Eduardo exports one pallet of wallpaper and carpets for a small business owner every week. If this pallet is late, damaged or lost, the trader's occupation is at stake. Risk is therefore relative, and the ethos of Morrison Express is to take both extremes into consideration. Supply chain risk management must also be aligned to geographical subtleties. Whereas standardization of processes across large countries (US, China, Brazil) is important when there are multiple facilities and offices, there are differences across countries that must also be considered. For example, regular domestic trucks move containers of electronics goods from US airports to container freight stations in a safe environment at a cost of $500 per truck. The same trucks and products move for the same price and similar distances in Mexico. But trucks in Mexico disappear. Therefore,

Eduardo must send two armed escorts with each shipment, at a cost of $450 each. Logistics in this case compensates for a lack of public safety.

Supply chain disruption *can* be caused by policy. One of Eduardo's major customers when employed by a previous organization was in the top-three automotive manufacturers in the United States, with a significant divisional operation in Colombia. The US HQ implemented an internal policy of holding two weeks of production materials (2WOS) at any one time and heavy penalties for late shipments were imposed on its transportation and logistics partners as a form of risk avoidance. On one occasion, an ocean container to Colombia arrived two weeks late. The plant stopped production and the supply chain disruption caused by the transportation delay attracted a penalty for Eduardo. Case closed? Not quite.

Each week, an ocean shipment departed Nhava Sheva Port near Mumbai, India, containing consolidated parts such as bumpers and plastics from eight suppliers. The largest supplier accounted for 80 per cent of the volume and 50 pallet spaces, whereas the remaining products could be anything from two to 10 pallets. The process was that the Colombian plant issued purchase orders to the various Indian suppliers and planned the weekly consolidations according to completion dates, including detailed vanning layouts (theoretical distribution of pallets and boxes within a container; vanning layouts allow the measurement or estimation of container utilization). They then instructed Eduardo's company agent in Chakan to coordinate collections and to load the containers at their facility. A consol sheet was sent daily to Colombia (data of picked-up material: quantities, PO#, invoice #, date picked up, # pallets, fumigation compliance, stacking norm, cubic metres, photos, remarks), together with a warning communication when a supplier was not in compliance with agreed upon delivery dates. In turn, Colombia rescheduled collection dates directly with the suppliers. Most suppliers were same-day collections and others in Haryana and Gujarat ranged from three to six days. Many steps were to be in place one week prior to sailing. The Chakan agent confirmed the feasibility of the estimated time of departure (ETD) in terms of pending supplier receipts and the probability of recovering the missing pallets on time. In turn, Colombia approved the ETD and sent the vanning layout for confirmation. The agent then booked containers with the ocean carrier and warned of any issues with the granting of space, in which case it was escalated to Colombia to resolve. Containers were then collected from the ocean carrier container freight station (CFS). At a rate of 10 per day, the agent stuffed and optimized the containers based on the agreed upon vanning layout, reported to

Colombia the number and type of containers utilized and transferred the batches of 10 to the CFS for customs clearance and inspection.

The goods were customs cleared by the agents' Mumbai office and if an inspector required physical inspection, containers were unloaded and reloaded. Mumbai then transferred the containers to the ocean carrier and warned Colombia of any port congestion that would impact the ETD. Again, Colombia was tasked with resolving this directly and requesting the next earliest departure. The vessel departed and now the local shipping agent in Colombia coordinated approval and compliance of the BOLs with the customer plant, monitored the progress of the shipment, giving notification of any issues that arose during the voyage, and then ensured that all documentation was physically prepared and handed to the customer for customs clearance. Once customs clearance had been completed, scanned copies of the documentation were sent to the Indian suppliers through the local shipping agent. All of these steps were outlined in a comprehensive standard operating procedure (SOP). The Colombian manufacturer was directly involved and responsible for most of the shipment planning. On this occasion, there was an Indian holiday that caused major port congestion, hence the delayed arrival by two weeks. The plant was at risk of losing millions of dollars per minute, air freight was a solution that was being demanded, and this was escalated to the supply chain director within the US HQ. Eduardo was tasked with negotiation and demonstrated that the detailed SOP outlined above included just as much detail about the Indian holiday schedule as it did container planning (21 events in total). Eduardo's organization was not at fault but paid a nominal penalty as a gesture of goodwill. The real cause was a *lean inventory policy* that had no built-in redundancy, and the resulting planning strategy either did not factor in the full spectrum of variables such as holiday seasons or was operating within the confines of a policy that was not fit for purpose. Case now closed.

Chapter 2 suggested that the policy failure of the International Monetary Fund to support developing nations due to their inability to contain multinational organizations (and private producers and investors) has led to disruption in nations whose leadership does not have the political will to raise the standards of its citizens. Consider emerging Brazil and the strategic approach of its customs authorities to have zero tolerance regarding inaccurate shipping documentation. In a previous company, Eduardo was booked to move a hot shipment of four solar panels on one pallet for a leading North American solar manufacturer, from the US to an important trade show in Sao Paulo. This was recovered from San Francisco and trucked the eight hours to Los Angeles, whereupon the agent cut the house air waybill, including the pallet weight and dimensions, as normal, before being flown to Brazil via Miami.

Enter Brazilian customs, desiring to be the Switzerland of South America, and a weight check reveals that the documentation had stated the wrong weight. Shipment on hold. The customer trade show ruined. Only heavy penalties would have released the pallet. That was two years ago, and any other jurisdiction would have enabled a resolution. Not a great policy for a developing country reliant on international trade, one would assume. But are the high fees and penalties strategic? The ill-fated solar panels now reside in the largest airport logistics complex in Latin America, TECA GRU, within a self-proclaimed 'expressive' 97,000 square metres industrial and commercial park in Guarulhos city, servicing 29 countries from its prime fully automated location. Further investment of R$45 million will see improved airport infrastructure and greater capacity. A deliberate customs policy to create supply chain disruption? You decide. Eduardo suggests ways in which the top management team can align with SCM goals:

- Supply chain risk mitigation should be built into human resource management. Life and business are not perfect, but in both cases, nothing replaces willingness and passion to deliver, and an anger to succeed. Detailed standard operating procedures or manuals are not required if people are aligned for success. Personal goals (tuition for kids, car, mortgage, professional growth, etc) must be aligned with company goals (more sales, better service, lower costs, etc).

- The top management team must understand that there are forces that derail departments and business units from achieving their objectives. However, organizations need to be nimble enough to foresee and adjust the chain of actions required to get the same or similar outcomes. It is almost as if Eduardo read Chapter 2: 'It is this friction, which makes that which appears easy in SCM difficult in reality. The top management team must be aware of this friction so that, where possible, it can be overcome, and must learn not to expect a precision in results because of this friction. Know friction and triumph over it. Friction cannot be learned theoretically, but experience and tact will enable the supply chain manager to make decisions based on situational needs, whereby they decide and determine suitably to the occasion.'

- Strategies (similar to budgets) are theoretical. Execution requires the experience of supply chain management and an intense thought process in order to avoid disruption and achieve desired outcomes. The strategic renewal process is critically important in this business but should never take long. Alleviating supply chain disruption has a cost. However, we must be categorically selective with risk and safeguard against those events that are most likely to happen or that will hurt us the most.

From the Acropolis to the Port of Rotterdam now to meet Jeroen van Beek, District Manager of Morrison Express. Covering an expanded area of 105 square kilometres and enclosed by autonomous robotic cranes and computer-controlled chariots, Europe's largest port is unrecognizable compared to its 14th century incarnation. Office blocks oversee the annual throughput of 29,650 seagoing vessels. Jeroen was previously positioned within one such block, the now-empty offices of Hanjin Shipping Company of South Korea, which was declared bankrupt in February 2017, with a total debt of $10.5 billion, and the subject of the first disruptive event that we discussed. Hanjin was in the top 10 container carriers globally and transported 3.7 million container equivalent units (TEUs) annually. The collapse of Hanjin was the most significant in the history of the container transport industry and left up to 24 vessels stranded at ports because stevedores and other port authorities and services demanded cash payments to offload their containers. To rectify the situation, the vessels were forced to leave maritime-law protected territorial waters in search of free havens. The inventories held onboard caused major disruption for Hanjins' customers, but also caused a capacity shortage in Asian deep-water seaports such as Hong Kong, where panic demand transferred to air freight, whose operators in turn dramatically increased their rates. Major brands such as Nike were impacted, but it was mainly small to medium sized firms without redundancy strategies that suffered most.

There are a number of causes of the Hanjin bankruptcy. The 2008 global financial crisis reduced global demand and shipping costs were consequently forced to fall. This resulted in the formation of alliances and, under a conference system, pricing agreements were made, even amongst competing organizations. Greater efficiencies were sought such as more frequent hull-cleaning and slow-steaming to save on bunker costs, and artificially removing vessel capacity from the market. These strategies had limited success due to customers incessantly demanding further price reductions, even continuing to exploit Hanjin when it was known six months prior that the company was in trouble. In addition, shipping lines were frequently forced to loop empty vessels in order to keep alliances going. Nevertheless, everything was being kept afloat, as it were. Enter the European Union, and a policy to abolish the conference system. Shipping lines were now aggressively competing against each other again to drive down costs in a highly capital-sensitive industry. This ultimately led to the bankruptcy of Hanjin. Supply chain disruption caused by this new policy did not end there, however, and this discussion will be continued in the Rotra section.

Firstly, we travel to Eindhoven to see MEC's impressive, newly acquired 4,500 square-metre distribution centre, where Jeroen mentions another source of disruption not generally found in academic literature. Chinese New Year (CNY), or the Spring Festival, which begins at the turn of the traditional lunisolar Chinese calendar for a period of 15 days, supposedly causes significant supply chain disruption due to manufacturing and transportation capacity issues and delays, together with consequential price increases. There *is* one element of CNY that is outside our control. Resident factory workers who return home for the festivities generally do not come back to work, and this results in a recruitment and training dilemma (re-start problems). Outside of this, CNY, the largest human migration in the world, happens annually, and has done for centuries. Hardly a cause of disruption, then? I am in agreement when Jeroen suggests that logistics providers are held accountable for delayed and expensive shipments. Similar to logisticians blamed for poor container utilization (you can only ship what is front of you). The real source of disruption is organizations not having a strategy in place to prepare for this known event. Jeroen advises firms to begin planning six months in advance rather than the typical seven days of panic as CNY booking deadlines approach. A change in mindset is needed, to improve forecasting and prioritization of critical and seasonal products.

Woodland Group

Woodland Group are a large, privately owned global supply chain and logistics provider with offices in the UK, USA, Hong Kong and Ireland. They offer multi-modal transport services from sea, air and road freight to end-to-end 3PL supply chain solutions. Globally, Woodland employ over 600 people who all share the same determination to deliver quality and value to their customers. Founded in 1988 by Kevin Stevens, CEO and Chairman of Woodland Group, their team of experts have been providing innovative and bespoke logistics, e-commerce and supply chain management services since, having earned a reputation for being reliable, honest, hard-working, solutions-driven and fast to react. Rapid expansion has been a cornerstone of the company with office openings such as New York (1991), London Heathrow (1996), Newcastle and Dublin (1997), Chicago (1999) and Los Angeles (2000), leading to recognition in

2003 as being in the top 100 fastest-growing businesses by Deloitte & Touche in the *Independent on Sunday*. This accolade was repeated by *The Sunday Times* in 2012, proceeding the openings of Atlanta (2003) and New Jersey (2010). A Hong Kong presence was subsequently established in 2014. The British International Freight Association (BIFA) has made Woodland a multiple award-winner including for training and staff development (2006), air freight services (2012) and supply chain services (2015).

Cyber security, Government of China factory closures, dangerous goods policy implications

When it comes to disaster recovery plans, cyber security is at the forefront of Woodland Group's mitigation strategies. A culture of continuous coaching and paranoia has been adopted in the aftermath of the 27 June 2017 NotPetya ransomware attack on Ukrainian government and business computer systems. Data could not be accessed unless a payment of $300 in bitcoin was made. The purpose was to disrupt Ukraine's anniversary of divorce from the Soviet Union and the establishment of the 1996 Constitution. However, this gathered momentum and caused significant chaos to a number of major organizations internationally, most notably for our business, the Danish container shipping conglomerate AP Moller Maersk. This mainly impacted their Maersk Line, APM Terminals and Damco divisions, and cost the company up to $300 million in lost customer bookings over a two-day period. TNT Express, now a division of FedEx, also lost revenues to the value of £221 million. This type of malware had not previously been encountered and therefore existing patches were ineffective. This also affected US pharmaceutical giant Merck, a Cadbury chocolate factory in Australia, and the Chernobyl nuclear plant, where operators had to manually monitor radiation levels when their computers failed (Perlroth *et al*, 2017). Continuous organizational vigilance is critical. Someone just needs to innocently open an e-mail. Woodland Group intercepts thousands of rogue e-mails on a weekly basis.

Kevin Brady, Managing Director of Woodland Group Ireland, described recent disruptions that continue to directly impact his customer network. There is an increasing trend of manufacturing plant closures and forced business holidays in China ahead of major events to ensure the subsidence of emissions so that visiting dignitaries can enjoy blue skies. For example, Beijing shut down scores of chemical producers, construction material factories and textile manufacturers within 300km of Hangzhou for 12 days before the G20 Summit in September 2016. This was repeated in 2017 for a military parade to mark the end of the Second World War (*Times of India*, 2016). One assumes that President Xi Jinping of the People's Republic of China would not have considered the impact of this instruction on international traders, given that China had up to recently considered environmental policies as a Western plot to subdue their economic progress. But this policy does indeed cause significant and abrupt supply chain disruption, arising without warning or communication, and is therefore very difficult to prepare for. However, risk mitigation should be in the form of not just being satisfied with manufacturing costs of existing or potential suppliers, but rather requesting Chinese Ministry of Environmental Protection (MEP) inspection history, certification and licensing, waste management practices and indeed demanding the same of their supplier base.

Factory disruptions are not just for cosmetic reasons. 'As much as 40 per cent of China's manufacturing plants have been closed temporarily by safety inspectors since 2016, with up to 80,000 officials charged with criminal offences for breaching emissions limits' (Dockrill, 2017). Government policy is enforcing an escalation of inspections in their drive to reduce the 'concentration of hazardous fine particulate matter from 47 micrograms per cubic metre in 2016, to 35 micrograms by 2035'. One must acknowledge this as a positive policy in the long term, of course, but in the context of supply chain disruption, organizations must consider it an ongoing threat to their global operations. One Woodland client is an importer of stoves, who experienced significant disruption as a result of factory closures in China, causing a major loss of orders and customers. Returning to Chapter 1, resilience needs to be developed so that organizations, whether it is systems and processes, or resources and skills, have the ability to either return to their original state or evolve to a new and more desirable state after being severely disturbed. The characteristics of resilience include robustness against initial disruption, redundancy, resourcefulness and rapidity of the recovery process. In this regard, Woodland Group assisted its client with an alternative solution of sourcing from India, and this has resulted in a new and more desirable state.

Dangerous goods also threaten our global supply chains. There was a series of catastrophic explosions in August 2015 at Tianjin, the largest man-made port in China, tragically causing the recorded death of 173 people. This began with an overheated container of dry nitrocellulose, and the almost simultaneous detonation of 800 tonnes of ammonium nitrate, held at a 46,000 square metre warehouse owned by Ruihai International Logistics. The blasts were equivalent to a 2.9 magnitude earthquake. Established in 2011, Ruihai had been illegally operating on expired government authorization to handle chemicals from October 2014 to June 2015, before their licence was renewed only two months prior to the disaster. This was in spite of inspectors later discovering discrepant customs documentation making it impossible to identify what substances were in storage. Government inertia therefore, and a policy for damage control rather than prevention, led to this situation. Another reason for such devastation was that China imposed a regulation in 2001 that mandated chemical storage to be 1,000 metres from public spaces. The adjacent city has 15 million residents and is increasing in proportion to economic growth. Therefore this regulation has become unrealistic and has been routinely violated by facilities such as Ruihai International Logistics. Fruit sellers operate alongside toxic rivers and the public were oblivious to the risks involved prior to the explosions (Woodside *et al*, 2017).

Quite often, how a government responds is the main cause of disruption rather than the actual event, such as closing borders, shutting down air traffic, or evacuating areas (Sheffi, 2001). The immediate response was to ban the loading and discharging of all dangerous goods (DG) materials at Tianjin, and the ports of Qingdao, Lianyungang, Dalian, Fuzhou and Xiamen also implemented new regulations to restrict the handling of certain hazardous goods. It took two years for the government to approve again the processing of Class 8 and 9 (corrosive and miscellaneous) items of the UN's International Maritime Dangerous Goods Code at Tianjin. One can imagine the untold damage to global businesses from the increased costs and transit times associated with the congestion and complexity of re-routing vessels to locations still accommodating these DG materials, albeit in a more limited capacity. Kevin has observed such disruption at the Port of Ningbo, the busiest in the world in terms of cargo tonnage, due to a change in government legislation to reduce the number of licensed DG facilities from eight to one.

While much of this remains invisible to the general populous, the launch of the Samsung Galaxy Note 7 brought the DG threat to the public due to the overheating and explosion of its lithium-ion batteries, costing the company $5 billion in recalls, and subsequently for the wider industry, the restrictions on the shipment of batteries has become a disruption in itself. Samsung management practices and a dual-supplier sourcing policy were cited as the root cause of the battery issues (Horwitz, 2017). Another impact of this event was the block-booking of China's air-freight capacity by a major Samsung competitor in order to exploit the opportune gap in the market. This of course then led to disruption for non-DG industries, who were unable to secure space with air carriers. It is interesting to see that globalization is so closely interlinked, and how one event can have such a widespread impact. Almost like a Carrington event, the geomagnetic solar storm of 1859, which, when repeated will shut-down the entire global supply chain network (it did happen in 2012 but missed the planet).

Royal Rotra Group

Established more than 100 years ago, the Dutch family business Rotra has in recent decades developed into a tried and trusted logistics one-stop-shop with over 860 employees in the Netherlands and Belgium. Rotra was founded in Doesburg by Hermanus Roelofsen. Four generations of the family have worked or are still working in the business. In the early days the goods were still carried by horse and cart, a situation that they can scarcely imagine now. Global forwarding by air, sea and land, warehousing, value added activities and supply chain management have been combined into one flexible organization. This has been built up steadily and carefully, with the result that Rotra is a stable company with a sound financial foundation and a reliable global network of logistic partners. Listen to the customer and respond swiftly with personal service is the principle they have applied from the start. It sounds simple, and simple is how they want to keep things for their clients. Organizing and managing logistic processes perfectly is intensive but Rotra makes this seamless. From a single consignment to integrated supply chain management, Rotra will handle it in a safe, reliable and sure manner. So much so that the Dutch Royal Family awarded the company Royal status, the only logistics organization to be honoured in such a manner. Quite impressive in the logistics hub of Europe.

Super ocean carriers and seaport congestion, and the threat of ecommerce on the 3PL sector

In the beautiful location of Doesburg, Michiel van Berkel, Sales Manager Netherlands, continues the saga of disruption in international waters. In response to the EU abolishment of the conference system, the industry moved to create multiple mergers that were legally posited with the United States Federal Maritime Commission (FMC) and the European Antitrust Policy.

For example, 2017 saw the formation of three major alliances. Shanghai-headquartered Cosco Shipping Holdings purchased Orient Overseas Container Line (OOCL) for $6.3 billion creating a combined fleet of 400 ships and a total capacity of 2.9 million TEUs. This preceeded a February 2016 merger of China Ocean Shipping (Group) Company (Cosco) and China Shipping (Group) Company (CSG), making Cosco Shipping the fourth largest alliance. On 24 May 2017, Hapag-Lloyd and United Arab Shipping Company (UASC) merged 230 vessels and 1.6 million TEUs, becoming the fifth largest operator. On 30 November 2017, Maersk acquired Hamburg Süd for €3.7 billion and together they have 19.3 per cent of global fleet capacity (4.15 million TEUs), with 773 vessels. In September 2016, French company CMA CGM completed its $2.4 billion acquisition of Singapore-based Neptune Orient Lines, combining 2.4 million TEUs across a fleet of 563 vessels, making it the third largest with an annual turnover of $22.3 billion. The purpose of these mergers was to stem the tide of plunging rates (Xeneta.com, 2018). A further significant measure to achieve economies of scale has been the introduction of super carriers, and arising from this, and of particular concern to Dutch 3PLs like Rotra, is that congestion in Rotterdam has escalated in recent months.

Take, for instance, the 400-metre long MV CSCL Globe, operated by China Shipping Container Lines, which can take an incredible 19,100 twenty-foot containers compared to 14,700 TEUs on the Maersk e-class ships. An unusually large on-board crew of 31 is needed and the largest ship engine ever built (standing at 56 feet high) moves its gross tonnage of 187,541 GT. This all sounds really impressive, but the problem is that they threaten a large number of small ports that cannot accommodate the size of these vessels, ports that are already at risk from increasing demands for digitization as they simply do not have the resources or infrastructures in place. It could potentially come to a point whereby a much smaller number of large seaports will be servicing entire continents. In simplistic terms, Hamburg, Frankfurt, Gdansk, to name a few, cannot offload these ships, and instead must wait for feeder vessels to arrive from Rotterdam. Therein lies the issue of Rotterdam congestion.

Control is somewhat back in the hands of the shipping lines, which have negotiated reduced rates with stevedores to offload (and load) containers. This puts the stevedores (longshoremen) under intense financial pressure in addition to placing a huge strain on operations due to increased vessel capacities. This causes peaks and arranging appointments for the unloading of specific containers is not possible with the now more-powerful carriers, who are not amenable due to having no competition. Ports are a triptych comprising a seaside panel, the port itself and a landside panel (Hintjens *et al*, 2015). Therefore, this in turn results in the congestion of inter-modal vessels such as barges both at the port and onward waterways, and also disrupts the container flow on the outbound road networks. Export freight is also impacted, with major Dutch companies such as Heineken and Royal FrieslandCampina paying additional costs and experiencing delayed sailings. As the global economy grows, so too will this problem. Rotra builds business cases based on its impressive Container Terminal in Doesburg on the Gelderse Ijssel River, one of the largest trans-shipment locations in the heart of East Gelderland, but its self-owned Barge is under-utilized due to the Rotterdam situation.

Are there other underlying policies to blame? Of interest is that European Union marginal social cost pricing policy decreed in 2001 that all external costs per tonne-kilometre of freight transported across the European Union, including imports and exports, would be directed to the carriers. This included infrastructure maintenance, traffic control, emissions, and traffic fatalities and injuries. In the same period it was predicted that Dutch governmental policy in relation to 'investment in infrastructure networks was insufficient to accommodate the future increase in traffic demand, inducing a strong increase in congestion' (Runhaar *et al*, 2002). That was the past. What does the future hold? Michiel advises that MSC CEO Diego Aponte acknowledges that the mega ships are a contributing factor to the unreliability of timetables and this will be addressed by the deployment of additional vessels and the closing of loss-making routes. Punctuality has deteriorated to the extent of one-third of vessels being late and Head of Sea Freight at Kuehne & Nagel, Otto Schacht, maintains that complaining is of no use due to the fact that there may not be enough vessels on a particular route or others may be relocated to align with new alliance scheduling. This dissatisfaction from shippers and logistics freight service providers increases the challenge of rapidly increasing fuel prices. MSC recently introduced an emergency bunker surcharge that could increase the cost of containers by €150, closely followed by Maersk Line, CMA CGM and Singapore's Ocean Network Express. Manufacturing companies such as Electrolux are not impressed. Bjorn Vang Jensen, VP Global Logistics, sees the bunker increases as a business risk. In his industry, they are faced with sudden increases in steel and transport prices, but they do not pass on a steel adjustment factor or freight increase surcharge to their customers. Michiel says that maritime analysts are also critical. Drewry and SeaIntel see the new surcharge as a desperation measure and argue for a complete overhaul of the system of fees.

As a side note, the transportation industry is responding to seaport congestion in other ways too. Whilst trade between Asia and Europe dramatically changed in the 5th century when intense competition between the colonial powers motivated the invention of large ocean-going ships, we are returning to the historical silk routes that became possible with the compass and

The Art of Responding to Disruption Through the Physical Supply Chain

domesticated camels between 200 and 400AD. Through its Belt and Road Initiative (BRI), China is investing $1 trillion in new rail infrastructure and trade agreements to link Beijing to Europe, with 34 cities in both continents already connected. Rail freight is expected to double its share of trade in the next decade. In 2016, rail carried just 1 per cent of total Asia–Europe trade and so it is not a threat to the shipping alliances in the immediate term, but it does provide organizations with a middle option that is significantly cheaper than air freight and faster than ocean freight (Hillman, 2018). Another development has been the introduction of Blockchain, which companies are reporting as resulting in shorter ocean transit times. This is made possible through a secure, shared and transparent digital ledger across the entire supply chain that can be used for any type of exchange, such as payments (without the need for a traditional bank), trade agreements, contracts, supplier sources, manufacturing data, environmental stewardship, shipping documentation, customs clearances, tracking, warehousing data, proof of delivery, all of which will enable greater network efficiencies and time and cost reductions.

Only a beer in hand would have made the sun-drenched setting by the Ijssel river in Doesburg more pleasant as the vastly experienced Paul Aerts, Benelux Logistics Manager, discussed e-commerce as a force of disruption. Global e-commerce sales are expected to increase from 1.3 trillion in 2014 to 4.5 trillion in 2021 (Forsey, 2018). When you consider that the major organizations in this industry have a policy of free shipping to influence consumer purchases, this puts an incredible strain on warehouse and logistics providers. Rotra operates in this space, having constructed the most advanced bicycle distribution centre in the world, which has been operational since 2005. This automatic bicycle warehouse (ABW) is located at its Container Terminal Doesburg and really is an impressive sight. Electronic data processing provides a direct line to its dedicated provider in Dieren (Koninklijke Gazelle) which has been manufacturing bicycles since 1892. From this most advanced solution in the area of bicycle logistics, Gazelle and their dealers offer consumers an e-bike option. On a daily basis, Rotra processes between 1,000 and 2,000 bikes both inbound and outbound, with between 30,000 and 50,000 in stock at any one time. A highly optimized robotic conveyor (carousel) system for put-away and picking means the absolute minimum of handling and negligible damage.

At a transportation and distribution industry level, the demand for ever-larger warehousing, including a potential 7km-long warehouse in Tilburg, is certainly a form of supply chain disruption, but this is quite a serious threat to 3PL companies and indeed the environment. Certainly, policy drives this phenomenon, but consumers have become incredibly entitled and expect products delivered in ever-faster times at ever-lower prices. Their IT savviness puts demands on 3PLs to invest in systems that can provide real-time shipment updates, but this must be achieved in an environment of unpredictable demand in a growing global economy that restricts warehouse automation, rapidly changing information technology capabilities across the industry that need to be adopted to remain relevant, and continuous re-engineering of warehouse processes to align with consumers who often have the power to design their own product specifications. Warehouse expansion leads to a personnel shortage, and this is resolved by on-boarding non-nationals with different languages and cultures, requiring applications, systems and documentation such as standard operating procedures to be multi-lingual, and of course, adherence to various religious practices. Paul has 43 different cultures in one warehouse alone. Another concerning trend is an older workforce in what is a labour-intensive environment, whereby the Dutch government has been gradually extending the retirement age (66 in 2018).

Larger buildings due to increasing e-commerce sales also impacts last-mile road transportation and courier capacity, a situation that has created an opportunity for non-asset owning shippers to enter the market, exponential organizations discussed in Chapter 1, that are often unlicensed. Additional vehicles cause urban congestion and increased air pollution. Another environmental concern is waste at the consumer end when customers receive unpractical packaging that must be disposed of. Schiphol Airport in Amsterdam is reaching capacity and the Transport Ministry was given approval in April to build a new airport in Lelystad. Dutch aerospace is in the process of re-organization, but this will not be completed until 2023. In the meantime, all aircraft bound for Lelystad must maintain a maximum height of 1.8 kilometres in order to avoid Schiphol traffic. Consequently, the aforementioned consumers (albeit mainly Lelystad residents) who expect products delivered in ever-faster times at ever-lower prices are ironically protesting against the increased noise pollution that this new development will bring upon completion in 2020.

Kuehne + Nagel

In 1890, August Kuehne and Friedrich Nagel founded a business in Bremen, Germany, that has since grown into one of the world's leading logistics providers. Today, the Kuehne + Nagel Group has some 1,300 offices in over 100 countries, with around 76,000 employees. Key business activities and market position are built on the company's truly world class capabilities, such as being the number one global sea freight forwarder due to the formation of solid partnerships with an extensive range of preferred ocean carriers. A holder of global cargo iQ phase 2 certification, the company is the number two global air cargo forwarder, a position also held in the provision of global contract logistics. Overland, Kuehne + Nagel is a leader in groupage, LTL (less than truck load), FTL (full truck load), intermodal transports as well as pharma transportation through its extensive own fleet and close partnerships with best-in-class carriers.

Protectionism and trade wars, and non-tariff policy measures

From Doesburg now to Amsteldijk in Amsterdam. Ian Truesdale, Global Senior Vice President of Logistics and Innovation, agrees that the policy of the top e-commerce providers to offer free shipping for the domestic last mile has been a complete game-changer. One would imagine that the surge in online customer demand would be good for 3PLs and parcel delivery companies. However, such demand has unpredictable patterns and specific requests to achieve as short as 30-minute delivery lead-times, amidst intensifying competition, has caused serious disruption. City Link was forced to announce its closure on Christmas Day 2014 with the loss of 2,500 jobs, and Yodel, owned by the billionaire Barclay brothers, reported consecutive annual losses recently, despite delivering 155 million parcels per year. UK Mail Group has absorbed some of the City Link business but has had to grapple with excessively high costs from having to spot-hire trucks to take the huge volumes. Mergers and acquisitions are taking place to combine resources, such as FedEx purchasing TNT for €4.4 billion.

Within this climate, Kuehne + Nagel are faced with having to balance customer expectations and escalating operating costs. This becomes all the more challenging when e-commerce giants both in the United States and Europe have strategically partnered with investors and property developers to construct their own warehouses and distribution centres, in the process pushing up the price of real estate. 3PLs simply cannot acquire land in Western Europe, thereby limiting their ability to expand. Warehouses that are positioned in close proximity to consumers are cost prohibitive, whereas more remote locations cannot support the 'need it now' generation. There was a time when delivering 50 stock keeping units (SKUs) to retail outlets was standard business. Now there are 150,000 SKUs held in stock and it is impossible to forecast how these will be consumed. Order picking becomes incredibly complex and difficult to align to warehouse management systems. The level of automation needed to resolve this requires significant investment, but clients are understandably reluctant to sign seven-year contracts, making such investment uneconomical. Related to this, Blockchain was mentioned earlier in positive terms, but Ian is concerned that the system will be open to hacking and fraud, and therefore a source of disruption. The automation of global freight is a major shift in the operating model of all freight forwarders. In fact, the rapid development of information technology and the Internet of Things in general is creating an explosion within our own four walls, whereby we are evolving to linkages to smart sensors that will replace barcoding and scanning, and data downloading or uploading will be in the past. Near-field communication will enable electronic devices to exchange data when coming within 4cm of each other. Similar to smaller ports without the infrastructure to grow with technological advancements, warehousing also faces a threat of serious supply chain disruption. A reminder of Thomas Friedman's force of technology accelerating beyond our ability to adapt.

Now we transition to the topic of protectionism and a recent policy implemented by US President Donald Trump. On 14 June 2018, the office of the United States Trade Representative (USTR) published a list of Chinese origin goods to be subjected to a 25 per cent tariff under Section 301 of the US Trade Act of 1974, becoming effective on 6 July. This represents a charge to the value of $34 billion on Chinese imports related to 818 tariff items and $16 billion on a further 284 items to be announced later in 2018, a punishment for intellectual property infringements, and a request by Trump to the USTR to 'address the acts, policies, and practices of China that are unreasonable or discriminatory, and that burden or restrict U.S. commerce'. This also aims to reduce the Chinese trade surplus by $200 billion within the next two years. Further measures include a 10 per cent tariff on imported aluminium products, mostly impacting Canada, and a 25 per cent tariff on steel imports, predominantly sourced from Canada, Brazil, South Korea and Mexico. Reminiscent of the Smoot-Hawley Tariff Act of 1930, which turned a recession into a Great Depression, China, Canada and the European Union will commensurately retaliate and enter into a trade war.

Making America Great Again is of course the strategy, but enforcing restrictions on the 95 per cent of global consumers who are residing outside the United States (export market), and on Chinese manufacturers still sourcing certain components from the US to produce the many consumer products that will be shipped back into the US (import market, including the most in-demand consumer electronics brand on the planet) does not seem sensible. Supply chain disruption then arises from the inevitable and significant demand unpredictability that will make it exceptionally difficult to re-negotiate long-term pricing agreements with air and ocean carriers. This will result in spot-buying, and both excess and deficit capacity issues that will ultimately lead to increased landed costs. The decision then becomes whether or not to pass these costs on to customers or accept the loss in profit. Mitigation of such disruption comes in the form of Kuehne + Nagel global world trade indicators (gKNi trade nowcasting), which help to forecast and understand macro disrupters more accurately than economists. This 'leverages the largest possible inventory of logistics and supply chain data, from both public and proprietary sources. Big data and predictive analytics are used to provide the most up-to-date insights to economic agents. Estimates for exports, imports, balance of trade (aggregated, by sector and by trade lane) and industrial production are provided' for clients and internal forecasting. 'gKNi covers the health of twelve countries, six sectors, accounting for 50 per cent of world trade. Trade is analysed globally across multiple industries or individual commodities' (logindex.com).

Non-tariff policy measures (NTMs) are another concern: 'all non-price and non-quantity restrictions on trade in goods, services and investment. This includes border measures (customs procedures) as well as behind-the-border measures flowing from domestic laws, regulations and practices' (Berden *et al*, 2009). This suggests that quotas and domestic subsidies are not considered NTMs, both of which would be categorized as protectionist or assistance policies. Specifically, Ian sees a rise in non-protectionist disruption such as strictness in the accuracy of harmonized system (HS) codes, packaging and labelling requirements (as an example, special requirements could necessitate a manufacturing process change for shipping otherwise-standard products to Saudi Arabia) and anti-dumping laws (attracting a surcharge). Sanitary and phytosanitary rules (a pallet without an IPCC stamp will be held by customs, as it is not known if it has been heat-treated, kiln dried and debarked), and food, plant and animal inspections can cause frustrating delays (an importer of electrical goods may be surprised to have their ocean container pulled at the port for a veterinary inspection, a risk of shipping LCL). All of these measures are of course necessary but must be factored in.

The Tianjin event has resulted in safety data sheets being a requirement for DG materials such as NI-MH batteries, and this can delay shipments if there is any concern about specific declarations. Exporting outside of the European Union can be troublesome, if on an ad hoc basis, involving the selection of the appropriate declarations to apply to commercial invoices, certificates of origin waiting for chamber of commerce approval, EUR-1 (movement) certificates needing long-term supplier agreements in order to be legalized, or admission temporaire roulette ATR.1 certification being a pre-requisite for Turkey. Global trade has also seen an increase in the number of ocean containers arriving at port with internal harmful gases, the severity of which is based on the cargo, temperature and duration of the journey. This can be a cause of random disruption due to customs inspections of contamination levels, especially in the initial stages of importation until you become known to customs, but the issue has a much more serious and dark side, with several reported fatalities. Toxic boxes.

Crane Worldwide Logistics

On 7 August 2008 Crane Worldwide Logistics opened for business with a group of former senior EGL executives, including founder Jim Crane, with a vision to become a global player in the competitive global freight management and contract logistics services sector. Nine years later, Crane Worldwide has very quickly grown to more than $680 million in revenues with locations all over the world, expecting this to reach $1 billion in 2018. From the onset, Crane Worldwide set out to be different from the other players in the market by making their clients' business smarter. They provide transparency to clients' global supply chains and provide the best service in the industry. These are the reasons why they are growing, because they challenge the norm, convinced that superior people coupled with game-changing technology would transform the industry through five value propositions: People, Service Execution, Information Technology, Compliance and Quality Programm, and Account Management. Crane Worldwide is a full-service air, ocean, trucking, customs brokerage and logistics company.

Loss of containers at sea, and the Calais refugee crisis impacting road haulage

Returning to Cork, Shane Bradley, Business Development Manager, discussed the additional administration of Verified Gross Mass (VGM) certification, implemented for all global ocean shipments since July 2016.

This calculates the total weight of products, packaging, stowage materials and container, and is another non-tariff measure policy to contend with. The reason for VGM is to mitigate the surprisingly regular loss of containers at sea, although not quite the 10,000 per year that is commonly alluded to. Contributing to this false number would be the two recent and most catastrophic ocean container events in history. In June 2013, the 8,110 TEU container ship MOL Comfort bound for Jeddah from Singapore encountered adverse weather and broke in two in the Indian Ocean (Jiang, 2015). The aft section sank before the fore section caught fire and eventually sank two weeks after the initial wave impact, taking with it 4,293 containers. The 2011 grounding of the MV Rena 3,351 TEU Greek container ship on New Zealand's Astrolabe Reef had a loss of 900 containers and was due to the 'failure of the master and crew to follow proper voyage planning, navigation and watchkeeping practices, and the ship managers' insufficient oversight of the vessels' safety management system' (Schuler, 2014). Policy does not come into this, but less prolific annual losses can be attributed not just to weather episodes (the sophistication of navigation systems can avoid almost all cases) but to strategic 'choices' in terms of pre-VGM weight declarations at individual company level. Excluding catastrophic events that lose 50 containers or more, the World Shipping Council has estimated an average annual loss of 612 containers between 2014 and 2016. This is less than the average of 733 units lost each year in the three years prior (Schuler, 2017). The majority of these cases are due to loading based on 'deliberately' inaccurate weight declarations, which cause vessels to pitch and roll against their natural rotations. Boxes then simply fall off.

Gerry Hall, Regional Logistics Manager, brings our attention to Calais in northern France. For almost two decades this port city has been a controversial staging area for refugees seeking asylum in the United Kingdom. The 2003 Treaty of Le Touquet (formally known as the Treaty between the Government of the United Kingdom of Great Britain and Northern Ireland and the Government of the French Republic concerning the Implementation of Frontier Controls at the Sea Ports of both Countries on the Channel and North Sea), signed by British Prime Minister Tony Blair and French President Jacques Chirac, transferred British border controls to the French side. This was created in February 2003, entering into force one year later. Both governments believed at the time that this would be a short-term problem, but in fact it escalated, and the French were left with the full burden of preventing illegal migration to Britain. Eurotunnel stopped 18,500 refugees trying to get across to the United Kingdom between 1999 (when the French Red Cross set up the initial camp, Sangatte) and 2001, a situation that had not improved 15 years later following, in particular, the Syrian refugee crisis, when 20,000 illegal attempts were thwarted. This was the coming together of two policies to create supply chain disruption, the Le Touquet Treaty and Syrian governmental policy that produced both terrorist insurgents and residents of the Calais 'Jungle'.

Returning again to Chapter 1. Consider Syria, the geopolitical superstorm of the age of accelerations and the rise of the Islamic State of Iraq and the Levant. A combination of simultaneous factors, such as a population explosion during the 1980s, President Bashar al-Assad's regulation of the agricultural sector to benefit large-scale farmers (who were also government officials) upon taking power in 2000, enabling the purchase of vast lands and water drilling rights, a catastrophic drought known as *jafaf*, and the subsequent migration of small deposed farmers and their families to cities such as Aleppo in search of food and jobs, politicized a young generation into civil war, whose cause grew exponentially through a global reach that was powered by technology (Friedman, 2016). Of course, on a wider scale, the influx into the European Union also included migration from Libya, and other parts of Asia and Africa, with 600,000 applications for asylum in the first nine months of 2015 alone (Catchpole and Coulombier, 2015). However, by October there were 507,000 EU-registered Syrian asylum seekers. This compared to four million registered with the Office of the UN High Commissioner for Refugees (UNHCR) in the Middle East, predominantly across Turkey, Lebanon and Jordon, and while there have been comparable events throughout history, it was the largest scale movement of people from the Middle East to Europe, creating strategic conflict between EU member states. Tensions were already high with the Greek economic crisis, the United Kingdom contemplating a divorce from the EU, and the growing security threat from ISIS. The Yugoslav wars do provide some precedent, but the movement of the 1.5 million Bosnian refugees into the EU in 1994 was more gradual and manageable. The earlier surge of 900,000 Kosovar refugees in 1988–89 was more sudden and abrupt but considered a short-term stay. Of a similar tempo and scale of 2015 were 'the *Vertreibung* (eviction) of the German-speaking population of Central and Eastern Europe at the end of the Second World War, the partition of India in 1947, the Palestinian *Nakba* (catastrophe) of 1948, and the displacement from the 1979 Soviet invasion of Afghanistan' (Heisbourg, 2015).

At the height of the Calais crisis, Gerry Hall had been contracted with a previous company to transport goods from Hungary to a major UK technology distributor. Failure to deliver within a three-day transit time attracted penalties. Similar performance targets became a huge challenge for all road hauliers as migrants secretly stowed away on trucks (perhaps also highlighting again top management team obliviousness to the 'invisible' challenges of the freight and logistics industry). Drivers were held responsible and heavily fined for any migrants found by police. Offending vehicles were then impounded for several days for forensic inspection, while replacement trucks added to the mounting costs. Food supplies and medical products were considered contaminated and destroyed. Long queues arising from migrant efforts to board containers cost EuroTunnel €9.7 million in 2015 against a Freight Transport Association estimation of £89 billion worth of trade passing through Calais each year. To mitigate transit delays (and costs, with a 44-tonne truck costing £1 per minute to run), the combined governments raised 29 kilometres of high security fencing, and the British Prime Minister spent £80 million on border security (Yarr and Smith, 2016). Road hauliers came together to move in convoys and use only certain safe and secure stops, ensuring no diversions from predetermined route plans, and security monitors were attached to vehicles. Early in 2018, President Emmanuel Macron committed to abolishing the Calais camp, but a migrant presence remains, and the focus has now switched to Ireland-bound trucks.

Aramex

Aramex has rapidly grown into a global brand, recognized for its customized services and innovative products. Listed on the Dubai Financial Market (DFM) and based in the UAE, Aramex is centrally located at the crossroads between East and West, which allows them to provide customized logistics solutions anywhere in the world effectively and reach more businesses and consumers regionally and globally. They are committed to continually enhancing their operations across the region while pursuing opportunities for business growth in emerging markets abroad. This approach is core to the sustainable development of their business and commitment to facilitating wider, global trade in an ever-changing world. Aramex have successfully introduced market leading express delivery and logistics services to the Middle East and other emerging economies. As a leading global provider of comprehensive logistics and transportation solutions, their breadth of services include express courier delivery, freight forwarding, logistics, supply chain management, e-commerce and record management services.

Their unique, asset-light business model underlies all of the strategic decisions they make. It has proved highly successful, allowing Aramex to swiftly adapt to challenging market conditions, execute last-mile delivery solutions and quickly respond to changing customer preferences. Innovation in technology is critical to maintaining their asset-light business model and leveraging the Aramex global network. Instead of investing heavily in infrastructure, they acquire or partner with domestic-focused logistics companies that have strong local networks, knowledge and transportation solutions already in place for efficient and effective last-mile delivery. This approach has proven to have significant benefits for both their business and customers and why they consider themselves a technology enterprise, selling transportation and logistics solutions without being encumbered by heavy investments in assets. They also believe that investing in and sourcing new technologies in the field of e-commerce in particular is core to a swifter, more efficient movement of goods and services globally and maintaining their market leadership position.

Aramex also recognize that to continue to grow a truly sustainable business they must serve and develop the markets and communities where they operate. Their 'delivering good' sustainability platform is active in over 180 educational, social and environmental projects worldwide and they have partnered with a number of international and local organizations devoted to similar causes. Aramex are proud of the close ties they have with the communities where they operate and the contributions they have made to their sustainable economic development.

Mitigating disruption through change-adaption, and policy controlling oil prices

Amsterdam again, and Frank Kilbride, Country Manager for Ireland, discusses supply chain disruption from the perspective of opportunity for positive change. *Change-adaption* is a more appropriate term than disruption in an industry that is continuing to transform and innovate. For example, greater clock speeds and forced efficiencies can help us all evolve and counter the challenges of e-commerce, embracing this niche as an opportunity to re-assess lead-times, usage of inventory and delivery models.

Since the original speculative crash of the 1637 tulip crisis during the Dutch Golden Age, more of a socio-economic rather than an economic phenomenon, men and governments have influenced global trade. Such a

The Art of Responding to Disruption Through the Physical Supply Chain

socio-economic movement is happening in present times with the advent of battery-powered electric vehicles. Consumer and commercial demand is increasing on the commendable premise that they are making a positive impact on the environment. This development brings challenges, of course, from an industry perspective, such as in Ireland where the flexibility in terms of range and payload available from these vehicles is restrictive outside of urban areas, something that must be addressed for revenue-generating cargo. These conditions are heightened in the United States and Europe on 24-hour routes and the general up-front costs for the infrastructure needed to charge vehicles are prohibitive. In addition, the launch of autonomous (driverless) vehicles also poses a teething issue for insurance companies. However, this will all change as the technology is refined and further adaption takes place. And this is the point. Organizations must embrace the new realities of global trade as a tangible opportunity for continuous improvement.

In the opening chapter it was mentioned that, through the embracement of risk, and continuous experimentation, the exponential organization has a greater capacity to respond to disruption through increased agility, also self-disrupting as a core strategy before others do so, unlike traditional firms that are rarely structured to counter unforeseen disruption. Ireland Inc and its leading technology sector is in a perfect position to embrace the challenge of electronic vehicles. The global market is expected to reach $180 billion by 2023 through the development of software and hardware services, and as this mode of transport becomes the norm Ireland could gain 100,000 high-end direct and indirect jobs. Intel predicts that an additional $7 trillion in economic activity could be provided by this new wave of technology solutions (Taylor, 2018).

China is already a perfect example of Frank's *'change-adaption'*, where a fleet of electric buses the size of London's entire fleet is launched every five weeks, in their mission to reduce pollution levels. This has been made possible through government-subsidized construction of brand-new transport networks using electric technology from the outset. But, most importantly, it was possible through a cultural shift in mindset in the response to disruption.

An opposing argument, one that cannot be in any way associated with the above viewpoint, is that the introduction of battery-powered electric vehicles may be 'problem-shifting' because they 'exhibit the potential for significant increases in human toxicity, freshwater eco-toxicity, freshwater eutrophication, and metal depletion impacts, largely emanating from the vehicle supply chain. Their (Chinese) production phase has proven to be substantially more environmentally intensive' (Hawkins *et al*, 2013). Time will inform us if the production, use and disposal of lithium ion batteries has a more beneficial effect on the excessive retention of solar energy in the atmosphere, compared to internal combustion engine cars. Currently, 95 per cent of transport relies on liquid carbon fuels derived from crude oil and due to the fact that emissions from this sector are on the rise, up 35.8 per cent between 1990 and 2006 (Hacker, 2009), it will be challenging to determine the true impact of electric vehicles. The major contributor of the battery to the environmental burden is the supply chain surrounding copper and aluminium collector foils for the production of the anode and the cathode, in addition to the cables for the battery management system (Notter *et al*, 2010). It has already been discussed how ever-increasing sales (indirectly of batteries) will have an exponential impact on Chinese port congestion due to the reduced capacity in dangerous goods processing.

Frank considers another opportunity for *'change-adaption'*. Prior cases mentioned increasing bunker costs as a business risk, but another perspective is that organizations that factor fuel price as an input cost that allows for a high degree of volatility, rather than simply a disruptor, have an advantage. History informs us that this volatility is an ever-present and should be part of planning processes, akin to Chinese New Year: profits in the oil business are driven by market prices, governed by political stability, weather and economic growth, which are outside the control of production companies, and also by production costs, which the industry can control to a degree. There are higher numbers of wells to drill since the 1980s, but extraction costs are rising because the easy oil has reached saturation. Therefore, companies must explore deeper and more complex reservoirs (Brent *et al*, 1995).

An event in October 1973 is the best example of policy controlling prices. The Organization of the Petroleum Exporting Countries (OPEC) was established in 1960 with five founding members (Iran, Iraq, Kuwait, Saudi Arabia and Venezuela) 'to coordinate and unify the petroleum policies of its member countries and ensure the stabilization of oil markets, in order to secure an efficient, economic and regular supply of petroleum to consumers, a steady income to producers, and a fair return on capital for those investing in the petroleum industry' (OPEC.org). Another objective of course was to protect Middle Eastern producers against the dominance of United States multinationals. Today it has 15 members, Saudi Arabia being the clear leader, and is a major influencer of pricing, with almost half of global oil production under its remit, and over 80 per cent of global reserves. In the decade up to 1973, global production per capita had peaked, and control shifted from countries such as the United States and Germany, who were

The Art of Responding to Disruption Through the Physical Supply Chain

now becoming dependent on Middle Eastern suppliers, where production was on the increase. Prices escalated. The 1973 Yom Kippur War led by Egypt and Syria against Israel in October created an oil crisis when the US supported the Israeli military. The Arab nations of OPEC responded by proclaiming an embargo on oil exports, lasting until March 1974. This created a perceived shortage and soaring prices.

There was further US disruption in 1979 when it supported the Iranian revolution, and again in 1980 when Iraq invaded Iran, significantly halting production in both countries. Other countries began to bridge this gap in supply, and prices began to fall again. In fact, this coincided with a general decline in global economic growth, which created a temporary oil surplus. Market prices into the 1990s were relatively stable, but production costs were continually increasing and the number of barrels of oil per day (BOPD) per well had fallen accordingly. The present climate is not so stable. Brent crude oil pricing, the industry benchmark, finally plunged in 2014 following the global financial crisis, reaching a low in December 2016. OPEC then implemented a production-cut quota of 1.2 million BOPD, with complete member-compliance, which resulted in the doubling of prices. Today, OPEC's reversing of this decision in June 2018, when its technical committee recommended a supply increase of one million BOPD, will send pricing soaring again, simply on the basis that new measures will not create a surplus, or a 'glut' as coined by *The New York Times* in the 1980s. Saudi Arabia and Russia are expected to benefit the most from this latest policy to address a global supply deficit (Mazodila, 2018).

Such political, economic and socio-economic volatility is creating significant bunker fuel surcharges for the industry and a parallel demand unpredictability that challenges long-term pricing agreements with the now-consolidated shipping lines. The business decision then becomes whether or not to pass these costs to customers. Therefore, the challenge becomes one of transparency. Ocean alliances are not the only network-protecting mergers and acquisitions impacting supply chain management. Oil production companies are also seeing an increasing trend, with the west-Texas Permian basin attracting the most activity in 2017, including the ExxonMobil purchase of the Bass family companies ($6.6 billion), Parsley Energy acquiring Double Eagle Energy ($2.8 billion), and Noble Energy purchasing Clayton Williams for $2.8 billion (Bandz, 2017). Another significant announcement in June 2018 was the biggest oilfield service provider, Schlumberger, combining forces with the largest provider of fracking services, Halliburton (blasting water, sand and chemicals underground to release trapped hydrocarbons), 'for an onshore production sharing deal with Brazil's state-controlled Petrobras' (Alper and Hampton, 2017). These policy-driven developments point to a changing business model but can and should be an opportunity to re-assess and improve.

Conclusion

The aim of discussing the challenges of the freight and logistics industry has been to demonstrate the disruptive policy-driven supply chain forces that are seemingly invisible to the senior management team strategic-formulation-process of global organizations. Insights from highly experienced professionals have shown that Friedman's premise that the forces of globalization, technology and climate change are accelerating beyond our ability to adapt is valid. This is due to political and economic policies but is also arising from socio-economic trends. Supply chain managers must be just as cognisant of these challenges, instead of routinely demanding cost and transit-time reductions from their 3PLs in monthly scorecards and quarterly business reviews. Instead there needs to be a recognition that (corporate) organizations must take greater ownership of these new global challenges and align internal processes accordingly. Corporate inventory-holding policies and Chinese New Year planning strategies are illustrations of this.

Organizations must factor in port congestion, and the limited power that service providers have over the situation, origin delays in China due to factory closures and dangerous goods processing, which crosses into manufacturing strategy within supply chain management, and non-tariff measures that lead to additional time and costs. Greater clock speeds and forced efficiencies can help us all evolve and counter the challenges of e-commerce, embracing this niche as an opportunity to re-assess lead-times, usage of inventory and delivery models. Alliances on the ocean and oil fields will ensure that disruption from the more widely encompassing problems of security and fuel charges, and the dilemma of absorbing these costs or passing them on to their clients, will continue. Returning to the aims and objectives now, with these new findings:

- *Determine how supply chain managers operationally identify, predict, cope and recover from supply chain disruptions.* Many events are unpredictable such as China's factory closures, and freight companies are also exposed to client-organization disruptions, which are not under their direct control. However, planning for disruption can include:

- *Avoidance:* Discovery (this can be personal goods that require complex documentation and thereby open to customs events, or high value cargo that is not covered under client insurance as the risk is too great), information (it is critical for freight forwarders to gather all information on cargo, such as in the case of client non-disclosure of dangerous goods, which could lead to additional charges, customs events, and losing control of the cargo entirely), security, preparedness (safeguarding the cargo prior to shipment to minimize risk).
- *Containment:* Indirect investments (insurance certificates can be created for each shipment to cover the full value), supply chain design, redundancy, operating flexibility, security, preparedness.
- *Stabilization:* Supply chain design (optimizing routes for clients, offering hub solutions and advising on air and ocean combinations), redundancy, operating flexibility, preparedness.
- *Return:* Operating flexibility, preparedness (this can take the form of assisting clients in sourcing alternative solutions to return to a more favourable state, such as the Woodland case of stoves now being procured in India).

- *Identify which phases in the supply chain disruption process require engagement with top management to implement strategic solutions aligned to business goals.* In the case of freight and transportation companies, this becomes an internal business decision on whether to absorb the additional costs of fuel and security or pass them to their clients. Despite the competitive nature of the industry, the growing challenges must be highlighted to client management in order to improve alignment.
- *Consequently, determine whether a categorization of supply chain strategy exists, such as a tier consisting of strategies that can be implemented autonomously by the supply chain division, and a tier or tiers that requires 'negotiation' across the top management team prior to implementation, to collaboratively mitigate risk.* It was discussed that disruptions can be light (such as a misunderstanding on fees), which can be responded to autonomously, or severe, which require team-work to solve (such as vessel accidents, or a $5 million case with customs authorities in South America due to wrong documentation). External policies (political, economic, social, technological, climatic) can be placed within the negotiation categorization. Internal policies within the boundaries of supply chain management belong to the autonomous categorization.

Supply Chain Disruption

Policy: the source of supply chain disruption

External policy: political, economic, social, technological, climatic
Protectionism and trade wars; political cyber-security breaches; political migration;
Socio-economic customer demand: e-commerce and environment-driven decisions;
OPEC production management, military-driven oil embargoes, oil and gas mergers and acquisitions;
China government manufacturing plant closures; culture of CNY non-returning work-force;
Holiday schedules in China and India, week-long port closures and resulting back-logs;
Major consumer-brand product launches, reducing ocean and air capacity

Internal industry policy: supply chain management
E-retailers consuming warehouse real-estate; non-licensed exponential logistics companies
entering the market; Blockchain: risk of hacking and fraud; accelerating force of technology such as NFC;
Customs documentation restrictions and non-tariff measures including VGM;
Ocean alliances and mega-ships; containers lost at sea due to weight declarations;
Slow-steaming and artificial removal of vessel capacity; mergers of logistics providers;
Sea-port congestion including inter-modal inbound road and waterway delays;
Fuel and bunker surcharges; China government dangerous-goods processing;
Security measures including convoys and restrictions in route-planning

**Internal organizational policy:
top management team strategic renewal process**
Lean inventory holding; CNY planning

Supply Chain Disruption

Macro: impacting supply chain network design
TMT negotiation based on pre-determined investment threshold of the organization

Micro: supply chain friction
HRM policy: anger to succeed and passion to deliver

Supply Chain Disruption:
Black Swan Crises and Disasters
Grey Swan Breakdowns
what we do inside the bubble of our profession

Supply Chain Strategies:
both TMT negotiation and autonomous

Supply Chain Friction:
Petty circumstances
Blind natural forces
know what we do inside the bubble of our profession and triumph over it

Supply Chain Strategies:
autonomous

- *Determine how supply chain managers engage with the top management team in the process of aligning business and supply chain strategies, thereby identifying key enablers and inhibitors.* The threshold for top management team involvement is based on the investment value and therefore the simulated costing of network redesign is critical to engagement. It was also found that the demonstrable value of people above process is key to negotiation. Supply chain risk mitigation should be built into human resource management. Life and business are not perfect, but in both cases nothing replaces a willingness and passion to deliver, and an anger to succeed. Detailed standard operating procedures or manuals are not required if people are aligned for success. Personal goals (tuition for kids, car, mortgage, professional growth, etc) must be aligned with company goals (higher sales, better service, lower costs, etc).

- *Develop a process model that establishes the phases of supply chain managers' engagement in dynamic business to supply chain strategic alignment.* The policy schema from the end of Chapter 2 (page 37) can now be expanded: see previous page. The top management team strategic renewal process remains noticeably lean in terms of disruption sources, but this was to be expected given that this chapter was not so much about business to supply chain strategic alignment, as it was about sources of policy-driven supply chain disruption at an industry level, and how logisticians respond through their art of movement.

References

Alper, A and Hampton, L (2017) https://www.reuters.com/article/us-petrobras-schlumberger-exclusive/exclusive-schlumberger-halliburton-ready-bids-for-petrobras-output-sharing-deal-idUSKCN1J222U

Bandz, K (2017) https://marketrealist.com/2017/09/these-have-been-the-top-5-energy-ma-deals-so-far-this-year

Berden, KG, Francois, JF, Thelle, M, Wymenga, P and Tamminen, S (2009) *Non-tariff Measures in EU–US Trade and Investment: An economic analysis*, ECORYS Nederland BV

Brent, A, Dole, S, Chmilowski, W, Harmon, H, Vernon, G, Lewis, R, Vinson, M, Thompson, J and Watson, T (1995) Alliances in the oil field, *Oilfield Review*, 7(2), pp 26–39

Catchpole, M and Coulombier, D (2015) Refugee crisis demands European Union-wide surveillance! *Eurosurveillance*, 20(45)

Dockrill, P (2017) https://www.sciencealert.com/china-shutting-40-factories-massive-effort-cut-pollution-carbon- pm2-5

Forsey, C (2018) https://blog.hubspot.com/marketing/ecommerce-trends

Friedman, TL (2016) *Thank You for Being Late: An optimist's guide to thriving in the age of accelerations*, Farrar, Straus and Giroux

Hacker, F, Harthan, R, Matthes, F and Zimmer, W (2009) Environmental impacts and impact on the electricity market of a large-scale introduction of electric cars in Europe: Critical review of literature, ETC/ACC technical paper, 4, pp 56–90

Hawkins, TR, Singh, B, Majeau-Bettez, G and Strømman, AH (2013) Comparative environmental life cycle assessment of conventional and electric vehicles, *Journal of Industrial Ecology*, 17(1), pp 53–64

Heisbourg, F (2015) The strategic implications of the Syrian refugee crisis, *Survival*, 57(6), pp 7–20

Hillman, JE (20180) https://www.csis.org/analysis/rise-china-europe-railways

Hintjens, J, Vanelslander, T, Van der Horst, M and Kuipers, B (2015) The evolution of the economic centre of gravity and the consequences for gateway ports and hinterland connections: The case of the Flemish–Dutch Delta, *Proceedings of the IAME Annual Conference 2015, International Association of Maritime Economists, Kuala Lumpur, 24–26 August 2015*, pp 1–23

Horwitz, J (2017) https://qz.com/892221/samsung-ssnlf-finally-explained-what-caused-the-galaxy-note-7-explosions/

Jiang, X (2015) What happened to MOL comfort? *SWZ/MARITIME*, pp 13–16

Logindex.com (2018) https://logindex.com/products/gkni/

Mazodila, S (2018) https://oilprice.com/Geopolitics/International/The-OPEC-Agreement-Puts-A-Floor-Under-Oil-Prices.html

Notter, DA, Gauch, M, Widmer, R, Wager, P, Stamp, A, Zah, R and Althaus, HJ (2010) Contribution of Li-ion batteries to the environmental impact of electric vehicles, *Environmental Science and Technology*, 44(17), pp 6550–56

OPEC.org (2018) http://www.opec.org/opec_web/en/about_us/23.htm

Perlroth, N, Scott, M and Frenkel, S (2017) Cyberattack hits Ukraine then spreads internationally, *The New York Times*. [Online] https://www.nytimes.com/2017/06/27/technology/ransomware-hackers.html

Runhaar, HAC, Heijden, R and Kuipers, B (2002) Flexibility of freight transport sectors: An Exploration of carriers' responses to external pressure on prices and service, *European Journal on Transport and Infrastructure Research*, 2(1), pp 19–40

Schuler, M (2014) http://gcaptain.com/rena-grounding-final-report/

Schuler, M (2017) http://gcaptain.com/number-of-containers-lost-at-sea-falling-survey-shows/

Sheffi, Y (2001) Supply chain management under the threat of international terrorism, *The International Journal of Logistics Management*, 12(2), pp 1–11

Taylor, C (2018) https://www.irishtimes.com/business/technology/irelandcould gain 100-000 jobs by embracing driverless technology 1.3456820

Times of India (2016) https://timesofindia.indiatimes.com/ world/ china/Chinese-cities-shut-down-factories-ahead-of-G20-summit/articleshow/53913311.cms

Woodside, J, Chen, S, Wenjuan, X and Huilan, L (2017) https://www.theguardian.com/cities/2017/may/23/city-exploded-china-growth-tianjin-disaster-inevitable

Xeneta.com (2018) https://www.xeneta.com/shipping-line-mergers-timeline

Yarr, H and Smith, MH (2016) *Dealing with Supply Chain Disruption: How businesses are managing their supply chains through the migrant crisis in Calais*

The challenges of humanitarian logistics   05

After the Great War, the League of Nations mandated the partition of Greater Syria under French control into the countries of Lebanon and Syria (independent since 1943), where the Irish Defence Forces now face tensions (UNIFIL Sector West and Golan Heights) that can only be fractionally appreciated by road hauliers passing through Calais border checkpoints. One sector of our profession who can certainly relate to these tensions are the noble and exceptionally brave humanitarian logisticians who are deployed in areas such as the home of the Calais refugees of Syria.

The clandestine and underground manner in which these humanitarian logisticians are forced to operate in certain circumstances is the epitome of supply chain disruption in action. Geopolitical polices and interests have completely failed to support both the victims of the continuing 2011 Syrian popular uprising, and the medics and logisticians coming to their rescue, who are systematically targeted by government forces. The age of capitalism unleashed demonstrated inadequacies in international institutions and the non-attendance of Doctors Without Borders (*Médecins Sans Frontières*) and other organizations at the World Humanitarian Summit in May 2016 showed their disapproval of the indifferent handling of Syria by agencies such as the UN Security Council, and in fact European nations in general who opted for a push-back policy (Boulet-Desbareau, 2016).

A similar situation has arisen with African refugees departing from Libya, whereby European governments in the Central Mediterranean are blocking the disembarkation of people rescued by agencies such as SOS Mediterranee in partnership with *Médecins Sans Frontières*. International maritime and humanitarian laws prohibit these boats from returning to the unsafe haven of Libya, and in the four weeks up to mid-July 2018 alone, over 600 refugees including toddlers have drowned. What makes this worse is that the EU-supported Libyan Coastguard intercepted around 10,000 people in the first half of 2018 and returned them to detention centres in Libya where their lives are in grave danger (MSF, 2018). At the start of the decade, the continent of Africa was impacted by remote climatic forces in Russia with the Black Sea drought, excessive rains in Canada and the American Midwest, and massive flooding in Australia and Pakistan, all major wheat exporters. Combine this with the price of oil moving towards US$125 per barrel in the Middle East, making the operation of tractors and the use of fertilizers prohibitive in Africa, and the resulting serious bread shortage prompted an Arab Spring that began in Tunisia in December 2010 to challenge authoritarian rule, and included the 2011 expulsion of Egyptian President Mubarak where protestors cried 'bread, freedom, dignity' (Friedman, 2016). The almost exact conditions that led to the 1789 French Revolution.

Humanitarian agencies legally entering a disaster situation do so under the authority of the government and local authorities, but thereafter generally do not control where their supplies and resources are distributed. In Damascus, the Government-led Syrian Red Crescent therefore assigns foreign aid to defenders of the Bashar Assad regime, forcing some humanitarians to covertly engage with opposition groups in order to reach the true victims of this conflict, trapped in besieged zones. The Syrian Government has disregarded Geneva Conventions that protect medics and patients through their policy of large-scale destruction of hospitals, and execution of doctors and surgeons, mainly to prevent the severity and number of Bashar Assad atrocities being recorded. A double-tap bombing of hospitals has been adopted to ensure the minimum of survivors. Once ambulances have arrived and taken on victims of the initial rocket attack, a second wave is launched on the nearest medical facilities. In 2015, eighty *Médecins Sans Frontières* members were killed, and between 2011 and 2016, 720 Physicians for Human Rights died while performing their duties.

It is estimated that for the death of every one medic, two logisticians have been killed through sniper fire and mine explosions when crossing siege borderlines. This has somewhat been alleviated through temporary Russian–US cease-fires, such as in February 2016 when the International Syrian Support Group authorized the United Nations and the International Committee of the Red Cross to move goods to non-critical areas. However, the bombing of hospitals has remained a constant, even during these reprieves. Within this context, medical points have been established in bathrooms and hidden rooms, and mobile hospitals set up in mosques, basements and caves. Success in this environment demands a focus on innovation rather than efficiencies, a balance between humanitarian risk and impact, and complete transparency across the entire network (Boulet-Desbareau, 2016). Against this tense backdrop of political and military supply chain disruption, we meet two professional humanitarian logisticians.

LogAid Humanitarian Logistics Consultancy

Supply chain disruption in Afghanistan and East Africa: a military and humanitarian perspective

During a 28-year military career with the Royal Logistics Corps of the British Army, David Duddy MSc CMILT commanded the AFNORTH Multinational Transport and Maintenance Company in Brunssum, Netherlands and in Kabul, Afghanistan, and was Second-in-Command of 17 Port and Maritime Regiment, RLC in Southampton. David is now Managing Director of LogAid, based in Scotland, providing preparation, deployment and direct support to crisis response organizations across the globe. Our respective doctoral research brought us together at the Logistics Research Network in Southampton Solent University. Having experienced both spectrums, David first explains that military supply chain disruption can be defined as any force that leads to an impediment in the flow of goods along the supply chain and can be grouped into internal action, external action and environmental conditions. In the case of NATO partner land forces, military objectives are achieved through the projection of combat power, and this is facilitated by any combination of land combat troops, direct air engagement, and direct maritime engagement. These elements are supported by indirect combat action-and-enabling support services, such as engineers, intelligence units, strategic communication units, helicopter weapons platforms and artillery units, and of course by combat-service-support (CSS) troops such as transportation and supply units.

The CSS commander must ensure that support is provided to front-line combat troops exactly when and where they need it. The challenge of this includes the contextual and situational nature of war, in addition to disruption caused by economic, commercial, political, diplomatic and environmental issues. There can also be blue on blue incidents such as a coalition attack helicopter mistakenly identifying a friendly forces ammunition convoy for an enemy strategic move, or indeed a President situated remotely not authorizing convoy protection because the loss of military personnel would damage an upcoming election campaign. Modern military operations are increasingly supported by civilian contractors, and if a freight partner fails to comply with international trade laws or a host nation's import legislation, the resulting disruption will have the same impact as the enemy bombing the only bridge across a river.

Afghanistan in 2003 provides a case for David to demonstrate this. Early in the attempt to stabilize the political and conflict situation, the International Security Assistance Force (ISAF I–IV) deployed fully integrated HQ-led force contingents to Kabul from NATO nations under the command of a general from a lead nation, on rotation between the UK, Germany and Turkey. David commanded a transportation and maintenance company (ISAF V) from Brunssum, Netherlands, comprised of 11 nations. Diesel fuel was essential to this operation in order to power vehicles, and for generators that provided light, heat, air-conditioning and electricity for HQ and outpost buildings, communications installations and troop accommodation. Local fuel storage depots were replenished by a commercial supplier, from where bowser trucks of the AFNORTH transport squadron distributed the fuel across Kabul city. Insurgents were of course aware of the importance of these movements and immediately caused disruption by targeting trucks through various means. NATO forces reduced this threat by changing routes and timings, running both convoys and single vehicle packets, and escorting tankers with heavily armed troops in armoured personnel carriers. This, however, did not completely suppress the imagination of the terrorists.

On one occasion, a single tanker moved along a wide, busy main street in Kabul that had been reconnoitred and given security clearance, every 100 metres passing under telephone cables and electrical wires elevated over the carriageway, using tall poles fixed in place in old oil barrels full of concrete. There were hundreds of these installations on almost every main arterial road. The escorted tanker driver noticed on approach that a telephone cable was at windscreen height and slowed down to avoid it snapping and cutting bystanders. However, this was actually steel wire and two lightweight oil barrels containing explosives hit the side protection bars between the tractor unit and wheels of the trailer unit. Fortunately the explosives did not detonate, and the driver's alertness averted a disaster caused by a crude tension device. A solution was identified and implemented for this temporary near-fatal supply chain disruption, allowing fuel supplies to resume and showing the terrorists that AFNORTH would not be easily stopped.

Let us discuss humanitarian supply chain management and the 2014 outbreak of the Ebola virus in West Africa. The three countries affected each had traditional links with three developed countries who provided the basis of their aid platforms, and although military personnel were deployed to assist, the response effort was commanded and controlled by their foreign affairs government departments, and not their defence ministries: France to Guinea, the UK to Sierra Leone, and the United States to Liberia. A donation of more than one hundred off-road motorcycles was made to one of the stricken countries and these were positioned in a United Nations-owned compound prior to registration for road use and assignment to direct engagement teams in up-country districts for the collection of valuable blood samples and transportation to testing laboratories. However, a large number of that country's civil servants were strategically redeployed into important Ebola response roles, and the vehicle registration and licensing office was consequently significantly under-resourced. The result was serious supply disruption of these essential motorcycle assets. This disruption was resolved, and the assets were moved to where they were desperately needed. The source of the problem was not so much the redeployment of experienced civil servants, but the disproportionate effort needed to negotiate with top management teams and re-align their political aims to the situation on the ground. *Gap of pain.*

Meanwhile, the foresight of an advisor working in one nation's Ebola response operations centre led to the procurement of Unimog all-terrain ambulances in preparation for the rainy season. Once received, the Unimogs were registered, and four months prior to expected heavy rainfall were positioned in front-line areas where Ebola was most prevalent, and where the transport infrastructure was known to be extremely difficult in wet conditions. The operation was disrupted when one of the ambulances went missing. A search was initiated, and it was eventually discovered that an individual had decided that since the vehicle would not be needed until the rains came, it could serve as his personal all-terrain camping wagon in the interim. Unfortunately, in preparing it for camping mode, many essential medical installations had been removed, damaged or destroyed. This renegade supply chain disruption later prevented infected casualties in some areas from reaching medical facilities until such time as the sojourning ambulance was repaired and returned to front-line service.

A compassionate perspective must be considered when comparing corporate and humanitarian supply chain disruption. There are some parts of the world where the values and ethics of Europe and North America are not necessarily understood, appreciated or tolerated, and where the people being exposed to conflict, extreme poverty and natural disasters may not see that their actions may be disrupting a humanitarian supply chain. If the procurement manager in a major corporate automotive assembly plant orders 100 gearboxes from a component manufacturer but only 86 actually arrive, there is an impact to production and profit, and penalties are imposed on the supplier for the supply chain disruption they have caused. However, if a humanitarian nutritionist in a disaster area estimates a requirement for 100 sacks of rice to feed the affected people, it is highly improbable that 100 would be delivered due to several factors:

- The contents of a sack could be scattered if a fork-lift truck pierces a sack in a European warehouse.
- One may fall off the delivery truck on the way to the port.
- Another may fall into the sea as it is being craned onto a ship.

Once inside the host country, the losses are likely to be considerably higher due to hungry dock workers, unscrupulous warehouse watchmen and unpaid policemen manning road check points. These all contribute to supply chain disruption in an academic sense, but an ethical judgement must be made as to whether these losses are tolerable and sustainable. The truck reaches its destination and only 86 sacks arrive. The nutritionist may concede that 100 would have been better, but at least the people have something to eat. Perhaps this is therefore not supply chain disruption in such a situational context since dock-workers are also victims and, through experience, the nutritionist may factor in such losses and order an additional 14 sacks in advance to ensure that the full demand is satisfied.

Humanitarian supply chains need to be bespoke in their design, reacting to the environmental, infrastructural and financial aspects of each response.

However, many UN agencies operate a generic supply chain design, which they adjust to better suit the situational needs of an operation. This approach risks internally created supply chain disruption. One particular UN agency has traditionally separated the logistics functions of supply chain management and procurement (noting here how the military places logistics as the higher-level function). Supply chain management is conducted by logisticians at a regional level and procurement by financiers in global HQ departments. The supply specialist's imperative is to position the right items at the right place at the right time and in the right condition, and it can be frustrating (but also fatal) when someone in a finance office on the other side of the world is asking you to be patient while they adhere to certain internal fiscal procedures. Procurement processes and procedures are essential when it comes to the distribution of food and medicine for human consumption, but in humanitarian supply chains, all stakeholders must fully understand the need to design and use these processes to create the conditions for the delivery of supplies at speed (reducing the *gap of pain*), just as commercial supply chain stakeholders need to design and use them for the delivery of profit.

Traditionally, humanitarian supply chains have been viewed as a subset of commercial supply chains, with soldiers operating military supply chains in a manner reflecting an armoured commercial supply chain. This is no longer the case. Military supply chains are now becoming less soldier-operated armoured supply chains and more civilian-operated unarmoured supply chains, while humanitarian supply chains are now seen as a distinct discipline, differentiating themselves through developments in the way donations and procurement are handled in disaster scenarios, together with changes in attitudes towards fiscal and performance aspects. A fundamental difference is that consumers control commercial supply chains as the customer, whereas in the humanitarian domain, the consumer is the beneficiary of aid, but the controlling customer determining commodity demand is the subject matter expert within the response operation. This individual varies demand depending on environmental factors, storage availability and medical priorities and, as the principal stakeholder in a flexible and adaptable supply network, can influence procurement and delivery channels, access alternative supply sources and choose between donated supplies or local purchase. This process is independent of the consumer who is at the mercy of the resulting outputs.

There is a saying in the British military that a lean unit can also be agile if it maintains an *all-informed-net*, whereby the most able and intelligent combat soldiers carry the platoon or squadron radio and listen constantly to the broadcasts of all the other callsigns on the network frequency, to keep their commanders fully informed of what is happening in the battle space. This *leagile* construct can be applied to humanitarian supply networks comprised of lateral supply chains, working in cooperation or collaboratively, each within the fully integrated vertical control and influence of strategic and regional decision-making management teams. Critical to the efficiency of this concept is that strategic managers have sufficient knowledge and experience so as not to cause delays and uncertainty throughout the chain.

David posits that his aforementioned sources of supply chain disruption (internal and external action, and environmental conditions) have further sub-categories:

Supply chain disruption: internal action

- **Management decision:** Delay in decision-making; change in supply strategy; misjudging the scale or nature of the supply chain operation; failure to design and control an appropriate supply chain; failure to appropriately man (experience, education and training) or resource the supply chain.
- **Management reconsideration:** Changes in financial or operational priorities; changes in manpower or personalities in authority; changes in the end-product, therefore a change in requirements; indirect impact of external pressures.
- **Information flow disruption:** Failure to communicate effectively and efficiently throughout the supply chain network; failure to communicate internal, external and environmental changes; failure to contingency-plan for potential future disruption.
- **Unauthorized act:** Deliberate operation of (or permitting the operation of) supply chain assets, such as equipment and vehicles, outside authorized parameters; failure to comply with legislative requirements.
- **Unintended or accidental act:** Human error; unable to control an external force, such as a road traffic accident; failure of infrastructure or equipment through wear and tear.
- **Intentional or incompetent act:** Negligent conduct; failure to control a controllable external force, such as failure of equipment through neglect; use of untrained or inexperienced manpower.

Supply chain disruption: external action

- **Political or governance intervention:** Decision of a governmental department or other such authoritative agency, which intentionally or unintentionally disrupts operations, such as restricting or denying access to resources or infrastructure; political or legislative conditions which impact on the effectiveness or efficiency of a supply chain to be established in a new jurisdiction.
- **Change in strategic priorities:** Changes in governmental or local authority priorities, such as: priority use of infrastructure; limited access to available resources; changes governing the use of non-domestic equipment, vehicles and manpower.

- **Criminal or unauthorized act:** Acts of sabotage, theft, extortion and bribery within an existing supply chain or ethically corrupt or unauthorized protectionist acts impacting on the ability to establish a supply chain; impact of conflict situations and, in military terms, enemy action.
- **Unintended or accidental act:** Unintended consequences of an action to address a particular problem not taking the supply chain into consideration; accidental or unavoidable act of an external agent, such as a transportation delay or illness of a key stakeholder; in multi-agency or military terms, unintended *blue-on-blue* actions by partner organizations and friendly forces.
- **Intentional or incompetent act:** Deliberate refusal of external agent to cooperate despite their organization's agreement to do so; an act of incompetence by an external agent, or incompetent decision by an external stakeholder organization, such as a decision to delay temperature-sensitive goods at a border post without the availability of air-conditioning or cold storage facilities.

Supply chain disruption: environmental conditions

- **Political, diplomatic, legal:** The political climate, including diplomatic relationships between stakeholder nations and the existing national legislation before a supply chain is established; changes to supply chain operations resulting from changes to the aforementioned.
- **Geographical, infrastructure, physical environment:** The state of existing geographical, infrastructural and physical environmental factors, or changes in features and facilities through natural forces including climate, weather, earth tremors.
- **Economic, commercial:** Disruption caused by external economic decisions, commercial pressures and competition for available resources.

Furthermore, and in conclusion, David summarizes the four supply chain disruption events of the ISAF fuel tanker, the Ebola motorcycles and Unimog, and the UN agency procurement process, under the criteria of impact, recovery, cause, business to supply chain strategic alignment, advice on how to reduce the *gap of pain*, and how the strategic friction of Carl von Clausewitz (petty circumstances or blind natural forces) influenced each case:

Supply chain disruption: ISAF fuel tanker

- **Impact:** Initial fuel rationing was followed by a spike in demand once the supply had been resumed. It is assumed that finding an immediate solution to the threat also sent a message of defiance to the terrorists.

- **Recovery:** A return to stability, and a deeper awareness of what methods of attack could be deployed against the supply chain.
- **Cause:** This was an unforeseen method of attack and therefore an unplannable disruption. The solution was determined and implemented in a short response time.
- **Business to supply chain strategic alignment:** Senior management functioned well when they were called upon.
- **Reducing the *gap of pain*:** It is difficult to foresee such disruptions in the military supply chain, but it is important to have an alternative modus operandi as part of a contingency plan to mitigate against disruption.
- **Supply chain strategic friction:** David agrees that this is part of everyday life for military personnel, including their supply chain specialists.

Supply chain disruption: Ebola motorcycles

- **Impact:** The testing of many blood samples was severely impacted and delayed the eradication of the virus. Without a doubt, this led to a further spread of the infection and increased loss of life. The reputation of the government department suffered, and the civil servants in the registration office were considered negligent and untrustworthy.
- **Recovery:** Vehicle registration returned to routine levels but, frustratingly, no priority fast-track was given for Ebola-response vehicles.
- **Cause:** A lack of understanding of the importance of the vehicle registration function for imported support vehicles coupled with a lack of suitably experienced or qualified staff. The lack of appreciation by office staff of the urgency for rapid registration was very frustrating and seemed lost on senior office managers and transport department officials.
- **Business to supply chain strategic alignment:** There was little evidence of alignment even though, given the nature of the assets being supplied, the registration office was effectively part of the supply chain. Lack of strategic management understanding.
- **Reducing the *gap of pain*:** A greater strategic understanding of logistics operations is required, and when confronted by logistics experts, senior management must acknowledge their credibility and have a willingness to listen. The implication is that the supply chain is supposed to conform to the greater operational plan rather than be an integral part of it. There was *no seat at the big boys' table for a logistician* (this alone sums up the entire premise of this book).

- **Supply chain strategic friction:** The often-frustrating difference in expectation and ethnic *weltanschauung* (world view), particularly between humanitarian responders from the developed world and local operatives in the developing world, gives rise to friction.

Supply chain disruption: Ebola Unimog

- **Impact:** The reputation of the individual who misappropriated the asset was severely tarnished, but he was able to continue due to the critical nature of his work in this area. The issue gave rise to the establishment of a 'Logistics Assets Inspection' regime by those allocating and controlling vehicle and non-medical equipment assets.
- **Recovery:** The vehicle was repaired and subsequently performed well in the deteriorating weather conditions.
- **Cause:** Greed, and the expectation that the individual could get away with misappropriating an essential medical transport asset.
- **Business to supply chain strategic alignment:** This issue was misappropriation of a supplied asset, which caused disruption to the reverse supply chain. Strategic management would not have anticipated such a bold act, and it responded correctly when it came to light, thereby enabling a quick resumption of the service.
- **Reducing the *gap of pain*:** Strategic managers must understand the value of performance measurement and proper accounting for assets. If a robust asset inspection regime had been put in place, from top management down through the organization, more scrutiny would have been applied to protecting assets, and misappropriation would have been discouraged. When an asset inspection regime was established, it was implemented by the senior logistician without buy-in from strategic managers, and therefore it was initially difficult to apply.
- **Supply chain strategic friction:** 'The African way' can be difficult to understand and can cause serious frustration, but NGOs and IGOs (non and inter-governmental organizations) must contend with it. Learning about each other's customs and ethos can help, but it does not stop the friction occurring.

Supply chain disruption: UN agency procurement process

- **Impact:** The impact has been tighter scrutiny (and therefore less waste) of budget spending and an acceptance that this is how long it takes. However, local and therefore faster procurement channels have now been formalized and subject matter experts are encouraged to make use of pre-scrutinized medical and non-medical items in catalogues to speed up supply.

- **Recovery:** The review of the UN agency's supply chain has resulted in considerable improvement, not only in the processes, but also in greater mutual understanding of the two departments: emergency supply chain operations and the finance procurement office.
- **Cause:** Lack of understanding of the integrated role of procurement as a logistics function. A belief that the control of finance is of greater importance than the emergency operations for which the organization exists.
- **Business to supply chain strategic alignment:** This issue has persisted for many years, despite experienced staff within the organization who have a full appreciation of how the system should work. There appears to be a lack of understanding by strategic managers of logistics functions, processes and procedures. They are not operationally aware.
- **Reducing the *gap of pain*:** The education of senior UN managers and directors in logistics is one approach, but surely the promotion of high-calibre logisticians to the roles of senior managers and directors is the most sensible way forward. For example, despite being responsible for the global provision of food and the lead for the UN's Logistic Cluster, no member of the World Food Program's management board is a logistician. The current executive director is a US politician, like many of his predecessors.
- **Supply chain strategic friction:** David suggests that in order to minimize friction, top management teams need to merge the behaviours and respective knowledge of long-term and institutionalized individuals adopting outdated work practices, with the more career-mobile individuals who bring greater best-practice efficiency and effectiveness to the organization. Unfortunately, some staff with entrenched views consider those with fresh thinking as disruptive. As a corporate logistician it seems incongruous to me that disaster-zone humanitarian agencies have such 'dinosaurs' on their teams, but that does appear to be the case, and points to the fact that senior management is not completely cognisant or engaged in reducing the *gap of pain*.

David Duddy MSc CMILT, Managing Director of LogAid, has provided a powerful contribution. Evidence that there is *'no seat at the big boys' table for a logistician'* is central to the main objectives of this research, which are, firstly, to increase our understanding of supply chain managers' engagement in the process of dynamic business to supply chain strategic alignment, within the context of supply chain disruption, and secondly, to contribute to the broadening of supply chain management to an integrated perspective across the top management team rather than a uni-dimensional and dichotomous view. This is both challenging and concerning in the humanitarian domain, where reducing the *gap of pain* is dependent on a customer (logistician) controlling the speed and appropriate accuracy of response to the consumer (disaster victim) against a culture of senior management decision-makers who lack understanding and are operationally unaware. Such decision-making (policies) inevitably causes supply chain disruption and this will continue unless we collectively make the promotion of logisticians our goal. This *must* take precedence over the education of management (politicians). The main concern of course must always be the consumers.

Emergency logistics team

Responding to the ISIS crisis in the Republic of Iraq

We now move to Erbil, in the Kurdistan region of Iraq, the base of Will Holden, Managing Director of the Irish Emergency Logistics Team, and one of Ireland's premier humanitarian logisticians, having been awarded the Operational Service Medal for Afghanistan, a campaign medal given by the Ministry of Defence of the United Kingdom for service by British Armed Forces personnel in support of the post-2001 Afghan War. Hundreds of thousands of Kurds in Erbil have been displaced from Kirkuk, Khanaqin, Khurmatu, Zummar and Rabea, which have become disputed areas under the military control of Iraqi forces, including the Hashd al-Shaabi, in opposition to the will of 92.7 per cent of Kurdistani people who voted for independence on 25 September 2017. Erbil was already a sanctuary for an estimated 250,000 Syrian refugees, who had fled the escalation of violence in the northern Kurdish regions of their country during the 2012–13 civil war, a situation that also produced a substantial number of internally displaced people (IDPs) who remain within their own border. Since the Islamic State of Iraq and the Levant (ISIS) began its onslaught on Iraq in June 2014, the group took control of Mosul, the second largest city behind Baghdad, with incredible speed. Mosul now also hosts Christians, together with the strictly endogamous Yazidi people, who were escaping a particularly gruesome ISIS extermination campaign in their ancient homeland of

Mesopotamia, the cradle of civilization that was established in 3100 BC, long before biblical times. This brought the number of people sheltering in unfinished buildings, public places, and camps (such as Kawergosk, Qushtapa, Darashakran and Basirma) to several million.

Such situations are supported by both military and humanitarian machines. The movement of the latter requires a very different mind set due to more modest numbers and the absence of small highly skilled specialist units. The logistics challenges faced by these agencies are 95 per cent of their own volition because many untrained agents simply do not have the credentials for this profession. This points to strategic misalignment and strengthens the notion that there is no room for logisticians at the top table. ReliefWeb, the self-proclaimed largest humanitarian information portal in the world, is a resounding testament to this. Under the instruction of senior management, NGO supply chain job advertisements are drafted, but they do not know what they are looking for. There is no comprehension of procurement and logistics, and these postings look instead for degrees and masters in accountancy and finance. Will also mentions, in concert with David Duddy, that in his decades in this field he has never found a supply chain manager on the board of any humanitarian agency. Government regulations are brilliant in their complexity, ensuring that the majority of positions are held by civil servants, documented processes do not reflect reality as they are formulated in remote locations such as Ireland, England and Denmark, and there are no practical standard operating procedures available for logisticians, who must continuously 're-invent the wheel', the latter reluctantly becoming their art form, and significantly contributing to the *gap of pain*. Before even coming to the aid of disaster victims, there is therefore internal policy causing supply chain disruption.

Consider a normal humanitarian response to the influx of Syrian refugees to Kurdistan in 2014, which involved the emergency distribution of food and water to thousands of people situated north of Mosul. Will initially hosted a low-level working group responsible for the formulation of strategic plans that established NGO tasks. When managing a refugee camp, various NGOs are intrinsically linked, and it is essential to have alignment. However, one week later, this particular situation became extremely challenging when the area was overrun by ISIS, thereby escalating to a humanitarian system-wide level 3 emergency declaration. The Kurdish authorities did not publicize the close proximity of ISIS, as they did not want to frighten the camp populations, but one can only imagine the abject fear amongst the humanitarians, and with ISIS at the gates it was a huge challenge to keep teams focused and motivated. The reality for these logisticians, especially international 'Western' aid workers, is that they knew very well that capture by ISIS would lead to either kidnap or a horrific death that would be filmed and broadcasted to the highest audience possible to promote widespread panic. This intense fear naturally spread to families at home, and Will maintains that the distraction of being worried, not only about themselves, but also about the welfare of their loved ones, became in itself a source of supply chain disruption as they responded to some of the most important humanitarian interventions since the end of the Second World War. This was heightened when an internal strategic decision was made to extract one of the largest and most critical NGOs from the response operational group, who withdrew overnight without any communication whatsoever. This NGO was responsible for the management of certain camps in Kurdistan and this gap was felt instantaneously as coordination crumbled at a critical time. This was similar to the Irish–Finnish Battalion case in Lebanon, but more sudden and exposing. Supply chain disruption in action.

This becomes so much more significant when you consider how markedly it contrasts to ISIS, whose recruitment drive has attracted highly educated international management and operational talent, including expertise in engineering and supply chain management. Coalition forces control Iraqi air space, but regardless, ISIS remained masterful at the clandestine transportation of people and goods under the cover of darkness, and accordingly it has taken the military substantial time to contain them, as their mission to emancipate the country from such an evil presence reaches a close. The June 2017 liberation of the ISIS-proclaimed Caliphate of Mosul after three years of conflict comes at a price, with eight million tonnes of conflict debris, and the number of unexploded devices that make it the most heavily contaminated area on Earth, costing $1 billion for its projected 10-year reconstruction (Williams, 2018). The main concentration of ISIS militants is now within Mount Qarachogh, near Makhmour, where a joint operation by Peshmerga and Iraqi security forces killed 14 terrorists on 16 July 2018. In an undisclosed region, one hundred ISIS prisoners are currently being held, of which there are 55 different nationalities, a demonstration of their global reach.

However, their most profound strategy was the re-development of expansive underground railroad tunnels that once connected Baghdad to Berlin, to serve their situational needs, further enhanced by digging a wider network of tunnels for stealth movement, all hidden from US warplanes overhead. Entrances were concealed, and tracks were removed to house all necessary facilities that included medical clinics, mosques and assault training courses designed for elite special forces. This prompted Israel to plan the construction of a large underground wall along its southern border to guard against ISIS infiltration, an extension of a barrier preventing the Palestinian militant group Hamas from entering through tunnels along the Gaza strip. The North Vietnamese adopted this strategy to much greater success during the 1955–75 Vietnam War, but this concept is an ancient one in the Middle East. For instance, 35 sweeping underground cities once protected the inhabitants of Cappadocia in central Turkey, the gateway to important trading routes, such as the renowned Silk Road.

Whilst not necessarily their responsibility, recompense for the unfortunate *gap of pain* caused by senior management not being aligned to supply chain needs is beginning with the humanitarian subject matter experts, through their education of logisticians on the ground. The Irish Emergency Logistics Team has established the first such training anywhere in the Republic of Iraq, its mission being to: deliver 'best in class' humanitarian and emergency logistics training, wherever it is required, build the capacity of supply chain and logistics professionals, support NGOs by building surge capacity, ensure the private sector is fully prepared to work in emerging markets, and build private sector engagement in humanitarian response. The Introductory Certificate in Procurement and Logistics (Humanitarian Context) has been held in Erbil, the University of Duhok and the University of Mosul, and is accredited by the Chartered Institute of Transport and Logistics International. All staff from five NGOs in the Kurdistan Region of Iraq have now completed the modular program consisting of procurement management, warehouse management, asset management, fleet management and distribution management. The collaboration with the University of Mosul has been really interesting as it was used as an ISIS base just one year prior and has been considerably damaged by both the insurgents and coalition forces. Delivering a lecture on how to complete a warehouse assessment in such surroundings of destruction, synchronous with the smell of burned asphalt, in what must be the most extraordinary setting anywhere for a supply chain and logistics course, can be challenging, but the University is rebuilding one room at a time. 'If these kids can continue their education in these conditions, then we have a responsibility to support them by bringing the course to them.' As an extension to this program, I personally implemented a Human Capacity Development Program in Erbil in December 2018.

Delivering aid to post-conflict areas also leads to some extreme supply chain disruption. For example, despite the successful removal of ISIS from Mosul, they still had an active presence in the more sparsely populated areas of Iraq. In December 2017, during Christmas week, a truck moving refugee housing units to an area near Tal Afar, west of Mosul, close to the Syrian border, hit a roadside improvised explosive device (IED). The road and adjacent area were swept and cleared of five more mines, four of which were freshly laid. An unexploded mine was found embedded into the roof of a small warehouse in February 2018. With the support of the United Nations Mine Action Service (UNMAS), Will managed to have this safely removed, but unfortunately the building still could not be used because removal trucks could not gain access to recover scores of dead civilians due to excessive debris.

Will described walking through the ruins of Mosul to assess the challenges he faced, an area that had endured the greatest bombing campaign in decades, as the definition of supply chain disruption. The stench of death was overbearing, with the remains of thousands of rebels and civilians still beneath the ruined buildings, but it was the real threat from unexploded ordnance consisting of IEDs, mines, bombs and munitions laying everywhere that predominantly concerned the humanitarian logisticians.

The Irish Emergency Logistics Team in Yemen

Now we move to the Republic of Yemen, where conflict spread to 21 of the country's 22 governorates, prompting a large-scale protection crisis and compounding an already-dire humanitarian crisis brought on by years of poverty, poor governance and ongoing instability. 'In September 2014, Houthi rebels took control of Yemen's capital, Sana'a, and proceeded to push southwards towards Aden, the second-biggest city. In response to the Houthis' advances, a coalition of Arab states launched a military campaign in mid-March 2015 to defeat the Houthis and restore Yemen's government. In 2017 alone, 50,000 children died, an average of 130 per day' (Al Jazeera News, 2018). In December 2017, it was estimated that 22.2 million people were in need of humanitarian assistance, including 11.3 million in acute need. Yemen had its worst 'cholera outbreak in 2017 with more than one million suspected cases, and a resurgence of the outbreak is likely in 2018 due to the prevalence of risk factors, such as rains, eruption or escalation of conflict, lack of safe water and sanitation' (Logcluster, 2018). The situation has led to a pseudo-blockade of the main port of Hodeidah, placing pressure on the other function ports and making the importation of medical and pharmaceutical items very slow, significantly impairing the Country Office Team in their ability to respond to sudden-onset crises and causing stockouts in essential supplies. It was within this context that Will Holden was tasked with performing a review in June 2017 to determine if the supply chain was being optimized to its full potential. It was also deemed necessary to review the operational structure of the Yemen team to ascertain if any improvements in efficiency could be made to the benefit of all stakeholders. This review included an analysis of international and domestic shipments over the previous 12 months and mapping of end-to-end processes in order to establish best practices.

Sources of supply chain disruption, actual or potential, were found to be structural:

- **Freight forwarding:** Processes were very specific but confusing, and with the level of spend on international procurement it was a concern that there was not a dedicated person in Yemen who was skilled enough to manage the intricacies of this key area.
- **Procurement planning:** A simple plan of action was needed to manage an approximate $40 million of funding that was in the immediate pipeline.
- **Framework agreements:** There was a danger of duplication of efforts due to several national and regional frameworks being developed simultaneously. Documentation of the process would help to eliminate this, and make implementation seamless.
- **Vendor management:** This can sometimes receive little focus during a conflict situation, but it is also an area that can be easily improved, and this was the case in Yemen. Will recommended that all departments should play a role, from programs, procurement and logistics, to finance, who must ensure the processing (and documentation) of payments in a timely manner, so that the establishment of a 'good name' in the business community would result in more vendors taking part in tenders and providing better bids. Will also recommended the vetting of suppliers to rule out non-compliant agencies, and the holding of regular meetings with pre-qualified suppliers to maintain service levels.
- **Procurement thresholds:** Separate thresholds did not exist for construction works, despite the norm being to have much larger thresholds for these types of projects, due to the high cost of equipment and goods. This needed to be changed, while remaining compliant with donor rules and humanitarian agency policies.
- **Increasing orders:** New tenders were being published because the quantities required increased from the original purchase requisitions (PR). Will advised that once there were agreed percentage increases allowed, such as 30 per cent on the original PR values, for example, then there is no need for new tenders and all the delays that then ensue.

- **Total information management (TIM):** This was considered to be a good information technology tool, but users had no 'helpdesk' to report issues to. In addition, there was an absence of documented procedures regarding data server backup, and no understanding of individual responsibilities to ensure the efficacy of this.

- **Procurement tracker:** Similar to TIM, corrupt cells and data were found but there was no pathway to report these issues, nor to receive assistance with training and support.

- **Job descriptions:** Not dissimilar to the corporate domain, a restructuring led to inconsistencies and lack of clarity of roles and responsibilities. These needed to be clearly defined and documented. Common understanding of positions is important, but this process also identifies gaps in essential skills.

- **Management control:** There was little evidence of management spot checks in relation to assets and stock disposal, procurement committees, tender standard operating procedures, staff shortages and internal auditing.

- **Program changes to purchase requisitions:** This is normal and understandable in the humanitarian domain, but the lack of communications that precede change requests, and the lack of understanding by program management of the complexity of changes, leads to frustration and fuels the *gap of pain*. The only way that this can improve is by making sure that there is a member of the top management team who is logistics and procurement focused. The supply chain team needs to work 'hand-in-glove' with programs, finance and security in order to be really effective.

- **Yemen best practice:** Investigating the routing from order entry to beneficiary receipt was a challenge because it was measured in months rather than weeks, and there was still a dependency on the 'Logistics Cluster Djibouti' despite commercial supply chains being open for business, which Will established after meeting with port authorities, shipping agents, a shipping company, medical suppliers, other INGOs and the World Health Organization. The Cluster facilitates access for humanitarian organizations to common logistics services such as overland transport, air cargo transport from Djibouti to Sana'a, sea cargo transport from Djibouti to Aden and Hodeidah, sea passenger transport between Djibouti and Aden, as well as Djibouti and Hodeidah, access to temporary storage facilities and fuel distribution. Delays at Aden port were due to the documentation procedures of the Ministry of Aden, but again also due to the absence of a dedicated person, experienced in freight forwarding, who would resolve any issues (such as incomplete documentation from INGOs) in a timely manner.

The Irish Emergency Logistics Team is generally faced with the ongoing challenges of warehousing and storage (where sparsely paid and untrained workers lack the processes, facilities, communications and motivation for any degree of productivity), safety and security in terms of vehicle movements and monitoring, load distribution preparation, and personal threats, and the holding of critical cluster meetings in extremely stressful locations. However, the one clear message is that humanitarian logisticians face substantial supply chain disruption from within their own organizations and it is therefore gravely crucial to have *a seat at the big boys' table* for our profession. This will reduce the *gap of pain*.

Conclusion

Humanitarian supply chains are now seen as a distinct discipline, differentiating themselves through developments in the way donations and procurement are handled in disaster scenarios, together with changes in attitudes towards fiscal and performance aspects. A fundamental difference is that consumers control commercial supply chains as the customer, whereas in the humanitarian domain the consumer is the beneficiary of aid, but the controlling customer determining commodity demand is the subject matter expert within the response operation. However, one constant across military and humanitarian organizations is that there is no supply chain representation on top management teams, a predetermined view from a corporate perspective that prompted this study. Therefore we can now begin to look at supply chain disruption as a collective phenomenon across the full spectrum of the profession. Returning again to the aims and objectives:

- *Determine how supply chain managers operationally identify, predict, cope and recover from supply chain disruptions.* Structural robustness can help the coping mechanism and reduce the *gap of pain* in crises that are unpredictable, contextual and situational. Emphasis should be on having: dedicated personnel in place to manage freight forwarding; procurement planning and tracking that includes agreed-upon thresholds for order increases without having to re-submit orders due to inevitable changes; well-documented framework agreements that have national and regional consistency; job descriptions that are understood and uniform throughout the organization; all departments should play a role in vendor management, from programs, procurement and logistics, to finance, who must ensure the processing (and documentation) of payments in a timely manner, so that the establishment of a 'good name' in the business community would result in more vendors taking part in tenders and providing better bids; technical support must be in place for users of IT systems, including training, and management controls must be implemented such as spot checks in relation to assets and stock disposal, procurement committees, tender standard operating procedures, staff shortages and internal auditing.

- *Identify which phases in the supply chain disruption process require engagement with top management to implement strategic solutions aligned to business goals.* This arises immediately during the response phase due to the fact that there appears to be a lack of understanding by strategic managers of logistics functions, processes and procedures. They are not operationally aware. For example, the integrated role of procurement as a logistics function is not appreciated. There is a belief that the control of finance is of greater importance than the emergency operations for which the organization exists.

- *Consequently, determine whether a categorization of supply chain strategy exists, such as a tier consisting of strategies that can be implemented autonomously by the supply chain division, and a tier or tiers that requires negotiation across the top management team prior to implementation, to collaboratively mitigate risk.* A negotiation categorization is impeded by the necessity to continuously educate senior UN managers and directors. This has included improving the procurement process through greater mutual understanding, but in general, given the critical operational circumstances, this is detrimental. Autonomous strategies such as the establishment of asset inspection regimes need management approval for smooth implementations.

- *Determine how supply chain managers engage with the top management team in the process of aligning business and supply chain strategies, thereby identifying key enablers and inhibitors.* The dominant conclusion is that senior managers are not operationally aware and that there is *no seat at the big boys' table for a logistician.*

- *Develop a process model that establishes the phases of supply chain managers' engagement in dynamic business to supply chain strategic alignment.* The updated policy schema on the next page now includes the new findings and demonstrates the emerging broad catchment of this topic.

Policy: the source of supply chain disruption

External policy: political, economic, social, technological, climatic

Protectionism and trade wars; political cyber-security breaches; political migration;
Socio-economic customer demand: e-commerce and environment-driven decisions;
OPEC production management, military-driven oil embargoes, oil and gas mergers and acquisitions;
China government manufacturing plant closures; culture of CNY non-returning work-force;
Holiday schedules in China and India, week-long port closures and resulting back-logs;
Major consumer-brand product launches, reducing ocean and air capacity;

Restrictions or legislative conditions on access to resources or infrastructure; changes in strategic priorities governing the use of non-domestic equipment, vehicles and manpower; acts of sabotage, theft, extortion and bribery within an existing supply chain or ethically corrupt or unauthorized protectionist acts impacting on the ability to establish a supply chain; Impact of conflict situations; unintended blue-on-blue actions by partner organizations and friendly forces; deliberate refusal of external agent to co-operate despite their organizations' agreement to do so; diplomatic relationships between stakeholder nations and the existing national legislation before a supply chain is established; external economic decisions, commercial pressures and competition for available resources

Internal industry policy: supply chain management

E-retailers consuming warehouse real-estate; non-licensed exponential logistics companies entering the market; Blockchain: risk of hacking and fraud; accelerating force of technology such as NFC;
Customs documentation restrictions and non-tariff measures including VGM;
Ocean alliances and mega-ships; containers lost at sea due to weight declarations;
Slow-steaming and artificial removal of vessel capacity; mergers of logistics providers
Sea-port congestion including inter-modal inbound road and waterway delays;
Fuel and bunker surcharges; China government dangerous-goods processing;
Security measures including convoys and restrictions in route-planning

Internal organizational policy:
top management team strategic renewal process

Lean inventory holding; CNY planning

Lack of TMT understanding and operational awareness; Management decision: delay in decision-making; change in supply strategy; misjudging the scale or nature of the supply chain operation; failure to design and control an appropriate supply chain; failure to appropriately man (experience, education and training) or resource the supply chain; Management reconsideration: changes in financial or operational priorities; changes in manpower or personalities in authority; changes in the end-product, therefore a change in requirements; indirect impact of external pressures; Information flow disruption: failure to communicate effectively and efficiently throughout the supply chain network; failure to communicate internal, external and environmental changes; failure to contingency-plan for potential future disruption;
Unauthorized act: deliberate operation of (or permitting the operation of) supply chain assets, such as equipment and vehicles, outside authorized parameters; failure to comply with legislative requirements;
Intentional or incompetent act: Negligent conduct; failure to control a controllable external force, such as failure of equipment through neglect; use of untrained or inexperienced manpower

Supply Chain Disruption

Macro: impacting supply chain network design
TMT negotiation based on pre-determined investment threshold of the organization

Micro: supply chain friction
HRM policy: anger to succeed and passion to deliver

Supply Chain Disruption:
Black Swan Crises and Disasters
Grey Swan Breakdowns
what we do inside the bubble of our profession

Supply Chain Strategies:
both TMT negotiation and autonomous

Supply Chain Friction:
Petty circumstances
Blind natural forces
know what we do inside the bubble of our profession and triumph over it

Supply Chain Strategies:
autonomous

References

Al Jazeera News (2018) https://www.aljazeera.com/news/2016/06/key-facts-war-yemen-160607112342462.html

Boulet-Desbareau, P (2016) Underground humanitarian logistics in Syria: The invisible driving force of medical care in besieged areas [Online]. http://emergency-log.weebly.com

Friedman, TL (2016) *Thank You for Being Late: An optimist's guide to thriving in the age of accelerations*, Farrar, Straus and Giroux

Logcluster (2018) Yemen: concept of operations, July [Online]. https://logcluster.org/sites/default/files/logistics_cluster _yemen_conops_180723.pdf

MSF.org (2018) Drowning skyrockets as European governments block humanitarian assistance on Central Mediterranean [Online]. http://msf.org

Williams, S (2018) https://www.standard.co.uk/news/world/mosul-to-mark-one-year-since-liberation-from-isis-but-experts-say-it-could-take-10-years-to-rebuild-a3892456.html

Corporate supply chain disruption

06

Aligning business strategy and supply chain tactics

Although very much interconnected, this chapter now transitions from the categories of crises and disasters to the protection of a $74 trillion global corporate economy. The complexity of supply chain management has been compounded by the force of globalization along the dimensions of replenishment, time and distance (Christopher and Towill, 2002). This feature of contemporary business practices certainly facilitates top management to supply chain strategic misalignment. From the learnings thus far we can begin to resolve that predicament:

- Top management teams are outsourcing mostly to China in search of cost reductions. However, trends such as the Chinese government *blue sky* policy, mandating widespread manufacturing plant closures without notice, restrictive verified gross mass and dangerous goods inspections, United States protectionism policy, and Chinese wage increases (wages in 1980 were 30 per cent of sub-Saharan Africa, but the reverse is true today), are all accelerating supply chain disruption. Alternatives must be explored. Perhaps this can be a *stove plan*, taken from the Woodland case (as discussed on page 106).
- Ocean freight (a global merchant fleet of 52,183 vessels) supports 70 per cent of all international goods moved towards the European Union and 95 per cent of goods to the United States. Top management teams need to have awareness of the present-day challenges arising from ocean alliances and mega-ships (construction on the worlds' next two biggest containerships, capable of holding 22,000 TEUs, began on 26 July 2018), containers

lost at sea, non-tariff barriers, port congestions, threats from digitization (Blockchain), and increasing bunker charges, in order to re-establish customer expectations and adjust planning strategies accordingly, such as *less*-lean inventory holding policies and better Chinese New Year preparations.

- The top management team approach to supplier relationships must be adjusted in regard to 3PL partners who are significantly impacted by e-commerce. Organizations must align internal functions to this *new reality*. Road freight capacity is at crisis point in the US, enabling truckers to choose the most profitable freight. Warehousing is at risk from the complexities of consumer ordering patterns, the introduction of new technologies, such as near-field communication, and the rapid depletion of real estate. Last-mile parcel shipments are being disrupted by unlicenced new entrants, outrageous consumer demands, and mergers such as FedEx–TNT, a partnership that has certainly not worked well in my experience of Europe-to-United States shipments. Both great companies, but the transfer of TNT parcels to FedEx stateside has not been systematic, but rather disruptive.

- It is widely accepted in our profession that supply chains compete, not companies. Therefore the strategic response to disruptions should not be uni-dimensional and dichotomous, thereby broadening supply chain management to a wider perspective (Wu *et al*, 2014). Supply chain knowledge and understanding has been found wanting among operationally unaware strategists. This can be addressed through top management team engagement: sharing data analysis and simulation modelling that *maps the benefits* to all stakeholders, generated to gain internal functional agreement and alignment, including customer advocacy. This can also apply to *retrospective* project reviews that show the actual impact of prior strategic decisions, which companies are generally neglectful of because the focus is on the next project. This should include alternative (reduced cost, shorter *gap of pain*) approaches had 'supply chain' been included in the strategic formulation process.

- It is critical that we nurture a culture of '*change-adaption*'. As examples, greater clock speeds and forced efficiencies can help us all evolve and counter the challenges of e-commerce, embracing this niche as an opportunity to re-assess lead-times, usage of inventory and delivery models, or to factor rising fuel prices as an input cost that allows for a high degree of volatility, rather than treating these events simply as supply chain disruption.

In the meantime... business breakdowns are at the operational level of supply chain disruption. Such disruptions can include uncertain customer demand, quality issues, transportation delays, poor supplier performance, equipment malfunctions, inventory and capacity issues, information systems breakdowns, increasing competitive intensity, and human-centred issues from strikes to fraud. These result in severe stock and operating underperformance and should be a high priority for senior management and shareholders (Kleindorfer and Saad, 2005; Sylla, 2014; Roh *et al*, 2014). Costs and other consequences, such as damage to a brand, can be even more challenging than terrorist acts because they have a greater cumulative effect over time and have a disproportionate effect on demand (Sheffi, 2001; Sylla, 2014).

Given the fact that disruption is increasingly threatening our global supply chains, together with the demonstrated reality that there is *no seat at the big boys' table* for the military and humanitarian logistician, it is critically important to test the prevalence of this fundamental source of supply chain disruption in the corporate domain. Some of the most prominent figures of our profession now help us in that regard and to consequently ascertain how much of a high priority this phenomenon actually is for senior management in practice. Schneider Electric provides the opening case, but first the scene must be set with John Gattorna's proprietary Dynamic Alignment™ model. This body of work has elevated supply chain management to a tailored and segmented approach grounded in science, and the voice of the customer, and has recently earned John the Council of Supply Chain Management Professionals' 2018 Distinguished Service Award, the industry's most prestigious accolade. Generic strategies in response to disruption have been explored, and this research is focused on strategic misalignment as the source. However, it is safe to posit that any organization that does *not* adopt the Gattorna Dynamic Alignment™ model is *encouraging* supply chain disruption.

A short history of the development of the Dynamic Alignment™ model

The search for a better theory to describe what goes on in a company's logistics network began in 1989. John Gattorna and co-researcher Norman Chorn set out to define a concept that would assist the enterprise to better 'align' with its customers and suppliers. In his unpublished doctoral thesis of 1987, Norman Chorn had already researched the linkage between business strategy and organizational culture. He joined Gattorna's consulting firm, Gattorna Strategy, in Sydney in 1988, and together they developed the first conceptual model, tying in Chorn's previous work with Gattorna's work on customers at the market end, and introducing leadership style at the other end. The result was what we called, at the time, Strategic Alignment.

The first academic paper on this concept was presented in 1990 in Stockholm, at the International Conference of the Strategic Management Society. We then set out to use this new conceptual model to answer the big question at the time, which was: If, as we posited, a 'one-size-fits-all' supply chain configuration was flawed, how many supply chains running through the business would be required in most product–market situations, to provide an 80 per cent fit with the market? This was the pivotal question.

We knew that the only way to attack this question was to start from 'outside-in', so we started by focusing on how best to segment the target market in order to best inform the design of enterprise supply chains. This was a fortuitous decision because not only did it lead us to the result we hoped for, our approach also turned out to be very consistent with 'design thinking' which came some years later. At the same time, we went in search of a common metric that would allow us to assess the alignment (or misalignment) of the enterprise [leadership/internal cultural capability/ and operational strategy], with the target market. The problem to date had been the different metrics used in all functions of the enterprise, which made a comparative analysis of alignment impossible. Building on Jung's seminal work on personality types [at the leadership level], and the later simplification provided by Ichak Adizes, we were able to develop a coding system that allowed us to use a common approach to describe what was happening at all four levels of our Strategic Alignment model. This was a real breakthrough because for the first time we had instruments to measure the behaviour of the human element in three of the four levels, and the ability to describe the fourth level in the same metric.

For the next three decades we have continued our field work, across many different industries and geographies, using the behavioural coding system that we developed in 1989. We soon found patterns in the data, and eventually we concluded that there were indeed sixteen behavioural archetypes present in the buyer markets, which by definition meant that in order to achieve a 100 per cent 'alignment' we would need sixteen corresponding supply chain configurations! This was a big shift away from the 'one-size-all' philosophy of old, which was built on conventional 'inside-out' thinking. Interestingly, SAP, who once were prime exponents of the 'one-size-all' philosophy because it fitted their ERP systems approach, has now gone to the other extreme and suggested that it should be possible in the future digital age for a 'Supply Chain of One', where every enterprise would have its own customized supply chain! Their argument is based on the continuing growth in analytics power, but we think it is impractical.

The most commonly observed behavioural segments and corresponding supply chain types are as follows; all of these have been observed and confirmed in practice, many times over:

    Collaborative segment............ Collaborative Supply Chain™
    Transactional segment .... Lean Supply Chain
    Dynamic segment................ Agile Supply Chain
    Project Accumulation segment ... Campaign Supply Chain™
    Innovative Solutions segment .... Fully Flexible Supply Chain™

We continued our field work with actual companies as our laboratories, and eventually came to the conclusion that for an 80 per cent fit to the target market, four to five dominant buying behaviours would suffice. The fifth one was only added in 2012 after extensive work with Schneider Electric, worldwide. What we discovered was the need for a new supply chain type to adequately service the Project/Construction market, which is very different from distributing manufactured goods.

In addition to establishing that (any) five dominant segments and corresponding five supply chain types would achieve an 80 per cent fit to the target market, we also found that customers could change their buying behaviour temporarily or permanently under certain market conditions. This caused us to change the model name to Dynamic Alignment™; we recognized that the customer was a moving target, and that this was the reason that the original 'one-size-fits-all' concept was causing so much grief and cost! Because, as the operating environment became more volatile, this conventional approach was causing an increasing number of exceptions due to the inherent misalignments, the consequence of which was over- and under-servicing, which gave the worst of all worlds result, ie, resources wasted on customers who did not appreciate the effort; and under-servicing of more deserving customers where the real revenue and margin opportunities were.

Prologue

Since we developed the original concept in 1989, and field tested it over the last three decades, our understanding of the value of the model to inform supply chain design and operations has increased logarithmically. During that time, literally hundreds of companies around the world have adopted this approach, some with spectacular results. There is still more work to be done inside the enterprise, as we seek to better understand how to shape and reshape the subcultures necessary to propel aligned operational strategies into the target market. And of course we are still testing various ways to undertake the actual 'transformation' from 'as is' to 'to be' on the ground in the midst of ongoing operations.

Sincerest thanks to John Gattorna for contributing this piece on Dynamic Alignment™ to this book, which is now represented diagrammatically in Figure 6.1, and available in *Dynamic Supply Chains* (Gattorna, 2015).

Figure 6.1   The John Gattorna Dynamic Alignment™ Model

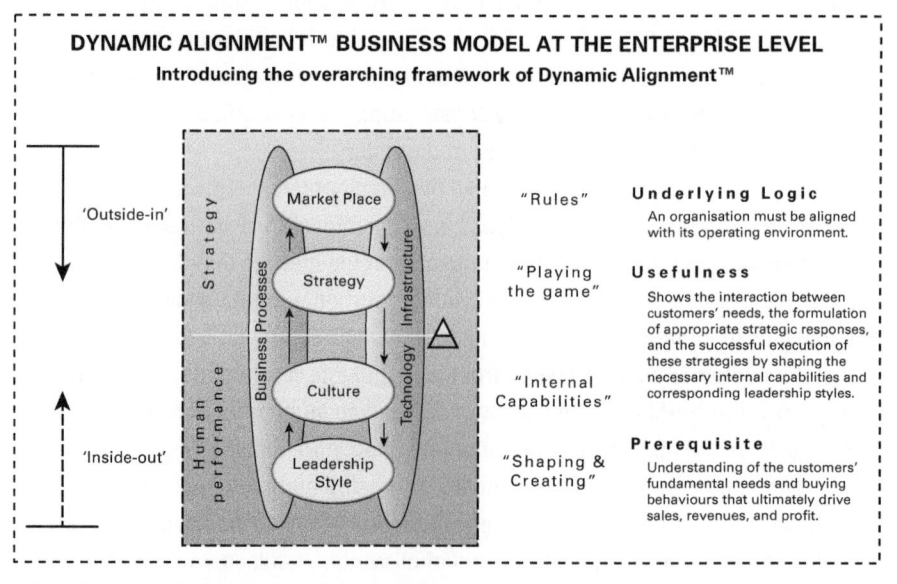

DYNAMIC ALIGNMENT™ BUSINESS MODEL AT THE ENTERPRISE LEVEL
Introducing the overarching framework of Dynamic Alignment™

'Outside-in'

'Inside-out'

Strategy — Business Processes — Human performance

Market Place — Strategy — Culture — Leadership Style

Infrastructure — Technology

"Rules"
"Playing the game"
"Internal Capabilities"
"Shaping & Creating"

Underlying Logic
An organisation must be aligned with its operating environment.

Usefulness
Shows the interaction between customers' needs, the formulation of appropriate strategic responses, and the successful execution of these strategies by shaping the necessary internal capabilities and corresponding leadership styles.

Prerequisite
Understanding of the customers' fundamental needs and buying behaviours that ultimately drive sales, revenues, and profit.

SOURCE Adapted from Gattorna (2015) p.25
© John Gattorna Trade marks: Dynamic Alignment™ Collaborative Supply Chain™ Campaign Supply Chain™ Fully Flexible Supply Chain™

Demonstration of the Gattorna Dynamic Aligment™ model in action: Schneider Electric

A global specialist in energy management and automation

Probably the most prominent demonstration of Dynamic Alignment™ in action was a Schneider Electric project to build a customer-centric logistics platform tailored to customers' buying behaviour. This was tasked to Stuart Whiting, Senior Vice President, Logistics and Network Design. In five years, the Schneider Electric logistics and network design team successfully doubled their customer satisfaction score on delivery, improved their on-time delivery to customers by 3.2 points and secured recurrent annual savings of €150 million on logistics (DC and transportation). Recognizing that a one-size-fits-all approach does not adequately deliver to customer needs, Schneider Electric's global supply chain organization designed their logistics network around their customers' key buying behaviours.

Starting with the customers' voice in mind, and through using advanced network modelling techniques, coupled with a suite of digitized logistics capabilities, they built tailored customer-focused logistics solutions. All of this was achieved without sacrificing the organizations' scale and efficiency, which makes its logistics and delivery network their key competitive advantage. Through consistent customer engagement, dynamic network modelling and design, and the adoption of digitization along with disciplined data governance, Schneider Electric evolved their operations to deliver successfully on 'differentiation' and 'right to win' capabilities, in collaboration with their Front Office (Sales) and Lines of Business (Products, Equipment and Services). These implementations were focused completely on the needs of their customers, and resulted in a disciplined global supply chain platform, aimed at delivering to customers with dynamic and significant results.

Background

For the 12 years prior to the project implementation, Schneider Electric's business more than doubled in size through mergers, acquisitions and organic growth. With a legacy of 125 different enterprise resource planning systems, and numerous warehouse management and transport management systems, a newly formed logistics and network design team was tasked in 2013 to transform a previously decentralized, productivity-driven organization into a truly customer-focused logistics network that provided tangible value to its customers:

- **Data:** With little connectivity between the various nodes, there was limited real-time visibility within the logistics network, their customers' service-level expectations and feedback, and the cost of delivery. A baseline perspective was required before they could prioritize, challenge or change, and they clearly needed to capture 'the voice of the customer'.

- **Customer satisfaction:** While some customers expressed dissatisfaction around delivery, Schneider had little granularity on the specifics. They needed to get closer to their customers, to truly understand their needs, their buying behaviours, their key attributes and expectations, to help define and shape Schneider Electric's demand chain. They required a built-for-purpose operations framework that could align both their supply and demand chains closely, while becoming more customer-focused.

- **Internal complexity:** The company had become a conglomerate of distinct 'ecosystems', with disparate processes, cultures, systems and distribution networks. The opportunity was significant, both internally and externally with the customer, to simplify and leverage these ecosystems into a single unified network, systematically reviewing the customer experience and aligning their supply chain to their customers' buying behaviours. This became the mission of the newly formed logistics and network design team.

Customer innovation

Innovation

Schneider Electric charted a path to capture structured and unstructured data from across the supply chain to drive innovation in the delivery of their products, services and capabilities. Developing an 'outside-in' culture attuned to listening and directing interaction and engagement with their customers required cultural change, to build trust and collaboration across stakeholders in the entire demand and supply chain, comprising both the supply chain and front office, as well as their customers and suppliers. They needed an agile yet structured process by which virtual teams could collect, assemble and analyse data, and then drive customer innovation aligned to insights from their current needs and future industry trends:

- **Customer buying behaviour research:** Customer surveys were used to identify 'dissatisfied' customers, with whom they engaged in interviews, customer forums and conferences to better understand the source of their dissatisfaction. The surveys did not identify buying behaviours, attributes that drove them, nor the dynamics of the demand chain. A research process to complement the surveys was put in place to determine customers' dominant and secondary buying behaviours, and the attributes (hard and soft) that drove these behaviours, and subsequently their demand chain. Based on this research, customer supply chain needs were categorized into five types: Collaborative, Lean, Agile, Project, and Fully Flexible.

- **Customer process capabilities:** Using the output of the surveys, 18 'customer process capabilities' were designed to improve the delivery experiences that needed to be prioritized, resourced, developed and implemented, and to drive differentiation in the market. Using the buying behaviour research, these customer delivery capabilities could now be configured based on customers' different needs and buying behaviours.

- **Commercial logistics offer:** Stuart and his team then triangulated the market (customer), business (Schneider Electric) and competitor analysis to gain insights on how they could realign their operations to deliver optimal service using the capabilities, in line with customer buying behaviours and expectations, creating a unique selling proposition for their customers through a 'tailored supply chain'.

Execution

Following the data-gathering processes, and an internal and external alignment process, a virtual cross-functional team developed scenario network models with clear objectives and attributes aligned to customer, business and supply chain objectives. Using supply chain optimization and simulation tools, the team evaluated these scenarios thoroughly testing the trade-offs between service, simplification and cost efficiency. This process follows eight key steps:

Step 1: Establish a baseline network model.

Step 2: Sign-off the baseline model.

Step 3: Run an unconstrained model.

Step 4: Run 'to-be' scenarios.

Step 5: The selected scenario(s) undergo validation to test 'viability'.

Step 6: Customer validation (advocacy).

Step 7: Business case validation.

Step 8: Execution and implementation.

Impact

- Customer net satisfaction score:
  29.4 per cent in 2017 versus 13.6 per cent in 2012.
- On time delivery to customer:
  95.8 per cent in 2017 versus 92.6 per cent in 2012.

Business win

Innovation

- **Digitization:** In parallel with customer innovation, the team focused on removing complexity from the network, aggressively reducing numbers of logistics providers globally from 1,450 in 2013, to 300 in 2017, of which 16 emergent major suppliers would manage the remaining 284 by 2020. The rationale for the reduction is their digitization strategy, calculated to create end-to-end visibility across their customer delivery platform. Starting in 2013, in collaboration with the 16 strategic partners, Schneider Electric successfully digitized their delivery platform from the 'outside-in' by leveraging their suppliers' technologies, helping to minimize cost, complexity and time-to-value realization. Additionally, they have re-focused internal resources and effort on building a common messaging platform and standardized message content across their systems. This platform and connectivity forms the foundation of their 'logistics control towers' where these entities, with their 16 strategic partners, are tasked to predict, sense, and event-manage the delivery experience for all physical product moves, allowing real-time tactical decisions to minimize negative customer impact.

- **Delivery complaint rate:** Building on the base of data, digitization and simplification (modelling), they could then standardize, adopt and leverage best-in-breed processes and tools across the organization, documented within global standard operating procedures (GSOPs). With adoption of and compliance to the GSOPs, all logistics processes are now clearly focused on delivering optimal quality, service, and efficiency, both internally and externally in the eyes of their customers. This is measured utilizing a metric called delivery complaint rate (DCR). Recorded on a monthly basis by entity and site, DCR focuses clear and immediate attention on process flaws, supplier issues, and other events that negatively impact customer delivery experience. Once root causes are identified, sustainable fixes are made to the processes and communicated out across the network.

Execution

- **Team:** The global logistics and network design team was formed in January 2013, tasked with developing the strategy and ensuring the enablement of the organization. The global team works closely with the regional teams who are ultimately responsible for the execution. Supported by clearly defined roles and responsibilities, the organizational structures in each of the regions are now standardized to facilitate greater coordination and teamwork on a global basis. The global and regional teams meet twice a year in the logistics steering committee. This committee agrees priorities, allocates resources, and ensures focus on the strategy and tasks, whilst also sharing best demonstrated implementations, practices, challenges and resources to enable success on a global basis

- **Process:** Global supply chain (GSC) sets out its vision in line with corporate change programs. These corporate change programs run from three to five years and are supported by the GSC strategic prioritization (or HOSHIN) process. Hoshin Kanri is a seven-step process used in strategic planning in which strategic goals are communicated throughout the company and then put into action. Cascaded throughout the organization, the priorities of each year are clearly communicated to every GSC employee and supported by their own domain priorities. Logistics performance against the HOSHIN, and of each transformation initiative, are measured through the global and regional project management offices. Disciplined in project management process (PMP), the teams utilize internally developed tools that are automated to manage projects, and measure progress and performance globally monthly, reinforced in quarterly reviews. GSOPs are dynamic documents that cover each of the logistics domains. They articulate the vision and objectives of GSC, logistics and network design, and of each domain, clearly linking each activity to customer value and company objectives. The internal Schneider performance system (SPS) is used to measure adherence to the GSOPs, lean processes, innovation, and people management.

Impact

- Digital delivery capability:
  >80 per cent in 2017 versus <30 per cent in 2012.
- Delivery complaint rate:
  2,000 parts per million in 2017 versus >2,865 parts per million in 2015.
- Recurrent identified savings: €150 million.

    (Distribution centres (DC) and transport only)

Social impact

Innovation

As the global specialist in energy management and automation, sustainability is at the core of what they do at Schneider Electric. The two key facets are their people and the environment, both of which are integral in ensuring the success of their transformation:

- **People:** With their move to a more digital and connected world, there is a strong focus on ensuring that their people, structure and role designs are evolving to meet these trends. Key to their success is ensuring that they are developing their people with the necessary skills, competencies and experience to operate in a more digitized and dynamic supply chain. To be productive in this increasingly fast-paced environment they also address well-being, looking not only at agile and enhanced work environments, but also at training, tools and guidelines to help their staff address various welfare topics.
- **Environment:** Network optimization naturally presents opportunities to reduce packaging and transport-related CO_2 emissions. The logistics regional and global team(s) are measured on optimizing container utilization, engaging in local initiatives to reduce 'fresh air' in last mile shipments, and overall improvements in CO_2 reduction. Key distribution sites are working to achieve zero to landfill, supporting a broader global supply chain initiative. Schneider Electric energy-efficient products and solutions are also being introduced into their sites.

Execution

The logistics 2.0 program was launched in 2015 to address the 'people' aspects of the transformation, which includes:

1 Redefinition and standardization of logistics roles, introducing new 'digital' roles focused on connectivity, driving end-to-end visibility, and enhanced roles related to customer delivery experience.
2 Development of comprehensive learning paths addressing specific competencies of logistics. These detail specific education, experience and exposure opportunities.
3 Comprehensive competency reviews and individual development plans.

Twice a year, a dynamic action plan based on the results of the employee opinion survey is launched to address the needs and concerns of the logistics team coupled with regular communication on the progress of this action plan. The environmental agenda is strongly championed by the chairman and CEO, coupled with strong support from senior management. Metrics have been put in place by which all logistics personnel are measured. In addition to bigger corporate programs to optimize the network, and introduce energy efficient products into distribution centres, the regions are encouraged locally to be agile and identify initiatives to drive improvements in their container load factors and remove 'fresh air' from their last mile shipments. Best practices are actively shared through skills networks with peers in other regions.

Impact

- Logistics and network designs' employee satisfaction has dramatically improved during this time, achieving its highest rate of 68 per cent in the first quarter of 2017.
- Similarly, their impact on the environment has improved with a 16 per cent carbon dioxide reduction between 2011 and 2015, with a further reduction of 12 per cent forecasted between 2016 and 2017 (to be determined).

Notwithstanding this tremendous success, which took three years to implement, and despite internal cross-functional stakeholder and customer advocacy at the front end of the project, through the application of the various simulation models, 80 per cent of the implementation phase was focused on gaining acceptance from the senior management team. This was a *gap of pain* that would have certainly benefited from *a seat at the big boys' table* for the logistician.

Zoop Mobility Network Inc

Justification for borrowing dynamic business to information systems strategic alignment academic literature

Esther Lätte is the Field Operations Manager at ZOOP Mobility Network Inc, based in Tallinn, Estonia, and manages the global supply chain campaign for Schneider Electric. This involves detailed analysis of customer feedback, and the resulting combined key performance indicator (KPI) data is captured on dashboards, enabling continuous real-time strategic decision-making at Schneider. 'ZOOP creates enterprise software and provides business process outsourcing services for primary use in the (Schneider Electric, in this case) customer experience arena'. Esther posits that supply chain disruption is in most circumstances unpredictable and regardless of the cause can have a financial effect on various aspects of the business. These events are categorized as internal (late deliveries, drastic demand changes, quality issues, production process issues) and external (accidents during transportation, natural disasters, terrorism, changing policies). Preparation strategies and risk management processes mitigate the impact of disruption. Experience has shown that the following strategies have enabled organizations to maintain operations and return to a steady state, despite financial loss through planning changes and late deliveries, and these validate the academic and empirical findings in previous chapters:

- Response to events begins with rapid and effective internal and external information exchange, including the continuous updating of demand requests.
- Quality control and auditing of processes (both internal and external): For example, additional steps and improvements in the production process (or packaging) may need to be immediately implemented.
- Safety stocks and shared demand between suppliers from various locations, using alternative sources to fulfil particular orders: Use offshore suppliers for the bulk of the procurement volume, and local suppliers to offset disruption (incremental costs of strategic redundant inventories are the *premium* for reduced risk). The cost depends on probability of risk, and a form of hedging and deployment of supplies to strategic locations could also be adopted. It was demonstrated how the Irish Defence Forces pre-position redundant supplies based on average consumption to mitigate supply chain risk. It was also previously mentioned that many organizations have adopted a lean approach such as a reduced supply base, just-in-time inventory systems, and vendor-managed inventories. In a stable environment, these strategies are extremely effective (Tang, 2006). *We do not operate in a stable environment*. In the event of supply chain disruption, the results of lean strategies can be devastating.
- Esther suggests that the challenge for internal strategic alignment is balancing lean inventory-holding, whereby adjusting to demand changes can be complex and unachievable, and the high impact on revenue streams of safety stocks that can again cause disruption within other

links of the supply chain, or indeed within the internal organization. The negotiation factor therefore becomes the degree of sustainable redundancy premium.

- 'Those who cannot remember the past are condemned to repeat it' (George Santayana): In the case of external disruption, strategic decisions can come from the historical experience of dealing with specific suppliers and shipping from specific locations. This is apt, given that history largely informs this research. Such experience can be captured in another form of redundancy, knowledge back-up, through the standardization of processes and practices.
- Various transportation modes, such as changing shipments from ocean to air freight: Depending on the product-line, air freight can resolve the disruption for the customer, but can obliterate profit margins.
- We are introduced to constant changes in the business environment as well as to technology improvements, all of which are potential threats to our supply chains: Constant market surveillance and continuous technology knowledge-acquisition are pre-requisites for risk management strategies.

Costed data analysis can be used in my two-tier categorization of supply chain strategies or tactics (one that requires negotiation with the top management team, and one that can be implemented autonomously), a distinction acknowledged by Esther. As already demonstrated, financial simulation of various options is the vehicle and threshold for engagement with the top management team, but this must be combined with market impacts, both of which have been the top priorities to consider in Esther's experience. Facts and figures, pros and cons for all potential options must be presented. In my own opinion, any aspiring supply chain manager must consider that expert-level Microsoft Excel and PowerPoint skills are key to advancement. However, a more obvious reason for negotiation is the seeking of advice from a more experienced group of business professionals. This latter point has been an omission of this research, consumed instead by the uni-dimensional aspect of supply chain management. It was indeed noted that my thesis is by no means a criticism of the top management team. As a supply chain professional, I have not been directly exposed to the many (economic, political and social) factors and pressures facing policy makers at the highest levels. Further perspectives include:

- In the pursuit and categorization of strategic alignment, we must also consider the level of criticality of supply chain management to the organization, which depends on the business and the market where the company is operating. If supply chain management is one of the key factors to a company's success (on-time deliveries, etc), then strategic alignment with the top management team will generate more transparency between internal stakeholders and encourage various improvements in the practice thereof.

- For autonomous strategic implementation, financial acumen is also important when determining the most economical solutions available when, for instance, changing transportation modes.
- A second acknowledgement of this research is the confirmed existence of strategic friction: Based on experience, small disruptions are a part of daily supply chain management, meaning that not everything can be controlled or managed from a human standpoint.

Esther *contributes* to the attainment of dynamic business to supply chain strategic alignment by suggesting that effective internal and external communication across the network (with a focus on rapidity to reduce the *gap of pain*), financial acumen and market knowledge are critical tools to be developed within our profession. First and foremost we must be business leaders.

From this and prior contributions, then, there is validation for borrowing business to information systems strategic alignment academic literature, to further our supply chain knowledge:

- Strategic alignment is based on two fundamental assumptions, economic performance, which directly relates to the strategic fit of external positioning, and internal arrangements, and that strategic fit is inherently dynamic: reaching dynamic capability depends on the organization's ability to exploit supply chain functionality on a continuous basis. Esther confirms financial acumen, and rapid information exchange, including the continuous updating of demand requests, as critical supply chain tools.
- Success depends on the development of a mechanism of shared knowledge integration across the top management team. Consider Esther's position as one such mechanism: detailed analysis of customer feedback, and the resulting combined KPI data is captured on dashboards, enabling continuous real-time strategic decision-making at Schneider Electric. Sharing of industry challenges is also important, such as freight and transportation disruptions, and Chapter 3 concluded that as the (alignment) model evolves, we can consider a military decision making type process at both the strategic formulation stage and the disruption response phase. We also need to include value creation as a proactive force rather than exclusively a reactive force.

- Consider the cross-sectional linkages within an organization and the temporal nature of strategic decision-making. Alignment is a continuous co-evolutionary process that reconciles top management team 'rational designs' and operational 'emergent processes'. Esther highlighted the financial impact of supply chain responses to disruption on various internal functions. It is therefore important to consider all stakeholders to ensure consensus and enhance the reputation of 'supply chain'.

- There is a process of user improvisation and adjustment, due to perception and understanding of supply chain features. Strategic plans are therefore resources for situated action that do not in any strong sense determine their course. Many of the case studies have shown that disruption is unpredictable and there is much evidence of adjusting to situational needs during the response phase, whilst staying inside the core competencies and strategic vision of the organization.

- A supply chain is not an external object, but a product of ongoing human action, design, and appropriation, which, over time, becomes imbricated, embedded, entangled and intertwined, subject to social negotiation and sense-making, materializing through anchoring and objectification. We need look no further than the Armaments and Equipment (AAE) and CS-41 documents that outlined the available resources to meet the Irish Defence Forces Nordic Battle Group mission objectives, and how the provisions therein led to 'constraints, restrictions, freedoms' that resulted in an evolving portfolio of personnel.

- Alignment must include setting goals, understanding the business to supply chain linkage, analysing and prioritizing gaps, specifying actions, choosing and evaluating success criteria, and sustaining alignment by developing and cultivating an alignment behaviour: This is the purpose of the ZOOP KPI Dashboards. The Irish Defence Forces military decision-making process analyses supply chain capabilities and tasks whilst simultaneously aligning with top management team strategy (the foremost consideration). In the humanitarian domain, structural robustness can help the coping mechanism and reduce the *gap of pain* in crises that are unpredictable, contextual and situational. Emphasis should be on having:

    o dedicated personnel in place to manage freight forwarding;
    o procurement planning and tracking that includes agreed-upon thresholds for order increases without having to re-submit orders due to inevitable changes;

- well-documented framework agreements that have national and regional consistency;
- job descriptions that are understood and uniform throughout the organization;
- all departments playing a role in vendor management, from programs, procurement and logistics, to finance, who must ensure the processing (and documentation) of payments in a timely manner, so that the establishment of a 'good name' in the business community would result in more vendors taking part in tenders and providing better bids;
- technical support must be in place for users of IT systems, including training, and management controls such as spot checks in relation to assets and stock disposal, procurement committees, tender standard operating procedures, staff shortages and internal auditing.

- Alignment can occur through supply chain transformation where the supply chain manager has the role of architect to the top management team's supply chain vision. This is enacted within the autonomous category of strategic implementation.
- Supply chain strategy can be the enabler, and has competitive potential, whereby the top management team is the business visionary to the supply chain manager's catalyst role of developing and exploiting emerging supply chain capabilities to impact new products: Esther has advised that market intelligence and thereby the need for supply chain managers to be business leaders is important for alignment, and of course, supply chains compete, not companies (we just need to convince the top management team of this!).
- A world-class supply chain organization can be developed if the supply chain manager enacts an executive leadership role, and the top management team accordingly prioritizes the allocation of resources: This is enacted through the negotiation category of strategic implementation. The Irish Defence Forces AAE and CS-41 documents provided the empowerment, through Deputy Chief of Staff support, to internally 're-distribute' equipment as needed.
- Business to supply chain strategic alignment enablers: Top management team support for supply chain; supply chain involved in strategy development; supply chain understands the business; business to supply chain partnership; well-prioritized supply chain projects; supply chain demonstrates leadership. There is strong evidence that there is *no seat at the big boys' table* for the logistician and that reversing this will have a significantly positive impact on increasing strategic alignment, and reducing the *gap of pain* in response to supply chain disruption.

- The supply chain manager must first and foremost be a business leader and must participate as a real general management peer, displaying such characteristics as a diplomat, visionary, leader, strategic thinker, relationship builder, and reader of markets and the tactics used for influencing top management team members. A close relationship between the supply chain manager and CEO is crucial and this extends to solidarity between the supply chain manager and all functional top management team members. The contributors to this research display such characteristics in abundance. The next phase for our profession is to broaden supply chain management to a wider perspective across top management teams. Esther has certainly helped in this regard.

Jon Bumstead

Thoughts on evolving corporate supply chain disruption

Jon Bumstead, a profoundly experienced supply chain consultant, advises that corporates have steadily used centralization over ever-increasing boundaries. Firstly on a national scale, such as retail distribution in the United Kingdom in the 1970s and 1980s, and the growth of Tesco and similar chains, then regionally from 1992 with pan-European logistics, and the globalization wave from the mid-1990s, to the global financial crash in 2008. The disruption or discontinuity factor then became accessing cheaper labour and free trade across boundaries. Since the financial crash, this has steadily unwound, starting the 'China plus one' sourcing strategies, which was finding a closer country to source from (for speed) in addition to China. Supporting Chapter 4 findings, the next phase is that of populist nationalism, such as Brexit and the Trump tariffs, which is moving us backwards in the direction we came from, and secondly the Amazon e-commerce effect of getting consumers to want everything now! This means that product distribution centres need to be much closer to markets they serve. The technology of factor of logistics automation could well be a supporting disruptive factor to lower the cost of expensive and increasingly rare resources (such as warehouse operatives and truck drivers).

When e-commerce launched in the late 1990s, the Oracle slogan was 'the internet changes everything', which it certainly did, but that change was to have a terminal effect on high-street retail. Jon remarks that it is fascinating to note that Marks and Spencer (M&S) first started noticing a decline from 1999 when it reached £1 billion in profit and never got close to that again in the 18 years that followed. The company had clearly triumphed in the previous epoch of high-street retail but continued to stumble over subsequent and persistent disruption factors. Their anti-change culture continues to be their Achilles heel as they attempt to adapt the older supply chain model to service the new requirements. This has made them slow to react and respond to market changes in such a fast industry as fashion and causes them to frequently miss the boat. When M&S started to source globally back in the early 2000s it simply asked its United Kingdom suppliers to source in Asia, bring the goods into the UK and store them in their existing warehouses, whereby they did not have to change systems. This added time and cost to the supply chain and dramatically led to their first-ever pre-Christmas sale in 2003, when they had failed to forecast market demand and had excessively high stock by early December that year.

Amazon has to be one of the greatest disruptors in recent times, in the sense that no one predicted their real disruption being in logistics, nor the scale of their business growth. Their desire to re-invent every aspect of logistics and supply chain demand is breathtaking in its audacity and has been more successful than the business magnate, investor and engineer, Elon Musk. Another fascination for Jon is that companies such as Amazon and Alibaba are now moving back to physical retail and he foresees international e-commerce as the next key disruption where anyone can play anywhere, although this prediction is tempered by the new wave of nationalism that is unfolding.

The force of sustainability is a key disruptor impacting us, which has gathered increasing velocity in the past 10 years. In 2007, when Jon started Neutral Group inside DHL, an organization aimed at strategic energy and carbon emission reduction in logistics and supply chain, many dismissed such a move. Now, the momentum of the regenerative system known as the circular economy means that supply chains must design for the 'after-next life' and material contents of products are being re-thought (plastics, in particular). Great examples of this are Phillips, who moved from selling light bulbs to selling light as a service (managing the complete supply chain lifecycle of the bulb) and Bavarian Motor Works (BMW) creating recycling centres. Research that Jon is doing involves finding a link between sustainability performance and brand value. Increasingly he predicts this trend to continue. There is an even stronger link to brand value if the corporate is also a supply chain grand master. All the more reason to find a *seat at the big boys' table* for supply chain managers!

Another pending supply chain disruption is the International Maritime Organization 2020-planned 0.50 per cent sulphur cap, down from the current cap of 3.5 per cent, which is seen as the most significant change in the industry since the removal of coal-powered vessels, and one that few have started to factor in. The majority of ships today use heavy fuel oil with an average sulphur content of 2.7 per cent. Those that do not have exhaust gas cleaning systems (scrubbers) will have to begin burning a compliant bunker fuel from 2020, estimated to be 81 per cent of the global maritime fleet. One challenge is that only major refining centres, such as Singapore and ARA (ports of Amsterdam, Rotterdam and Antwerp), will have the capability to create the blends needed to develop compliant 0.50 per cent sulphur fuel oil products, thereby restricting availability. However, this has led to a niche opportunity for suppliers of alternative compliant bunkers, such as for ships that have either been designed or modified to use liquefied natural gas. It is widely expected, though, that most will transition to marine gasoil, which will dramatically increase global shipping costs (ExxonMobil, 2018).

Gattorna speaks eloquently about cadence and clockspeeds increasing, when he suggests that contemporary supply chains must be designed for faster clockspeeds to cope with the increasingly volatile operating environment, and Jon believes that we will not be able to 'put the clock back' on this trend. If Zara made M&S look slow, Boohoo.com is now making Zara look ponderous! Gattorna (2018) wrote:

Designing contemporary supply chains for faster clockspeeds to cope with the increasingly volatile operating environment
John Gattorna

In 1998, Charles Fine published his groundbreaking book on *Clockspeed*. He based much of his research on the observation of fruit flies, which he called a 'fast-clockspeed species', evolving from eggs, through adulthood to death, all in under two weeks! Much of his research was concentrated on the industrial equivalents of these fast-evolving fruit flies. One of the companies that he focused on was Intel, which in turn had fast-evolving customers such as Compaq and Dell, whose products inevitably had short life cycles in the marketplace. Clearly, then as now, the real pressure was coming from the customer end of the chain, and that pressure has increased significantly in the two decades since Fine wrote his book.

Fine studied whole industries, noting the different *rates* that they evolved at. He called these rates 'industry clockspeed', which he defined as resulting from a combination of product, process, and organization clockspeeds, respectively. Fine drew the conclusion that any differences in clockspeed between businesses is manifested in the size or length of the decision-making window, and I agree with that. When it comes down to basics, enterprises under pressure from their customer base and/or competitors must, by definition, find ways to make faster decisions if they are to survive. Indeed, given that competitive advantage is now regarded as only 'temporary', the enterprise must continually re-invent itself to stay ahead. The old concept of locking in a 'sustainable advantage' is not possible in fast-moving industries and markets.

Fine defines a company as 'its chain of continually evolving capabilities', and by that he includes its own capabilities and those along the entire supply chain. In our terminology, he is referring to the extended supply chain. Of course, the old maxim of the weakest link applies. Fine cites Dell as a great example of a fast clockspeed company, mainly due to its early supply chain design which placed it in direct contact with consumers and users. This advantage receded in subsequent years as Dell was forced to engage in different distribution channels involving intermediaries. Interestingly, with the coming of the e-commerce era, and the direct access that this affords suppliers to their consumers and end users, coupled with digitization and the disintermediation effect of Blockchain, we are likely to see many more disruptions across industries that are dragging their feet on clockspeed.

Fine comments on the dynamics of extended enterprises, and in particular nominates two laws which he sees as pivotal, ie *volatility amplification* (or Bullwhip effect, by another name), which moves upstream in the chain, and *clockspeed amplification*, which moves downstream towards the final customer. Fine introduces his notion of clockspeed analysis, which begins by mapping existing supply chain *capabilities* in order to identify potential weak links as well as potential opportunities. So, in Fine's thinking, clockspeed is defined as the summation of capabilities along the extended supply chain, to which I would add the time taken for each element, across the full breadth of the total lead time, from supplier(s) through to end user or consumer. Further, he postulates that in order to improve the Clockspeed in an enterprise or indeed an industry, products, processes and capabilities have to be designed concurrently. He coined a phase for this: '3DCE' or 3D concurrent engineering.

Finally, Fine makes an initial attempt at measuring clockspeed, with the qualification that it is very complex, not dissimilar to cost allocation in that there are many areas where judgement is required. Time has moved on and we now understand the dynamics of supply chains a lot better than in the 1990s. For instance, the idea of 'one-size-fits-all' has been banished forever, and we have a clear guiding principle that supply chains must, by definition, be designed from the 'outside-in'. This is consistent with *Design Thinking*, and consistent with Fine's stated view that 'clockspeed amplification' emanates from the customer end of the chain. We also know that supply chains are not inanimate beasts, but are living ecosystems, propelled by people situated all along the chain, making decisions, for better or worse. Hence, the need to incorporate the study of organizational culture and leadership style in our analysis of supply chain performance.

So, when we talk about clockspeed we are not suggesting that the enterprise has to suddenly accelerate to meet volatile conditions. Instead, we are convinced that the entire organization has to lift its tempo and operate at that new higher level, ALL THE TIME. Once this is achieved, the internally generated clockspeed will hopefully match and indeed nullify the effect of volatile demand emanating from the customer end. Because we are now talking about achieving faster split times in each element of the overall lead-time, the time buckets are shorter, and this has the effect of reducing the risk of forecasting errors. As in the case of Zara, they are never more than three weeks away from the next cycle of product launches to stores, so markdowns become much less of a problem, and stock-outs become something of a virtue. How the world has changed!

And if we couple this phenomenon with our proprietary Dynamic Alignment™ model, involving an array of up to five supply chain types, each aligned with a particular customer buying behaviour segment, over and under servicing is virtually eliminated, as is the corresponding complexity and associated costs, both actual and opportunity based. In the end, it all comes down to developing and nurturing a defined range of *capabilities*, and then combining these in different *recipes* to underpin the engagement with customers (and suppliers) according to their preferred way of buying our product and service categories.

The important point here, especially for executives with a mandate to 'transform' the business, is that we are dealing with a 'whole-of-enterprise' phenomenon. In other words, in the process of transforming your enterprise supply chains, it is in fact necessary to transform the entire organization in order to achieve the faster rhythms inherent in faster clockspeeds. What this means in fact is that defaulting to lean processes in our enterprise supply chains is no longer the correct option, because a new default has arisen in the form of speed and agility in order to cope with the faster, more volatile operating environment. Companies operating in fast-moving consumer goods, hi-tech and fast-fashion markets are already experiencing this change in modus operandi, and similar conditions are heading in the direction of older, more established 'bricks and mortar' industrial companies. Their challenge is to embrace the change and, in the process, raise themselves to new, higher levels of competitiveness.

The enterprise-wide *capabilities* required for success in the new, faster clockspeed world are briefly:

1 New organization designs that promote speed of decision-making.
2 Process mapping and re-engineering along all supply chain types.
3 Adoption of appropriate KPIs to measure performance, free of conflicting demands.
4 Deploy IT systems that are genuine Decision Support Systems (DSS) in order to speed up decision-making.
5 Install effective Sales and Operations Planning (S&OP) regimes to focus the entire organization on agreed priorities to meet customer demand.
6 Shape a number of different 'subcultures' inside the business to underpin the different supply chain types. This will involve all of the above plus additional effort in areas such as defining roles, defining incentives, methods of internal communications, recruitment of specific types of personnel, introduction of a range of training and development programs, and role modelling.
7 Build in resilience to recover from a major unplannable disruption in our supply chain network.
8 Conscious development of an Internet of Things strategy and corresponding analytics capability, including customer and supplier sensing.
9 A blended combination of 'business as usual' and 'search' for new innovations.
10 Managing *capacity* at all points in our supply chain network at all times.
11 Considered and strategic channels selection.
12 Requisite collaboration with appropriate network members.

These internal capabilities should be supplemented by supply chain specific capabilities as follows:

- Product design: CAD, modular, supply chain friendly.
- Manufacturing: CAM, automation and robotics, AI, 3D-Printing, group technology, flexible manufacturing.
- Logistics: Postponement, insourcing and outsourcing mix, control towers, 3PL management, network optimization modelling.

There are many moving parts in contemporary supply chains, and many external factors that can potentially impact performance. Nevertheless, if we are able to increase the clockspeed of the entire enterprise and literally get in sync with the operating environment, complexity is materially reduced and operational and financial performance correspondingly increased. We know, because we have done it!

The final thought from Jon Bumstead is that technology always provides the opportunity disruption, but many introductions do not happen the way we envisage. Radio-frequency identification (RFID) did not really take off in the way that everyone predicted, but it looks like Blockchain might be pivotal. Throughout his 30-year career, there have always been tech waves (ERP, e-commerce, RFID, cloud, digital, etc) and every project starts off the same, with everyone over-focused on the technology, and remarkably the projects always end with the conclusion that more thought should have been given to the *people* aspect. This aligns to the first paragraph of my preface: one thing I have learned is that supply chain management is about people.

Conclusion

Reflecting on the main aims of this research, to increase our understanding of supply chain managers' engagement in the process of dynamic business to supply chain strategic alignment, within the context of supply chain disruption, and to contribute to the broadening of supply chain management to an integrated perspective across the top management team rather than a uni-dimensional and dichotomous view, this chapter has been of tremendous value. Adoption of the Gattorna Dynamic Alignment™ model secures top management team endorsement and operationalizes the organization for faster clockspeeds, thereby ensuring shorter *gaps of pain* in response to supply chain disruption, a fortunate by-product. Such endorsement may take time, as in the Schneider case, where 80 per cent of a three-year implementation was spent on negotiation with senior policy-makers. Greater alignment has now been achieved. The Schneider (logistics) environmental agenda for instance is strongly championed by the chairman and CEO, coupled with strong support from senior management. However, we must collectively ensure that this alignment is *natural* and *instant*.

But how? Schneider attained business to supply chain strategic alignment by gathering and analysing extensive data-sets, securing customer advocacy, simulation modelling that mapped the benefits to all internal functional stakeholders, prior to engagement with the top management team. This was then supported by continuous reporting of positive impacts in areas such as customer innovation, business wins and social well-being. Is it enough? There is still *no seat at the big boys' table* for the logistician (neither at Schneider or elsewhere) and there are just two more chapters to solve this dilemma, including a journey to the geographical heart of globalization, the People's Republic of China, before proposing a disruption-reduction process model. Supply chains compete, not companies, but why is it only supply chain professionals saying this? Marketing found a seat, despite few knowing what it was when I got my marketing degree in 1991 (certainly not in Ireland). Supply chain management was coined in 1982 by a Booz Allen Hamilton consultant. Why has it not reached the top after 36 years?

Concluding again with the extended research objectives:

- *Determine how supply chain managers operationally identify, predict, cope and recover from supply chain disruptions:* Schneider Electric informed us that, with adoption and compliance to global standard operating procedures, all logistics processes are clearly focused on delivering optimal quality, service, and efficiency, both internally and externally in the eyes of their customers. Reducing numbers of logistics providers globally from 1,450 in 2013 to 16 emergent major suppliers by 2020 has addressed complexity. Additionally, they have refocused internal resources and effort on building a common messaging platform and standardized message content across their systems. This platform and connectivity forms the foundation of their 'logistics control towers' where these entities, with their 16 strategic partners, are tasked to predict, sense and event-manage the delivery experience for all physical product moves, allowing real-time tactical decisions to minimize negative customer impact. This all reduces the risk of disruption. ZOOP added that response to events begins with rapid and effective information exchange, redundant-inventory and dual-supplier sourcing strategies, expeditious quality control and auditing of processes, and continuous market surveillance and technology knowledge acquisition are cornerstones for achieving this particular objective. John Gattorna advocates dynamic alignment to customer buying behaviours and the adoption of faster clockspeeds.

- *Identify which phases in the supply chain disruption process require engagement with top management to implement strategic solutions aligned to business goals.* Schneider Electric's global supply chain (GSC) sets out its vision in line with corporate change programs. These corporate change programs run from three to five years and are supported by the GSC strategic prioritization (or HOSHIN) process. Cascaded throughout the organization, the priorities of each year are clearly communicated to every GSC employee and supported by their own domain priorities. Logistics performance against the HOSHIN, and of each transformation initiative, are measured through the global and regional project management offices, reinforced in quarterly reviews. They articulate the vision and objectives of GSC, logistics and network design, and of each domain, clearly linking each activity to customer value and company objectives.

- *Consequently, determine whether a categorization of supply chain strategy exists, such as a tier consisting of strategies that can be implemented autonomously by the supply chain division, and a tier or tiers that require negotiation across the top management team prior to implementation, to collaboratively mitigate risk.* Financial simulation of various options has been re-confirmed as the vehicle and threshold for engagement with the top management team in the negotiation category, but this must be combined with market impacts, both of which have been top priorities to consider.

- *Determine how supply chain managers engage with the top management team in the process of aligning business and supply chain strategies, thereby identifying key enablers and inhibitors.* ZOOP suggests that the top management team must be viewed as a valuable resource of knowledge and experience, and their advice must be consequently sought during key events. Schneider Electric successfully used the sharing of data-analysis and simulation modelling that mapped the benefits to all stakeholders, generated to gain internal functional agreement and alignment, including customer advocacy.

- *Develop a process model that establishes the phases of supply chain managers' engagement in dynamic business to supply chain strategic alignment.* The policy schema on page 152 can now be updated once again from the new findings, which will influence the final model.

Policy: the source of supply chain disruption

External policy: political, economic, social, technological, climatic

Protectionism and trade wars; political cyber security breaches; political migration;
Socio-economic customer demand: e-commerce and environment-driven decisions;
OPEC production management, military-driven oil embargoes, oil and gas mergers and acquisitions;
China government manufacturing plant closures; culture of CNY non-returning work-force;
Holiday schedules in China and India, week-long port closures and resulting back-logs;
Major consumer-brand product launches, reducing ocean and air capacity;

Restrictions or legislative conditions on access to resources or infrastructure; changes in strategic priorities governing the use of non-domestic equipment, vehicles and manpower; acts of sabotage, theft, extortion and bribery within an existing supply chain or ethically corrupt or unauthorized protectionist acts impacting on the ability to establish a supply chain; impact of conflict situations; unintended blue-on-blue actions by partner organizations and friendly forces; deliberate refusal of external agent to cooperate despite their organizations' agreement to do so; diplomatic relationships between stakeholder nations and the existing national legislation before a supply chain is established; external economic decisions, commercial pressures and competition for available resources

Internal industry policy: supply chain management

E-retailers consuming warehouse real-estate; non-licensed exponential logistics companies entering the market;
Blockchain: risk of hacking and fraud; accelerating force of technology such as NFC;
Customs documentation restrictions and non-tariff measures including VGM;
Ocean alliances and mega-ships; containers lost at sea due to weight declarations;
Slow-steaming and artificial removal of vessel capacity; mergers of logistics providers;
Sea-port congestion including inter-modal inbound road and waterway delays;
Fuel and bunker surcharges; China government dangerous-goods processing;
Security measures including convoys and restrictions in route-planning

Internal organizational policy:
top management team strategic renewal process

Lean inventory holding; CNY planning; failure to evolve with and adapt new technology advancements;
Failure to consider the people aspect of technology implementations; anti-change culture;
Failure to engage in the circular economy; failure to adopt Gattorna Dynamic Alignment™

Lack of TMT understanding and operational awareness; management decision; delay in decision-making; change in supply strategy; misjudging the scale or nature of the supply chain operation; failure to design and control an appropriate supply chain; failure to appropriately man (experience, education and training) or resource the supply chain; management reconsideration: changes in financial or operational priorities; changes in manpower or personalities in authority; changes in the end-product, therefore a change in requirements; indirect impact of external pressures; information flow disruption; failure to communicate effectively and efficiently throughout the supply chain network; failure to communicate internal, external and environmental changes; failure to contingency-plan for potential future disruption;
Unauthorized act; deliberate operation of (or permitting the operation of) supply chain assets, such as equipment and vehicles, outside authorized parameters; failure to comply with legislative requirements;
Intentional or incompetent act: negligent conduct; failure to control a controllable external force, such as failure of equipment through neglect; use of untrained or inexperienced manpower

Supply Chain Disruption

Macro: impacting supply chain network design
TMT negotiation based on pre-determined investment threshold of the organization

Micro: supply chain friction
HRM policy: anger to succeed and passion to deliver; Chinese guanxi; Familistic collectivism; trust; dynamic business environment

Supply Chain Disruption:
Black Swan Crises and Disasters
Grey Swan Breakdowns
*what we do inside the bubble
of our profession*

Supply Chain Strategies:
both TMT negotiation
and autonomous

Supply Chain Friction:
Petty circumstances
Blind natural forces
*know what we do inside the bubble
of our profession and triumph over it*

Supply Chain Strategies:
autonomous

References

Christopher, M and Towill, DR (2002) Developing market specific supply chain strategies, *The International Journal of Logistics Management*, **13**(1), pp 1–14

ExxonMobil (2018) https://www.exxonmobil.com/en/marine/technicalresource/news-resources/imo-sulphur-cap-and-mgo-hfo

Gattorna, J (2015) *Dynamic Supply Chains*, Pearson Education Limited

Gattorna, J (2018) Designing contemporary supply chains for faster clockspeeds to cope with the increasingly volatile operating environment, LinkedIn. [Online] https://www.linkedin.com/pulse/designing-contemporary-supply-chains-faster-cope-dr-john-gattorna

Kleindorfer, PR and Saad, GH (2005) Managing disruption risks in supply chains, *Production and Operations Management*, **14**(1), pp 53–68

Roh, J, Hong, P and Min, H (2014) Implementation of a responsive supply chain strategy in global complexity: The case of manufacturing firms, *International Journal of Production Economics*, **147**, pp 198–210

Sheffi, Y (2001) Supply chain management under the threat of international terrorism, *The International Journal of Logistics Management*, **12**(2), pp 1–11

Sylla, C (2014) Managing perceived operational risk factors for effective supply-chain management, *AIP Conference Proceedings*, **1635**(1), pp 19–26

Tang, CS (2006) Robust strategies for mitigating supply chain disruptions, *International Journal of Logistics: Research and applications*, **9**(1), pp 33–45

Wu, T, Wu, YCJ, Chen, YJ and Goh, M (2014) Aligning supply chain strategy with corporate environmental strategy: A contingency approach, *International Journal of Production Economics*, **147**, pp 220–29

China 07
Supply chain disruption in the geographical heart of globalization

The complexity of supply chain management has been compounded by the force of globalization along the dimensions of replenishment, time and distance (Christopher and Towill, 2002), and therefore, where better to conclude my organizational case research, than in the geographical heart of outsourced production, the People's Republic of China. This region is of personal interest to me, due to certain historical figures whose artistry of war is beyond question, but who were also the early masters in supply chain management, whereby the efficient mass movement of people and supplies was the difference between success and failure, and from whom so much could be learned and applied to present day practice. For example, the Ch'in Dynasty was the end result of the warring states period (232–221 BC) that unified for the first time a collection of independent states into a single empire. This campaign was spearheaded by King Ch'eng, and the founding theorists in legalism, and he assumed the title Ch'in shih-huang-ti, or 'The First Exalted Emperor of the Ch'in'. Another is Genghis Khan (1162–1227) of Mongolia, widely regarded as history's greatest conqueror, who devastated most of Eurasia during his reign, relying heavily on yurtchis (logisticians) to do so.

Of course, I have also spent a decade visiting and building relationships across China and Taiwan and, notwithstanding the many challenges, have very much enjoyed the experience.

The challenges of globalization

Despite developments in technology that facilitate seamless communication and analytical sophistication, distance, a factor of globalization, remains a major challenge in the satisfaction of customer requirements due to increased lead-times. Globalization is primarily an economic phenomenon, involving the increasing interaction, or integration, of national economic systems through the growth in international trade, investment and capital flows, but has also involved a rapid increase in cross-border social, cultural and technological exchange. It has enabled profitable growth through the attainment of reduced costs and access to new markets, but this has been made possible only through the adoption of effective electronic processes that enable the timely flow of information, monies and products between a myriad of entities.

The geography of trade has changed unrecognizably to that of 20 years ago when, for example, Ireland (IBM, DELL, Apple), Scotland (HP, Compaq) and Holland were the dominant low-cost manufacturers, with 80 per cent of personal computers (PCs) being produced in these regions. A downturn in the PC market caused by factors such as a surge of sales in 1999 due to fears of the millennium bug, and a slowdown in technological advances, has resulted in PC original equipment manufacturers (OEMs) demanding an annual cost reduction of 15–20 per cent from its suppliers. To achieve this, companies continue to migrate towards locations with cost-saving benefits. In line with standard trade and comparative advantage theory, unskilled labour-intensive activities (such as PC manufacturing) tend to relocate to low-wage countries. Comparative advantage theory states that specialization is determined by the interaction between country and commodity characteristics. 'Since labour may be a small share of the costs of production there can be a large multiplier effect. If labour is 10 per cent of gross costs, then a 50 per cent difference in the productivity of all inputs will translate into a 500 per cent wage difference' (Venables, 2006).

The main beneficiaries have been China and eastern Europe, following the expansion of the European Union and introduction of the euro currency. The trade map has changed, but will continue to do so. The effect of supplying European customers, for instance, through production in China, has resulted in transport costs squeezing the producers' value. 'Trade costs should, of course, be thought of in much more general terms than just freight charges. Time in transit is costly (up to as much as 0.5 per cent of the value of goods shipped per day). This burden comes partly from the costs of carrying stock, and also from the likelihood that long transit times reduce the reliability and predictability of deliveries' (Venables, 2006). This *senior management strategic choice* also makes firms slower to respond to changing demand conditions or cost levels, and this is the (supply chain) argument for the alternative solution of domestic clustering of activities. 'Transport and trade cost savings are a direct benefit of proximity, but its full economic impact and value-add comes from economies of scale associated with operating in an area of dense asset-augmenting activities close to consumers, workers, and other firms' (Venables, 2006).

This close proximity is not a luxury afforded to organizations that have shifted production operations eastwards and this becomes one of the most substantial challenges in the satisfaction of customer requirements. 'Research at the Cranfield School of Management identified demand risk as a source of supply chain disruption, and this relates to potential or actual disturbances to the flow of product, information and cash emanating from within the network, between the focal firm and its market' (Sweeney, 2009). In the case of low margin products, ocean is the only cost-effective mode of transport, and this effectively means matching customer demand up to months in advance of the point of consumption. Adapting to cultural differences and business rules of foreign nations has become the norm. Instructions can become lost in translation, and invariably in developing regions there is a high turnover of operational contacts as new opportunities arise, resulting in re-training and re-establishment of relationships. Therefore the global model breeds inflexibility. Policy causes disruption.

Supply chain relational risk (SCRR)

The challenges of cultural differences and business etiquettes, or communications getting lost in translation, fall within the category of General Carl Von Clausewitz-championed (supply chain) strategic friction, and are causing myths and media headlines. The role of policy makers should be to acknowledge this friction during the strategic renewal process so that it can be triumphed over. Heidi Larsen, from Denmark, is the author of *(easily?) Made in China!* (2012) and *(easily?) Made for China!* (2016) and is perfectly placed to advise on how to reduce or eliminate these frustrations, through 'bringing the European results-orientated business culture closer to the relationship-orientated culture in China, thereby creating strong and sustainable business relations'.

Heidi is the resident 'China expert' on Danish TV2 News, is a European champion in public speaking, and founded a global supply chain consultancy (Plus7) to set up client supply chains in China, or to eliminate cultural challenges, hence overcoming frustrations in cooperation. This practitioner-based body of work perfectly complements the nascent dimension of risk management, supply chain relational risk (SCRR), introduced by the doctoral research of Fu Jia at the prestigious Centre for Logistics and Supply Chain Management, Cranfield School of Management, to mitigate cultural differences between China and the West. SCRR is defined as 'the risk to the supply chain of either party in a buyer–supplier relationship not fully committing to joint efforts due to either problems associated with cooperation or problems associated with opportunistic behaviour' (Jia and Rutherford, 2010). Specific guidelines are now explored in order to reduce our exposure to 'cultural supply chain disruption':

- **Guanxi:** During the development of collaborative relationships in China, we ourselves are potentially responsible for disruptions such as late shipments, documentation oversights, and product quality issues, when we do *not* consider *guanxi* (to give face), the most important term in Chinese culture. One secret to mastering this art form is to ensure that all questions are very specific and conclusive so as to avoid any ambiguity. Match expectations at every stage of the manufacturing and logistics processes (Larsen, 2012, 2016). There is no direct English translation, but Heidi says that the term also means the power of your network, something often not understood and therefore overlooked by Europeans. It is also like a bank account, whereby 'good *guanxi*' can be deposited through extensive nurturing across key business contacts. The Chinese character for *guan* means *fortress* and *xi* means interconnected, and a *guanxi* network is considered an extended family (Jia and Rutherford, 2010). There are three supply chain risks identified in relation to *guanxi*, the first being the fact that Westerners are generally driven by self-interest, or individualism, whereas, from birth, the Chinese are focused on familistic collectivism and positive group outcomes, as opposed to universal (national) collectivism, and therefore any business negotiations must be sensitive to this. A second risk consideration is our reliance on formal agreements, and the laws and regulations of multiple institutions, but the Chinese place greater importance on 'face' and 'familial sanction', and the hierarchical harmony within the *guanxi* network. Thirdly, relationship-building in China is based not only on 'face' but also on '*renqing*', which engages in informal, personal and long-term connections rather than our more formal approach, 'based on the interplay of competition and corporation'. All parties should consider international inter-firm learning and cultural adaptation (Jia and Rutherford, 2010).

- **Trust:** Building solid relationships, by investing significant time and patience, is critical in order to establish trust, something that is not a natural trait within the Chinese, who would otherwise transition to a better opportunity whenever it would inevitably arise. Establish the right chemistry, which, if lost, is irreparable. The commendable Chinese psyche is the elevation of the family group, and sometimes this can be at our cost (in the absence of *guanxi*). It is therefore important to go beyond Western boundaries to mitigate sudden disruption. Organizations should embrace a business-to-human approach by being fair, curious, humble, present and persistent, and acknowledge the literal meaning of 'out of sight, is out of mind'. WeChat is the most effective digital platform to maintain contact at all times and is a very easy and convenient communication method for impatient and results-orientated Europeans. Fortunately, once you have established trust in the relationship, you have a loyal friend for as long as you so wish (Larsen, 2012, 2016).

- **Dynamic business environment:** When Heidi first started doing business in China (ironically, we both first visited in January 2005), the cultural game seemed very black and white to her. Now she understands that almost everything is grey. 'Accept that nothing is linear and that things constantly change, anything that seems fixed and certain at first glance can be negotiated, even after signing'. Maintaining constant and open communication lines is therefore crucial. This again points to the need to take responsibility throughout, but it is of proportionate importance to never do so condescendingly, always treating the supplier as the rightful expert. Where other 'Western cultures' failed, *absolute respect* was the key to my own successes in the region, aligned to good *guanxi*. 'Proactivity is a European concept, not Chinese', but can be found there if an understanding of the 'why' is shared from the initial stages of projects. So many product designs and strategies that are formulated behind European desks do not involve the knowledge and expertise of Chinese business partners, to whom access is free, only to subsequently discover costly and time-consuming disruptions when the product does not 'come out of the mould' when testing commences in China. The 'German Auto Greater China' case later in this chapter illustrates this common circumstance.

- **Chinese New Year:** Forward planning is essential, as discussed in Chapter 4; shipments should be arranged one week prior if possible, or port arrivals scheduled two weeks after what is the most important holiday in China. Annual contracts are signed after the holiday and therefore it can take up to four weeks for normal production to resume while factory management wait for the return of workers who go home to their families, often a great distance away, or go in search of new hires for those who stay in their home province (Larsen, 2012, 2016). The one-child-only government policy is a factor (abolished in 2015, but still impactful), as it diminishes the attraction of factory-work, and the uncertainty for plant owners is reflected in reactive pricing, planning changes and deteriorating quality. Evil spirits are scared away by fireworks, but so too will your production orders if primary capacity loads are not moved to the low season.

The 'Chinese greatly treasure their history and ancestors', evidenced throughout the CNY celebrations when additional bowls of rice are laid out for those who have passed. It is understanding this sense of history, their greatest pride, and still present at the negotiating table in the guise of Sun Tzus' Art of War, written 500 BC, that is key to relationship-building and knowing the Chinese way of thinking. By extension, this mitigates supply chain disruption. Therefore it is of benefit to very briefly describe the last four significant dynasties:

- Jin Dynasty (1115–1234): One of the last to predate the Mongol invasion of China, arising from the rebellion against the Liao dynasty (907–1125), the Jin of the north launched a 100-year war against the Song dynasty in the south. A number of cultural and technological *advancements* marked this period, such as the fortification of the Great Wall, the revival of Confucianism and the development of gunpowder, but it was also the display of incredible *tenacity* that defined the Jin, when they suppressed Genghis Khan for 23 years before the Mongols formed an alliance with the Song to finally end the Jin reign.

- Yuan Dynasty (1271–1368): This was the first time the entire country was ruled by a foreign dynasty (Kublai Khan, grandson of Genghis), a period of rich cultural diversity and *innovation*, that introduced to the world, drama and the novel, significant advancements in algebra, medicine, astronomy, ceramics, printing and publishing techniques, road and water communications, geography, cartography (the latter four aiding the logistical power of the Mongol empire), and the rebuilding of palaces in Beijing, witnessed by the famous Venetian traveller Marco Polo.

- Ming Dynasty (1368–1644): This was the greatest period of governmental and social stability in human history, and although also famous for porcelain production, was marked by epic *journeys of discovery* as far as Africa, under the stewardship of Admiral Zheng He. However, what was sensational was that these journeys were made in expansive armadas including treasure ships and tens of thousands of sailors, the scale of which was not seen again until the Great War.

- Qing Dynasty (1636–1912): This was the last imperial dynasty before the establishment of the Republic of China, and the fourth largest empire in history. The population growth that we associate with the country began during this period to cultivate new world crops (doubling in the 1700s), together with the creation of land borders. This dynasty was also marked by foreign occupation. In the mid-19th century, foreign trade was confined to the port of Canton, through which European silver flowed, restricting the availability of tea, silk and porcelain, and to address this imbalance the First Opium War (1839–1842) arose when the British began to auction opium grown by the British East India Company to independent agents. This created opium addicts that drained the economy of silver and thereby reversed the Chinese trade surplus. The Chinese response was to blockade Canton trade and the British then used gunboat diplomacy to inflict a series of defeats, one outcome of which was the taking of Hong Kong as a British colony, also controlling Guangzhou and Shanghai waters. Of course, a Second Opium War broke out in 1956 when a British–French alliance successfully re-opened trade with the West under the Tianjin Treaty.

The point is that the social, cultural and business interpretations of the individuals that we outsource our manufacturing to are grounded in this history of innovation, tenacity and brilliance. Events have also nurtured mistrust towards the West, in particular the United States, who are comparatively viewed as teenagers against their own ancient past. In business terms, being without a history weakens your position and you must therefore engage mutual acquaintances in order to establish relationships. This is essentially using pre-made *guanxi*.

Conversely, the recent economic rise of China has created a class of Chinese consumers that are demanding US brands in unprecedented levels, provided the price is excessively high! With 1.3 billion consumers, China is also the largest market, not just the largest factory.

To understand the risk of supply chain disruption from the sudden transition to a better opportunity, one needs to consider the influence of Chairman Mao Zedong, who, during the Cultural Revolution in 1949, led the reformation of the country to the People's Republic of China, and wrote *Máo Zhǔxí Yǔlù*, known in the West as *The Little Red Book*. 'This is an important cornerstone in Chinese history, and many still refer to 'before and after Mao Zedong', his death coming in 1976. Mao is a symbol of the success that all Chinese are striving for, to be the maker of your own fortune.' He rose to leadership as a result of the strategic aims, and internal revolt, of the Communist Party of China (CPC), founded in 1921 in an alliance with Stalin and Moscow. Mao, a staunch communist, was in conflict with the founding party leader, Chiang Kai-shek, who wanted the party to continue as a nationalist group. This led to Mao retreating to the impassable mountains of Jiangxi province in 1927, where he started the Red Army, and after several unsuccessful attempts at defeating his troops, was eventually driven by Chiang on a 10,000-kilometre march to Yanan in 1934. Mao then assumed singular rule of the CPC when Chiang's peers mutinied in order to stand together against the Japanese threat, which manifested into the war of 1937–45. In the West there is a saying, 'Do not mention the war', but in all endeavours to build *guanxi*, Japan should never be a part of any conversation.

Defeat of Japan and the exhaustion of the Nationalist Party of China post the Second World War was an opportunity for Mao to gain complete power over the Middle Kingdom. The ensuing civil war ended with the flight of Chiang to Taiwan in 1949, and the inauguration of Mao as the leader of China. In 1958, he commenced the Great Leap Forward, a strategy to make the entire nation communist through enormous economic growth, which has instilled in the Chinese character to this day a determination to always reach their goals, which are controlled from the top-down, within five-year plans, and linked to the economy. This determination unfortunately resulted in extensive famine from 1960–61, and the loss of up to 40 million souls, due to Mao's relentless ambitions, but on balance he raised the standard of living (for those remaining) and is considered a national hero. *China reaches its goals*. Many of today's customs and convictions are rooted in his regime. The system is more important than the individual. Mao was succeeded by Deng Xiaoping, who opened China up to the West in 1978 (until 1997), tentatively enabling the growth of capitalism, but still controlled from the top-down, and who introduced zones where Western companies could produce under tight conditions. This began the economic rise that is evident today, under President Xi Jinping. When you consider the incredible history of this brilliant nation, one can begin to appreciate how misguided a top management team strategic renewal process is, which does *not* embrace the full understanding and mastering of correct business cultural etiquettes in China, and without the lessons from Heidi Larsen and academics such as Fu Jia it is clear how easily this deficient strategic mindset can lead to senseless supply chain disruption.

Contemporary China

To further our understanding of the national consciousness of China, let us consider the geo-political challenges of globalization and the construction of barriers, inspired by a rise in terrorism, violent conflict, refugees and immigration, and the increasing gap between rich and poor, particularly since the 2008 global financial crisis, causing people to cling more tightly to their groups, once the money was gone. Shock was expressed at the United States–Mexico wall proposed by President Donald Trump. Chapter 3 discussed the Blue Line, a border demarcation between Lebanon and Israel established by the United Nations on 7 June 2000, and Chapter 5 mentioned how underground networks in Iraq prompted Israel to plan the construction of a large underground wall along its southern border to guard against ISIS infiltration, an extension of a barrier preventing the Palestinian militant group Hamas from entering through tunnels along the Gaza strip. However, would it surprise you to know that 65 countries have 'walls' along their borders, half of which have been built in this century, and in Europe alone more miles of barriers have been erected in recent years than there were at the height of the Cold War?

Worldwide examples, which can only further intensify supply chain disruption, include:

- Greece and Macedonia, Macedonia and Serbia, Serbia and Hungary;
- Slovenia and Croatia, Austria and Slovenia;
- Sweden and Demark (to deter illegal immigrants);
- Estonia, Latvia, Lithuania and Russia (defensive fortifications against a pending attack);
- United Arab Emirates and Oman;
- Kuwait to Iraq to Iran to Pakistan to India to Bangladesh;
- Uzbekistan and Afghanistan, Tajikistan, Kazakhstan, Turkmenistan, Kyrgyzstan;
- Brunei and Malaysia, Malaysia and Thailand;
- China and North Korea, North and South Korea (Marshall, 2018);
- Perhaps Brexit policy negotiations will see a return of the North-South divide in Ireland, which will have inevitable militant ramifications, in addition to economic turmoil.

Just as the cyclical patterns of policies followed by economic crises, and then wars, are evident throughout history, Troy, Jericho, Babylon, Great Zimbabwe, Hadrian's Wall, Inca Walls in Peru, and Constantinople, tell us that the phenomenon of barriers is a repeating human behaviour. The Great Wall of China, their most prominent symbol, was 'a line of demarcation separating the steppe from the sown field, nomadism from agriculture, and barbarism from civilisation' (Fairbank, 1992). *Symbol* is the best description because it was not impregnable and therefore militarily deficient, it displayed an attitude of Sinocentrism, the 'belief that China was the cultural centre of the earth and the most advanced civilisation' (Marshall, 2018), and most Chinese visit the structure to show 'Chairman Mao spirit'. In his march to Yanan, Mao said that to *not* reach the Great Wall, would make you *not* a hero. *China reaches its goals*. Reaching it is one thing, but if you marched from the East to West coasts of the United States, and back again, twice, you still would not have made it to the end of this logistical marvel!

The Great Wall was constructed during the warring states period (232–221 BC), by Ch'in shih-huang-ti, or 'The First Exalted Emperor of the Ch'in. The Chinese believed that their Emperor was the only leader mandated by Heaven and therefore he was the legitimate ruler of the globe. Another clue to their psyche. The merging of the various states was on the premise that the Emperor could completely control the various factions within. Yet another clue, because 2000 years later, the 'Core Leader', President Xi has used a different barrier, the Great *Fire*wall of China, or the 'Golden Shield', as it is known internally, to maintain complete control over the flow of information within its 23 provinces, four municipalities, five autonomous regions and two special administrative regions. This is China's *wangluo anquan*, cyber security policy, ensuring that only 'positive energy' is shared online (Marshall, 2018). It is safe to say that this policy is a form of supply chain disruption, given that our profession is built on the flow of products, monies and *information*, but it is a price China is prepared to pay in order to suppress organized opposition to the one-party dictatorship, in the process becoming the ultimate purveyors of risk management.

Beijing has contained such opposition in the Mao-annexed Xinjiang region, home to Uighur Muslims and ISIS fighters, by sending one million communist Han officials to stay with local families as a form of reconnaissance, and half the population of Buddhist-Tibet is now home to six million Hans of the Middle Kingdom. Both act as strategic buffer territories, and therefore are worth the infiltration, but three additional policies make China an economic ticking-bomb.

Firstly, despite China's *one-child-only* policy being abolished in 2015, the country faces a labour shortage crisis, and a significant financial burden, to support a change in demographics from 200 million elderly increasing to 300 million over the next decade (Marshall, 2018). An ageing population is a potential supply chain disruption that must be considered.

Second is China's *urbanization* policy. Trade in the 19th century reversed economic priorities from internal land routes to the sea lanes of the Pacific Ocean. The eastern coast flourished, and foreign countries gained power through their superior militaries forcing favourable terms on China, but this alienated the interior population due to the consequential extreme poverty and neglected infrastructures ending their trading prospects. Mao brought equality and gained control over the entire nation once again, but this was achieved by cutting trade links with the developed world, while neighbours such as Japan, South Korea and Singapore began to leave China behind. This threatened not just China's economic status, but also their military and defensive security capacity, and of course internal cohesion once people realized what was happening (Marshall, 2018).

Deng Xiaoping re-opened trade with the West and this in turn created a pressure to ensure that the interior advances, not at the same rate as the Pacific coast (where wages are three times higher), but sufficiently to prevent the alienation of the past. Notwithstanding that hundreds of millions have indeed been lifted from poverty, China must relentlessly manufacture products, keep the factories going, subsidize the banks, and keep the system moving at all costs, or else the country might stop. Chinese income inequality is among the highest in the world. To address this situation through government policy, the urban areas of coastal China are being expanded to create a larger consumerist population. This in itself causes disruption because the estimated mass migration of 250 million additional urban dwellers will mainly comprise men, leaving behind their families to tend to farms, and the construction of megacities, roads and high-speed railways will destroy villages. As a result, rural China will also become increasingly illiterate in its composition (Marshall, 2018). The system is more important than the individual.

Thirdly, a policy that predates the Great Wall, the *Hukou system*, is an ancient method of registration and classification of the population. For example, this enables 'non-agricultural Shanghai'-registered people to access the best of education through funding 12 times higher than rural farmers. This classification will not change for the aforementioned 250 million migrants, who will continue to be treated as second-class citizens when they move to cities and will be unable to obtain social services. Although urban wages are higher regardless of your *Hukou* classification, many migrants may return again to the countryside if the net gains (both financially and socially) are not enough, similar to factory workers staying in their villages when they return home for CNY. Another consideration for long-term outsourcing strategies.

An important (albeit subtle) aspect of supply chain disruption was unearthed during my own experiences in China. On the surface, my colleagues were exceptionally professional, efficient, intelligent, warm, brilliant and linguistically advanced. However, below the surface was a hidden chaotic stress caused by a cultural inability to say 'No' to divisional peers perceived to be 'superiors' (in relation to supply chain and logistics management), such as marketing or product engineering. This resulted in an intense workload behind the orderly front that was displayed. On one occasion, from candid conversations with me to determine their operational practices, it was discovered that a department in Hsinchu, Taiwan, was tasked with performing 84 weekly manual transactions that were requested by their sales office in Taipei. It was out of their social control to change this. As a result, I then met with the Taipei team, and immediately either eliminated or redistributed all transactions across other (more appropriate) functions, and the supply chain group were free to focus on value-add activities, such as a more agile response to supply chain disruption. Food for thought: the *gap of pain* could also be caused by process congestions arising from senior management indiscriminately assigning tasks that are not a true fit to a particular functional area. It therefore pays to periodically perform in-depth analyses of cross-functional roles and responsibilities, especially in China where it may not always be possible to detect issues on the surface.

Supply chain disruption is a sensitive topic, policy as the source almost controversial, and the insights of professionals in the previous four chapters are very much valued. Disruption has now inevitably reached this research and it could be suggested that no amount of *guanxi* could breach the Golden Shield, and the need to have nothing but positive energy cascade outside the borders of China. Therefore, given an almost universal raising of barriers to participation that would make the Great Wall envious, the supply chain managers that now share their experiences must be commended for their openness. Their companies shall remain nameless. Just one offered full disclosure, only to then retract at the final moment. This of course, is also further validation of the earlier perspectives of Heidi Larsen and Tim Marshall (Sky News foreign affairs editor).

Collective understanding of the intricacies of Chinese customs practices as a means of mitigating disruption

Li (Lucia) Huang is a master's graduate in logistics and supply chain management from the Cranfield School of Management, home to the most prominent academics in our profession, and an e-commerce global supply chain and project manager based in Shanghai. Her *innominate* firm, whose identity remains within the Great *Fire*wall of China, is an online boutique featuring emerging women's apparels, chic dresses, fashion clothing, shoes and accessories. Since their inception in 2008 they have developed a strong partnership with industry insiders and collaborate intensively with mainstream manufacturers in China. Their elite multi-lingual customer service team selects the most reputable import and export companies, warehousing, logistics and after-sales providers to support a global customer base of two million. When asked what supply chain disruption means to her, it is interesting that Lucia sees the phenomenon as increasingly common in the present climate of global political and economic uncertainty, and also attributes it to geopolitics, the trade war with the United States being a highly sensitive topic in China, and senior management decision-making. Lucia has therefore observed that policy transcends the operational taxonomy of disruption that is found in mainstream research.

Generic risk mitigation strategies in the company include a high rate of procurement from local suppliers, while also sourcing from other regions to ensure product differentiation from competitors in the domestic market. Selection of products must be very precise for smooth importation. However, there is an inexplicit sense from Lucia that this smoothness is a nirvana, and that Chinese organizations view customs issues almost as a given. Whilst most of us shy away from the intricacies of customs, it is imperative that we analyse the inbound and outbound flows of our Chinese manufacturers and suppliers. Perhaps we are endemically causing disruptions that are resolved directly by our partners in China under the calm surface. It is our duty to understand these processes in order to eliminate such practices.

The collective West cannot be held entirely accountable, and Lucia attributes customs delays as the main source of supply chain disruption, pointing to top management team lack of awareness and understanding as the cause. The Islamic world is a major consumer and they have very specific restrictions on logos. The financial impact of shipping forbidden items has been significant for the company in terms of delayed shipments, order cancellations and damage to brand reputation. This should most certainly have been resolved at the market development stage, but the executive team is finally engaged in the recovery to an improved state. A third-party agent now handles clearances, and shipments are arranged in advance to avoid issues. Technically supply chain disruption, but undoubtedly a senior management oversight. This also indicates that disruption garners attention in the upper echelons only when sales are impacted, and this does not lend itself to strategic alignment. A further case of the supply chain department not being involved in the strategic renewal process is the top management team negotiating pricing and terms with logistics providers at a company level. This has contractually restricted business units from achieving logistics cost reductions and service improvements at a functional or operational level from the same providers, the very purpose of establishing such units. Lucia advises that management must *think first* and discuss strategies with their supply chain professionals *before* moving forward.

The power of sudden government environmental regulations to disrupt industries

Another supply chain manager who requests company anonymity is Suzhou-based Chunming Gu, a random, albeit strategic, participant, who it turns out shares the privilege with me of having a signed copy of John Gattorna's *Dynamic Supply Chains* from his attendance at a conference in Shanghai (at the risk of sounding fanatical, the fact that I have three can remain a secret). Even amongst a China population of 1.4 billion, it is a very small world sometimes. Prior to his present position, Chunming spent almost a decade at a €14 billion global technology company whose 92,000 employees deliver high-precision automotive components and systems, as well as solutions for a large number of industrial applications, and to whom the disruptive events are attributed, the first arising after his tenure there.

Disruptions can be categorized as commercial, logistical, information-based and *force majeure*. A major commercial crisis occurred in September 2017 when a new policy issued by 'the Communist Party of China Central Committee and the State Council established a comprehensive damage-compensation system to protect its environment in the next three years. Individuals or companies that cause environmental damage would have to help restore the environment or pay compensation if the damage is beyond repair' (Sit, 2017). Authorities shut down a key vehicle parts supplier (needle bearings) by turning off their water and electricity without notice. The estimated economic impact was $43 billion when 49 automobile producers in China were unable to complete planned orders for three million vehicles, given that it takes three months to replace a supplier in this industry.

The Communist Party blamed the incident on a management decision of the key supplier not to inform its customers, given that letters of a potential shutdown were issued in late 2016 and early 2017. A case of 'positive energy' perhaps, but either way, policy was the disrupter. The advice here is to determine if any new supplier is compliant with governmental regulations. The company subsequently redirected all sourcing to India, a second time this action has been seen in this research (the *stove-plan* of the Woodland Group). A second similar event arose from a *conflict* amongst the key shareholders of a supplier that caused a dedicated production line to stop, and this resulted in significant air freight premiums to procure the components from original European sources. Neither of these events could have been planned, but Chunming does advocate contingency plans in the form of standard operating procedures (SOPs) and work instructions, managed by group processes. He goes beyond SOPs, however, with a powerful suggestion to generally regulate supply chain management in the same way as banking and finance, given the critical nature of risk management. Financial law forms a substantial part of commercial law and provides a sound and clear legal policy foundation related to financial transactions across the entire global economy. This would certainly engage the top management team in terms of organizational compliance and strategic alliance. Perhaps Blockchain will have this same outcome. Materials Management Operations Guidelines (MMOG) is a comprehensive measurement of SCM maturity, but for risk evaluation or indicators (especially pre-indicators) there is no 'law'. In general terms, supply chain management (let alone strategic alignment) is seen as a low priority for senior executives in China, who assign little importance to it. The best we can do in such a climate is to align our strategies (or tactics, in reality) closely to company goals, whilst maintaining sufficient flexibility and discipline to fine tune our direction in response to supply chain disruption, maintaining cognisance at all times of management targets so that we can demonstrate our contribution to the bottom line.

China initiatives to reduce transit times to Europe, minimizing the demand challenge of globalization, and location as a critical factor in risk mitigation

Emily Yan is based in Dongguan and manages the global supply chain for specialists in LED profiles, strip lights and plastic extrusion profiles for international leaders in the lighting industry. The company offers extensive services to customers, ranging from raw material development, product design and manufacturing across a network of seven factories in Asia, Africa, Europe and North America. Emily believes that the United States–China trade war is the greatest threat to the global economy. In September, Alibaba chairman Jack Ma said that his Chinese e-commerce giant is no longer going to create one million jobs in the United States due to the conflict. At risk to the West is exportation to the largest market for cars, cell phones and seafood, the fastest growing market for luxury goods, air passengers and nuclear power.

Today's auto industry has a complex supply chain. A car assembled in the United States might have its engine manufactured in Germany, its transmission system from Mexico and its GPS from South Korea. Such sophisticated supply chains have formed through decades of globalization, which is difficult to unwind. In her own industry, Emily has seen a 40 per cent reduction in sales to the United States in comparison to 2017, and this has been largely linked to household appliances, in particular refrigeration products, which comprise LED components. What is refreshing to hear is that this situation is not leading to a sense of animosity towards the United States, rather a business threat that needs to be responded to in the same manner as any other. Business people in China therefore see this solely as a business issue and look beyond the political ramifications, and Emily takes the *change-adaption* approach of Aramex: it is an opportunity to re-assess and continue to transform and innovate. Greater clockspeeds and forced efficiencies can help us all evolve and counter the economic impact of protectionism.

Location is also a critical factor in risk mitigation. For example, the Pearl River Delta Economic Circle encompasses nine cities along the Pearl River, including Guangzhou, Shenzhen, Foshan, Zhuhai, Dongguan, Zhongshan, Huizhou, Jiangmen and Zhaoqing, and should be at the forefront of any supplier negotiations and selection. Proposed 2020 infrastructure is such that any manufacturing plant will be able to reach major ports, and indeed any destination in the circle, within one hour through the Metropolis Rapid Transportation. This is a direct result of the China open-door new revolutionary policy that has attracted substantial foreign investment in the economic zones. Through its Belt and Road Initiative (BRI), China is investing $1 trillion in new rail infrastructure and trade agreements to link Beijing to Europe, with 34 cities in both continents already connected. Rail freight is expected to double its share of trade in the next decade. The topic of disruption can certainly benefit from a degree of balance, and it is evident that the ancient brilliance of China continues to this day.

The enforcement of 'mother-ship' control over subsidiaries disrupting cultural integration, and the challenge of the localization of globalization

Established in January 2001 and headquartered in Beijing, 'German Auto' Greater China Limited is responsible for the operations of vehicles, financial services and leasing, spare parts and research and development (RD) centres in mainland China, Hong Kong, Macau and Taiwan. This is a subsidiary of 'German Auto' AG in Stuttgart, Germany, whose founders made history with the invention of the automobile in 1886. Raymond Gao, Supply Chain Manager, generously gives us an insight into disruption within the RD division, comprising procurement, warehousing, import and export, and vehicle management.

'German Auto' RD has been in China for the past 10 years and is therefore a relatively new and growing division. Vehicle development is a 55-month process that includes marketing and competitor analysis. The first 37 months are handled in Germany and this involves model design (exterior and interior), parts and software validation, supplier tooling, prototype development and the assembly of a 'B-car' for testing, after which the final design is frozen. This prototype vehicle is then shipped to China to begin the final 18-month project phase. In Beijing, local suppliers are sourced, and tooling is developed accordingly. All supplier parts are then warehoused, and undergo validation, functional testing, certification and release by RD. Quality assurance then approves the project for the plant to begin trial production, and thereafter mainstream production assembly begins.

Raymond is at the end of the entire process and must contend with supplier tooling delays and engineering design adjustments, but a systemic disruption is that parts are never set up on the 'dialog stair-lock IS system' upon handover from Germany. This reminds me of a previous European new product introduction manager who would inform the supply chain group that parts were available to procure, but at best this meant that customers had approved the samples, and a myriad of part number set-ups were still needed before orders could be placed on our plant in Suzhou, China. When I later moved into this position, I used this prior experience to develop a green-light dashboard, ensuring that all system tasks were completed before handing over projects. I felt that this was my responsibility, but it also showed respect for the supply chain personnel. When 'German Auto' engineering in Stuttgart transition the B-cars to Beijing it is indeed the case that part numbers, product data and drawings are at different phases of development and certain supplier assembly parts are not known to the company system. However, again not explicitly stated, I did detect a sense of elitism and disrespect not just towards China colleagues, but also towards a less powerful supply chain group that deals with less volumes than Stuttgart. Senior management should redistribute the responsibility of dialog set-ups to engineering to avoid unnecessary disruption that contributes to the *gap of pain*.

Closely related to this issue is a lack of communication between engineering and suppliers (who are negotiating componentry procurement independently) and RD warehousing. On a regular basis, unidentified parts that are not pre-alerted arrive at the warehouse and it takes considerable time to assign these to the appropriate SKU locations, once inbound checks have been completed. The China plant must also take some responsibility to further define dialog product descriptions to include testing purposes and (supplier) addresses, and also the inclusion of drawings on part labels. This will be resolved through the planned creation of a domestic subsystem over the coming years that will have linkages to procurement, finance and supplier portals. Part of the problem at the moment is that RD is governed by strict SOPs, but these are not extended to peripheral functions.

Effectively, Beijing RD must be an extension of Germany. Their work practices must be in the same step as Stuttgart, and the same know-how must be engrained. Staff must consist of 20 per cent German experts, who spend four years in China. China staff are also seconded to Stuttgart for one to two years. It was really amusing to hear Raymond's thick German accent, but there is an underlying disruption at play. Heidi Larsen earlier advised to always treat the supplier as the rightful expert. In this case, RD is not China. They cannot express their own style and this conflicts with other functional areas such as auto-logistics, manufacturing, after-sales support, etc, who remain Chinese. Germans are known for their engineering brilliance. But is this 'mother-ship' control over Beijing RD failing to draw on 3,250 years of even greater brilliance?

Another disruptive force is that Stuttgart organizational functions and silos are all under 'German Auto' AG ownership (RD, plant production, sales), whereas Beijing must fuse with various joint-ventures, such as Beijing Benz (an alliance between BAIC Motor and 'German Auto' AG), each with different contractual nuances, and this can be a problem for seamless information flow. With such a low budget and short project timelines, flexibility and discipline are traits needed by Beijing RD in this environment, in order to stay inside the boundaries of the core competencies of 'German Auto' AG. A pending challenge described by Raymond for his company is that the current staff of 700 is to be increased to 1,000 in 2020 due to three car lines ramping up to five. This will become an interesting test for cultural integration as 200 Germans will now need to be accommodated, but the RD organizational chart also needs to expand its supply chain capabilities, such as the positioning of prototype cost-engineering, procurement cost-planning, supplier quality assurance management, and project management teams.

Consider also the *localization* of globalization, and certain human resource factors that cause supply chain disruption. In the opening chapter, it was mentioned that invariably in developing regions there is a high turnover of operational contacts as new opportunities arise, resulting in re-training and re-establishment of relationships, and we have since seen the impact of CNY and the Hukou system on staff retention. However, in the case of 'mother-ship-controlled-subsidiaries', such as 'German Auto' Greater China, the promotion of indigenous staff to senior positions is not common practice. Think of the thousands of young graduates who were seduced by Beijing during the 2008 Olympics, who went there, as a result, to find their dreams within organizational power-houses, only to have these same dreams shattered a decade later once a certain level had been reached within the company (Wen, 2016).

Compounding this has been a 30–40 per cent increase in property prices since 2016 (Wen, 2016), not just in Beijing but also in Shanghai and the metropolis of Shenzhen, and consequently you have a significant exodus of supply chain talent. Rents, and indeed home ownership, are out of the reach of most professionals, who have to commute long distances just to put their heads down for the night. For example, the first conversation with Raymond was on one of his train journeys, and due to the noise, we resumed again when he arrived home at his midnight. It is of course a vicious circle, as these major cities cannot then attract replacement talent. This also does not bode well for the aforementioned government urbanization policy. No doubt we do not help the situation, continuing to demand cost reductions as a justification for our global outsourcing policies.

Conclusion

The insights from the geographical heart of globalization are now applied once again to the research objectives:

- *Determine how supply chain managers operationally identify, predict, cope and recover from supply chain disruptions.* Similar to prior domain case studies, identification and prediction of supply chain disruption is all but impossible when government policies such as the environment damage-compensation system are enacted. From a Western perspective, identification and prediction comes from understanding the concept of positive energy as the cornerstone of information exchange (thereby a need to take responsibility for communications and purchase order details), appreciating that behind a composed exterior, it is important to analyse tasks, roles and responsibilities, the relentless nurturing of *guanxi* and building trust with a culture that values collectivism, almost everything is grey and negotiable, even after signing, things are constantly changing, and respecting suppliers as the experts. It is also important to understand that demanding relentless cost reductions is short-sighted and ultimately damages relationship-continuity with key personnel when they are forced to relocate. Remember that our profession is all about people.

- *Identify which phases in the supply chain disruption process require engagement with top management to implement strategic solutions aligned to business goals.* The dominant message in this regard from Heidi Larsen and Raymond Gao is that Chinese expertise must be harnessed at the early stages of the strategic renewal process or indeed the design phase of new product introduction. When we outsource to China, it is critical in the context of *guanxi* to trust that the selected suppliers can add tremendous value if they are involved from the outset of the relationship. Failure to adopt this approach through 'mother-ship control' leads to supply chain disruption.

- *Consequently, determine whether a categorization of supply chain strategy exists, such as a tier consisting of strategies that can be implemented autonomously by the supply chain division, and a tier or tiers that require negotiation across the top management team prior to implementation, to collaboratively mitigate risk.* There is little evidence that such a categorization exists at a local level in China. The calm exterior that we are exposed to in the West hides an environment of managerial control and an absence of autonomous decision-making. It was also highlighted that senior executives do not assign much importance to supply chain management, and the failure to promote indigenous supply chain managers, coupled with crippling real-estate costs, suffocates individual growth, perhaps reflected in China being ranked 27 in terms of logistics performance (Germany, Netherlands and Sweden form the top three).

- *Determine how supply chain managers engage with the top management team in the process of aligning business and supply chain strategies, thereby identifying key enablers and inhibitors.* In addition to contingency plans and SOPs, Chunming Gu suggested the introduction of a SCM law akin to the banking, finance and accounting domain, which will undoubtedly be addressed when Blockchain becomes a norm.

- *Develop a process model that establishes the phases of supply chain managers' engagement in dynamic business to supply chain strategic alignment.* The cumulative policy schema on the page is the final instalment in the categorization of policy-driven supply chain disruption. It seems to be irrefutable that the strategic renewal process is the snake's head of disruption, a claim made in the opening chapters and validated through discussing the topic with professionals across the full spectrum of supply chain management. Now that this has been established, the impending *pièce de résistance* is to determine *how* dynamic business to supply chain strategic alignment can be accomplished. The *so what?*

Policy: the source of supply chain disruption

External policy: political, economic, social, technological, climatic

Protectionism and trade wars; political cyber-security breaches; political migration; Socio-economic customer demand: e-commerce and environment-driven decisions; OPEC production management, military-driven oil embargoes, oil and gas mergers and acquisitions China government manufacturing plant closures; culture of CNY non-returning work-force; Holiday schedules in China and India, week-long port closures and resulting back-logs; major consumer-brand product launches, reducing ocean and air capacity; Chinese staff turnover; Golden Shield; urbanization policy; Hukou system; one-child policy; ageing population; Environment damage-compensation policy; promotion ceiling for Chinese managers; Major Chinese cities: real-estate prices; fusion of joint ventures; shareholder conflict; Restrictions or legislative conditions on access to resources or infrastructure; changes in strategic priorities governing the use of non-domestic equipment, vehicles and manpower; acts of sabotage, theft, extortion and bribery within an existing supply chain or ethically corrupt or unauthorized protectionist acts impacting on the ability to establish a supply chain; impact of conflict situations; unintended blue-on-blue actions by partner organizations and friendly forces; deliberate refusal of external agent to cooperate despite their organizations' agreement to do so; diplomatic relationships between stakeholder nations and the existing national legislation before a supply chain is established; external economic decisions, commercial pressures and competition for available resources; EU–US mother-ship control in China; China localization of globalization

Internal industry policy: supply chain management

E-retailers consuming warehouse real-estate; non-licensed exponential logistics companies entering the market; Blockchain: risk of hacking and fraud; accelerating force of technology such as NFC; Ocean alliances and mega-ships; customs documentation restrictions and non-tariff measures including VGM; Distance, demand risk, time in transit costs; containers lost at sea due to weight declarations; Slow-steaming and artificial removal of vessel capacity; mergers of logistics providers; sea port congestion including intermodal inbound road and waterway delays; Fuel and bunker surcharges; China government dangerous-goods processing; Security measures including convoys and restrictions in route planning

Internal organizational policy: top management team strategic renewal process

Lean inventory holding; CNY planning; failure to evolve with and adapt new technology advancements; Failure to consider the people aspect of technology implementations; anti-change culture; Failure to engage in the circular economy; failure to adopt Gattorna Dynamic Alignment™; Lack of TMT understanding and operational awareness; management decision; delay in decision-making; change in supply strategy; misjudging the scale or nature of the supply chain operation; failure to design and control an appropriate supply chain; failure to appropriately man (experience, education and training) or resource the supply chain; management reconsideration: changes in financial or operational priorities; changes in manpower or personalities in authority; changes in the end-product, therefore a change in requirements; indirect impact of external pressures; information flow disruption: failure to communicate effectively and efficiently throughout the supply chain network; failure to communicate internal, external and environmental changes; failure to contingency-plan for potential future disruption; Unauthorized act: deliberate operation of (or permitting the operation of) supply chain assets, such as equipment and vehicles, outside authorized parameters; failure to comply with legislative requirements; Intentional or incompetent act: negligent conduct; failure to control a controllable external force, such as failure of equipment through neglect; use of untrained or inexperienced manpower

Supply Chain Disruption

Macro: impacting supply chain network design
TMT negotiation based on pre-determined investment threshold of the organization

Micro: supply chain friction
HRM policy: anger to succeed and passion to deliver; Chinese guanxi; Familistic collectivism; trust; dynamic business environment

Supply Chain Disruption:
Black Swan Crises and Disasters
Grey Swan Breakdowns
what we do inside the bubble of our profession

Supply Chain Strategies:
both TMT negotiation and autonomous

Supply Chain Friction:
Petty circumstances
Blind natural forces
know what we do inside the bubble of our profession and triumph over it

Supply Chain Strategies:
autonomous

References

Christopher, M and Towill, DR (2002) Developing market specific supply chain strategies, *The International Journal of Logistics Management*, **13**(1), pp 1–14

Fairbank, JK (1992) *China: A new history*, Belknap

Jia, F and Rutherford, C (2010) Mitigation of supply chain relational risk caused by cultural differences between China and the West, *The International Journal of Logistics Management*, **21**(2), pp 251–70

Larsen, H (2012) *(Easily?) Made in China! From 0 to 100 in cultural understanding*, It's Passion Darling

Larsen, H (2016) *(Easily?) Made for China!* It's Passion Darling

Marshall, T (2018) *Divided: Why we're living in an age of walls*, Elliott and Thompson Limited

Sit, S-S (2017) https://www.cips.org/en/supply-management/news/2017/december/china-to-make-polluters-pay-for-environmental-damage/

Sweeney, E (2009) *Supply Chain Management and Logistics in a Volatile Global Environment*, Blackhall Publishing Ltd

Venables, AJ (2006) Shifts in economic geography and their causes, Centre for Economic Performance, London School of Economics and Political Science

Wen, P (2016) https://www.smh.com.au/world/beijing-shanghai-shenzhen-the-cities-where-house-prices-rose-by-30-to-40-per-cent-20161003-grtwe6.html

Engaging in the process of business to supply chain strategic alignment

08

Here, then, is a chronicle of Supply Chain Disruption... Since time immemorial, the strategic renewal process has universally comprised the trinity of politics (strategic formulation), chance (strategic implementation) and hatred (consumer reaction). Formulation can either be through cunning and deception, or through strong force, and implementation is impeded by blind natural forces (strategic friction) that are *tactically* resolved depending on situational needs (Freedman, 2015). Irrespective of the circumstances, a disproportionate presence of any one element of the trinity leads to supply chain disruption. Given that our response rather than the event itself is the disruption (Sheffi, 2001), my research posits that, whilst remaining critical, the generic academic response mechanisms contained within supply chain risk management, or the taxonomy of disasters, crises and disasters should not be the main focus.

Our dominant concentration must instead be on the true source of elongated response times to disruption, framed herein as the *gap of pain* (Heaslip and Barber, 2014). Policy is that true source, caused by the strategic misalignment of politics (external, supply chain industry and business goals) and chance (supply chain management tactics). So what? When considering this position across the full spectrum of supply chain domains, as this research has done, monetary and brand-reputation damages of disruption are compounded by potentially *fatal* consequences of policy-driven *gaps of pain*.

Therefore, engaging in the process of dynamic business to supply chain strategic alignment protects not just corporate profitability, but most certainly saves human lives. Death and taxes. Policy matters.

Strategy is the central political art of creating power. From the Battle of Heaven to the escape of the Jews from Egypt, God has used both deception and strength to demonstrate His brilliance as a superlative strategist. He has also allowed the *sensation* of choice and free will, enabling individuals to 'shape the game', and when this ultimately leads to *disruption* through disobedience (akin to strategic implementation without political support, actions that go outside the boundaries of the core competencies of an organization), He uses this arena to restore balance to the trinity and His divine plan (Freedman, 2015). Let me explore free will for a moment by referencing a brief extract of an assignment I submitted to Oxford University.

Categorizing supply chain management through the philosophy of determinism

Society and, indeed, Roman Catholic teachings have engrained in me the concept of free will. We apparently have the freedom to act as we wish within the confines of religious and cultural norms, societal rules and laws. I suggest that this may *only* be true in relation to a category of seemingly insignificant actions such as whether you order an americano or cappuccino in a café. This sits fine with me, because our existence is dynamic and not static, or, as Heraclitus observed, a man cannot step into the same river twice (Rescher, 1996). He taught *panta rhei* (everything flows). The next time you might order a flat white without upsetting anyone! The German philosopher Arthur Schopenhauer (1788–1860) proposed a definition of freedom as 'the absence of all necessity' and this is where I place the categorization of cappuccino or any decision made at a 'consciousness of ordinary things that belong to the outer world in space and time' (Guttenplan *et al*, 2008). These are contingent actions and do not impact on the mechanics of the universe or indeed our existence. This correlates to the supply chain category within which autonomous tactics can be implemented based on situational needs. Edward Luttwak (2001) suggests that tactics ascend to the operational level and I therefore posit that *strategy* is the preserve of senior management. Tactics are autonomous actions.

For actions that shape our existence and challenge us, *determinism* is the dominant force, where every event has antecedent causes (Blackburn, 1999).

These are contained within the inner depths of self at a metaphysical level and manifested through our self-consciousness. Our innate knowledge and settings guide our actions. In this case, hard determinism, known also as incompatibilism, suggests the non-existence of free will and indeed (moral) freedom, *liberum arbitrium*. We act in a certain way that is determined, only through conformity with our inner will. We do not consciously know in that moment that it is determined, and therefore as humans we are prone to surprise, excitement, disappointment, resentment, both towards others and towards certain outcomes. This gives us an *illusion* of free will. I suggest that the manner in which we respond to these outcomes is a clear demonstration of determinism.

For instance, *a priori* knowledge that God exists means that you must reconcile your actions with His teachings, whatever your religion or God, and any proposed changes to the mission or goals of the CEO must be negotiated with the top management team (the second supply chain category). The element of hatred (consumer reaction) manifests in people concluding that if God actually existed, there would not be so much suffering on Earth (although there are no atheists in the trenches), and consumers can exacerbate supply chain disruption through disproportionate product demand in response to an event. Balancing the trinity in our profession means engaging in the process of dynamic business to supply chain strategic alignment. However, before we can begin this critical conversation with senior management, it must be demonstrated that policy *is* the source of supply chain disruption and, for many reasons, we begin with a self-proclaimed God, Napoleon Bonaparte, and the Age of Revolution.

The historically cyclical nature of supply chain disruption

The period circa 1800 was carefully chosen to commence this research into demonstrating the source of supply chain disruption. Of course, '1800' is used in the interest of simplicity. In the same vein as Friedman (2016) wondering about the revolutionary innovations of 2007, *what the hell happened in 1800* from a strategic supply chain management perspective?

- France was in a precarious position in 1799. Replacing the absolutist monarchy of Louis XVI and the Society of Orders (nobility class) a decade prior during the French Revolution had led to a number of pretenders to the seat of governmental power. The National Assembly, the Legislative Assembly, the First Republic and the Directory, were all deficient in gaining widespread approval from the large population. Remaining, were conflicting views such as republic versus monarchy, prioritizing individual rights over the sovereignty of the nation, and whether voting rights should be based on property or open to all adult men. There was no functioning legal system or stable currency, public order was in a state of chaos, and an absence of economic regulations stagnated commercial growth. Fresh from military success during the Italian Campaign of 1796–97 and a less victorious 1798 Egyptian expedition (but a venture that shaped a charismatic and persuasive leader), Napoleon Bonaparte was to bring the stability that the country desperately needed and was determined to build an empire in the process (Sperber, 2014).

- The Napoleon Code was introduced, and this has had a permanent legacy on continental Europe and beyond. This was designed to introduce civil and legal equality, abolishing labour dues forced on the Third Estate (French peasants) and enabling career advancement based on merit rather than on noble birth (Rapport, 2005). Napoleon founded the Banque de France, abolished the Guild of Merchants and Craftsmen to facilitate entrepreneurship and established the Order of Chivalry to encourage civil and military achievement. This remains the highest decoration in France. In order to manage European occupation, Napoleon implemented a highly efficient prefectural system of administration, and a more commanding *gendarmerie* police force. Napoleon legalized divorce, influenced religious tolerance through a reconciliation with the Roman Catholic Church despite the secularization and sale of church property, proclaimed the equality of Jews, including the closing of Jewish ghettos, disbanded the Holy Roman Empire, thereby creating a 39-state German confederation, later leading to a unified Germany in 1871, and ended the Inquisition, which had been in place since the 12th century. A more logical and practical legal code was the most defining introduction, as it remained in use, and indeed firmly established, after Napoleon's demise in 1815, areas such as the German states favouring this over a return to the highly complex medieval systems that had been in place. The creation of this new legal and administrative code demonstrated Napoleon's deep understanding of the initial aims and objectives of the 1789 French Revolution and displayed a vision of the political landscape of parallel brilliance to that of his military brain. Napoleon said: 'My true glory is not to have won forty battles... Waterloo will erase the memory of so many victories... but... what will live forever, is my Civil Code' (Schwartz, 1998).

- Napoleon Bonaparte used the theories of Frederick the Great, Jacques Antoine Hippolyte, Comte de Guibert, and Lazar Carnot to introduce and implement a strategy of annihilation (*Niederwerfungsstrategie*), a ferocious warfare of movement and surprise in overwhelming numbers (employing 'on-the-move' and 'off-the-land' troop replenishment), made possible through the rapid development of road infrastructures and modes of transportation (logistics), and indeed cartography. This enabled the establishment of the First French Empire (thus named because the French colonial empire established since the 17th century did not have an imperial ruler).

- Logistics was also used during that time in the strategy of exhaustion (*Ermattungsstrategie*) to overcome seemingly hopeless situations through *attrition* rather than direct engagement. In 1780, for example, the fortunes of the American War of Independence swayed from Lieutenant General Charles Cornwallis and the British, when the Americans unconventionally introduced guerrilla tactics to tease their superior enemy away from their supply base in Yorktown. Another infamous case, under the tentative leadership of Tsar Alexander, the Battle of Borodino in September 1812 saw Napoleon's Grande Armée lured deeper into Russian territory and further from supply lines, with fatal consequences for the French.

- Two prominent and competing observers of Napoleon's art of war, General Antoine-Henri Jomini (1779–1869) and General Carl von Clausewitz (1780–1832) founded modern strategy. Strategy of course existed before 1800. However, at this time, logistical support changed strategy due to a rise in republicanism and nationalism, which altered battles from a 'chance of arms' to total annihilation, and the need to mobilize, motivate, move and direct mass armies (Freedman, 2015). Transport and supplies now heavily influenced what could be achieved.

- Prussian General Carl von Clausewitz developed several principals, such as: war is a continuation of policy by other means; politicians have an authority over the military; policy is shaped by a trinity of primordial violence, hatred and enmity; strategic plans are based on a series of connected steps (process); flexibility must be maintained, opportunities seized as they arise; a calculated culminating point of victory must be kept in mind. All this, however, is restrained by friction, minor unforeseen incidents causing delays and confusion, resulting in generals being doomed to disappointment.

- Also founded was the discipline of economics, or political economy as it was known then, when Adam Smith published the seminal *Wealth of Nations* in 1776, later supported by David Ricardo (1772–1823) with the introduction of comparative advantage theory (producing and exporting the goods that you are much better at to a country you are engaged in trade with, and importing the 'other' goods from this country), further enhanced by Marx (1818–83), who advocated accelerating global expansion to increase value, the development of multinational companies, and the promotion of imperialism so that governments could protect indigenous organizations. The policy of capitalism and free trade was consequently established and replaced feudalism in Great Britain, and the dynamism of this policy led to pressure to expand beyond borders (Michie, 2017).
- What enabled this expansion? As part of the industrial revolution, a transportation revolution emerged in the early 1800s when American Robert Fulton (1765–1815) launched the first steamboat for commercial use, almost simultaneously as the British engineer Richard Trevithick (1771–1833) constructed the first railway steam locomotive. Long-distance international integration was now possible, and further policy changes to break down monopolies were implemented. Steamboats and railroads made it so much easier to trade and move bulk goods across continents cheaper than domestic prices.
- These latter two developments brought other nations such as Russia, India, West Africa and the Ottoman Empire into the global economy and established true globalization, despite this not becoming a defining term until the early 1990s (similar to supply chain management, which was not coined as such until 1982).

We therefore have a *perfect storm* of various practices emerging at the one time, such as modern strategy, modern logistics management, industrial transportation advancements, economics and globalization, and … with a storm comes… disruption. A perfect place to start.

Policy: historical source of supply chain disruption

When considering historical policy-driven disruption that has shaped us since the Age of Revolution, General Carl von Clausewitz has been chosen

Engaging in the Process of Business to Supply Chain Strategic Alignment

as the strategic influencer because the teachings of General Antoine-Henri Jomini did not consider politics, tactics, logistics or historical contexts. Both have equal status, but you are either in one camp or the other. Clausewitz introduced strategic friction, minor unforeseen incidents and petty circumstances that cause delays and confusion, which really resonates with logisticians. Friction must be factored into the strategic renewal process so that it can be triumphed over. The trinity concept of politics (business, top management team), chance or violence (military, supply chain management) and hatred or enmity (consumer reaction) is also from the Clausewitz stable and this section provides evidence that misalignment across the elements of politics and violence is the source of disruption. Consumers can compound disruption, but this is more reactionary and much less of a threat if the back-end alignment is reached, and their satisfaction is assured by proponents of Dynamic Alignment™, such as Schneider Electric.

- The decision of Louis XVI of France to engage in the American Revolution (1765–83) by signing the Treaty of Alliance on 6 February 1778 (the War of Independence dates from 1775), thereby recognizing the United States of America, was a face-saving act of revenge on the British, who had defeated him in Québec, Canada in 1763 (thereby relinquishing his colonies). This lacked strategic substance for a country that was already facing economic ruin from continuous military campaigns and climatic events that were destroying the crops of the peasant class (Third Estate). This precipitated the storming of the Bastille on 14 July 1789 and a French Revolution that would cause terrific bloodshed and disruption, including 'The Terror', for the next decade (Rapport, 2005; Sperber, 2014).

- The Napoleon Bonaparte strategy of war of movement in numbers amassed an empire in continental Europe (1799–1815) and the death of seven million people. However, this same strategy led to the disruption of the empire because it was *inappropriately* applied to the vast land of Russia, too far from supply chain support, in conditions too perilous for in-transit replenishment, and without political endorsement. It was a display of vanity misaligned to the strategic trinity of Carl von Clausewitz, and the Battle of Borodino in September 1812 was ultimately the end of Napoleon as a military force.

- Once Napoleon was finally banished to St Helena island after defeat at Waterloo in 1815 (a defeat that was uncertain until the last moment, and only because he lacked numbers), Europe was saturated with continuous attempts of revolt, but all failed because of strategic misalignment.

For instance, liberalism and nationalism challenges in 1848 did not adopt the theories of Clausewitz. Italian revolutionaries did not have a concerted *political* foundation because there was no alignment as to what nationalism meant in Italy, and without a defined political purpose they could not succeed. In terms of *military* performance, they were no match for the power of the Austrian army to the north. In addition, there was a miscalculation by the liberalists in assuming that the officer class would be sympathetic to their cause, whereas they were in fact absolutist conservatives. And with the final piece of the trinity, *citizens* were indifferent because they had received no benefit at any stage throughout the myriad conflicts since 1789 despite many promises to the contrary. By direct contrast, the most dominant leaders between 1850–70, Piedmontese Prime Minister Emilio di Cavour, French Emperor Napoleon III and Prussian Prime Minister Otto von Bismarck harnessed nationalism to great success by using war as an instrument of policy (Sperber, 2014).

- The Great Famine in Ireland (1845–52) was a direct result of the New Poor Law of 1834, a policy that denied relief to pauperism, arising from a concern that population growth could exceed resources. There was no shortage of food, of course, and Ireland was the most technologically advanced farming nation in Europe at that time. The 39 states of the German Federation and France also had identical potato crop failures, but in these cases the governments came to the immediate assistance of their citizens. Around 1.5 million Irish people died needlessly (Rapport, 2005). Policy-driven disruption.

- In what could be described as a tsunami, building momentum, the policy of capitalism and free trade with the gold standard linked to the British pound replaced feudalism in Great Britain. This led to conflicts such as the First Britain–China Opium War (1839–42) for trade rights (Michie, 2017). Subsequently, a huge increase in global trade and a scramble for Africa ultimately led to the great disruption, the First World War (1914–18).

- The First Lord of the British Admiralty, Winston Churchill, used Clausewitz's land-based strategy which caused disruption in the Dardanelles in February 1915 and the death of 110,000 people. In defence of Churchill, and I do defend whom I consider to be the greatest Briton in history, naval strategy was non-existent from the Battle of Trafalgar (1805) to 1914, simply because Britain had complete dominance at sea and any attempts at strategizing were just ineffective borrowings from Jomini and Clausewitz (Freedman, 2015).

- In March 1918, General Ludendorff, the Chief of the German General Staff, ordered the 'Spring offensive'. This was initiated by Operation Michael, which was intended to advance on allied forces through the use of the French railroad system from a starting point of the Hindenburg Line. This failed catastrophically because rail tracks only went so far and, ultimately, supplies could no longer be maintained for the German troops. Prior logistical intelligence would undoubtedly have influenced or altered this strategy.

- Policies in the 1919 Treaty of Versailles such as German reparation payments, loss of German territories, Allied blockades on Germany, Churchill's policy to re-establish the gold standard linked to the British pound (despite advice to the contrary from John Maynard Keynes, the brilliant British economist) led to another tsunami of events such as the 1929 Wall Street Crash and the 1930s global depression, the rise of fascism in Italy, Spain and Portugal, militarism in Japan, and the Japan–China war (Michie, 2017), ultimately leading to the next great disruption, the Second World War (1939–45).

- French policies to ignore Charles de Gaulle's lectures and four publications between 1924 and 1938, to construct (and have unreasonable reliance on) the Maginot Line along the French–German border, and to enable the lame German invasion (and, more significantly, the return) of General Maurice Gustave Gamelin, resulted in severe disruption for France. To compound and further demonstrate this strategic miscalculation, tragically, Adolf Hitler was an avid reader of de Gaulle's works, and used these concepts, based on the work of Carl von Clausewitz, against the French.

- The deranged policy of Hitler to invade Russia, Operation Barbarossa in 1941, failed for the same reasons as Napoleon's bid. This was exacerbated by a strategy to source oil in Maikop and Grozny. From the outset this lacked the logistical infrastructure or capacity to transport the oil back to Germany (Hayward, 1995).

- The Franklin Roosevelt policy to become the arsenal of democracy and to implement an embargo on Japan that included aviation equipment, fuel, steel and iron materials led to disruption in Pearl Harbor and the US entering the Second World War (December 1941)… and the use of atomic bombs over the cities of Hiroshima and Nagasaki in August 1945.

- In 1958, Chairman Mao Zedong of the People's Republic of China commenced the Great Leap Forward, a strategy to make the entire nation communist through enormous economic growth. This unfortunately resulted in a great famine from 1960-61, and the loss of up to 40 million souls, due to Mao's relentless ambitions (Larsen, 2012, 2016). On balance he raised the standard of living (for those remaining) and is considered a national hero, but you cannot discount the horrendous policy-driven interim fatal disruption.

- Despite a 10-month cease-fire of peace and tranquillity, Israel bombed Palestine Liberation Organization positions in Beirut in 1982. There was no political cause for the strike. It was a military action. This was in complete contrast with the teachings of Carl von Clausewitz: 'The subordination of the political point of view to the military would be unreasonable, for policy has created the war; policy is the intelligent factor, war only the instrument, and not the reverse' (Davis, 1995). The conflict persists to this day.

- The Margaret Thatcher (and Ronald Reagan) policies of deregulation, privatization, outsourcing, demutualization and financialization, combined with the free movement of capital across the globe, ultimately resulted in the 2008 global financial crisis, further great disruption. Enabling this was also the fact that the establishment of the International Monetary Fund in July 1944 to stabilize the preceding global chaos, which did indeed lead to a golden economic age up to 1975, did not go far enough in adopting the policies of Keynes (again) such as advocating investment during a recession, not during economic prosperity, and that austerity policies are bad for innovation and growth, and simply do not work. One just needs to reflect on Greece and the policy of EU-imposed wage reductions to discover collapse and disruption (Michie, 2017).

- Without the authorization of a United Nations mandate, the United States and British policy to invade the Republic of Iraq in March 2003 instead of implementing a diplomatic solution, due to Saddam Hussein's alleged development of nuclear and biological weapons, led to the death of up to 7,500 civilians, and later proved to be controversially based on manipulated evidence.

- The prioritization by the leading nations of trade negotiations, nuclear weapons negotiations, migration and human rights negotiations over climate-change agreements is causing accelerating disruption in our environment, and by extension our supply chain networks (Helm and Hepburn, 2009).

- A global policy deficiency to contain the accelerating force of technology and the skill-biased technical change hypothesis has led to increased domestic inequality through disruption in the low-skilled sector and a corresponding decline in the supporting trade unions. Technology is not exogenous, determined by the Gods, but endogenous, determined from within the economic and social system (Atkinson, 2016).
- President Bashar al-Assad's policy to regulate the agricultural sector of Syria to benefit large-scale farmers (who were also government officials) upon taking power in 2000 enabled the purchase of vast lands and water drilling rights, and the subsequent migration of small deposed farmers and their families to cities such as Aleppo in search of food and jobs, politicized a young generation into civil war, whose cause grew exponentially through a global reach that was powered by technology, and gave rise to the Islamic State of Iraq and the Levant (Friedman, 2016).
- The policy failure of the International Monetary Fund to support developing nations due to their inability to contain multinational organizations (and private producers and investors) has led to disruption in nations whose leadership does not have the political will to raise the standards of its citizens. Global inequality has decreased but domestic inequality has increased. The International Monetary Fund admitted in 2016 to damaging developing nations through strategic choices (Michie, 2017).

Certainly not an exhaustive list, but sufficient evidence that policy leads to disruption, more specifically, policy that does not engage in strategic alignment across institutions. The next phase is a demonstration that the same phenomenon applies at the organizational level. To achieve this, and to represent the profession of supply chain management in a balanced manner, the full spectrum of domains was explored to include military, humanitarian and corporate participants, together with the transport and distribution firms that interconnect each of these elements. Additionally, given that globalization has compounded the complexity of supply chain management, the geographical heart was consulted. People's Republic of China.

Policy: empirical source of supply chain disruption

From the Irish military to trade in China, 21 supply chain professionals across multiple organizations participated. Semi-structured interviews gleaned many powerful contributions, not just to the theory of strategy being the source of disruption, but also conversely demonstrating the significant benefits to dynamic business to supply chain strategic alignment.

Empirical discussions are grouped here as a collective for the simple reason that, if our response rather than the event itself is the disruption, then the policy-driven *gap of pain* has more relevance to our treatment of the topic than the actual domain or event taxonomy. It is important also to display the findings within the proposed dual categorization of supply chain strategy and tactics, which can now be put forward as *determined* and *autonomous*, since God has given me the free will to do so. Within the category of *determinism*, three levels have arisen, including:

- *external policy:* political, economic, social, technological, climatic;
- *Internal industry policy:* supply chain management;
- *Internal organizational policy:* top management team strategic renewal process; and strategic friction is featured in the *autonomous* category.

Supply chain category of determinism: External policy, beyond supply chain management

- Humanitarian policy-driven *gaps of pain*: Restrictions or legislative conditions on access to resources or infrastructure; changes in strategic priorities governing the use of non-domestic equipment, vehicles and manpower; acts of sabotage, theft, extortion and bribery within an existing supply chain or ethically corrupt or unauthorized protectionist acts impacting on the ability to establish a supply chain; impact of conflict situations; unintended *blue-on-blue* actions by partner organizations and friendly forces; deliberate refusal of an external agent to cooperate despite their organization's agreement to do so; diplomatic relationships between stakeholder nations and the existing national legislation before a supply chain is established; external economic decisions, commercial pressures and competition for available resources.
- Transport and distribution and (thereby) corporate policy-driven *gaps of pain*: Protectionism and trade wars, such as the United States and China; political cyber-security breaches (NotPetya ransomware attack on Ukraine); political migration (Calais crisis); socio-economic customer demand: e-commerce and environment-driven decisions (the problem-shifting

Engaging in the Process of Business to Supply Chain Strategic Alignment

element of electric vehicles); OPEC production management, military-driven oil embargos, oil and gas mergers and acquisitions; China government manufacturing plant closures (to ensure blue skies for visiting dignitaries); culture of CNY non-returning work-force; holiday schedules in China and India, resulting in backlogs due to week-long port closures (known events that are not planned for); major consumer-brand product launches, reducing ocean and air capacity, and thereby significantly increasing transport costs (Apple iPhones is the most prominent example); high Chinese staff turnover due to an abundance of opportunities arising from an expanding economy; distance, time in transit costs (up to as much as 0.5 per cent of the value of goods shipped per day) and demand risk of globalization.

- Policy-driven Chinese *gaps of pain*: Golden Shield cyber-security policy that ensures that only positive energy penetrates its border (it is therefore important to be cognisant that information may hide reality); an ancient *Hukou* system is a source of disruption to the urbanization policy that is itself disruptive to entire villages; one-child policy that was abolished in 2015 but still impacting an ageing population; environmental damage-compensation policy and shareholder conflicts leading to sudden factory disruptions and the search for alternative suppliers; promotion ceiling for Chinese managers and exorbitant real-estate prices in the major Chinese cities of Beijing, Shanghai and Shenzhen, exacerbating the disruption of staff turnover; forced fusion of joint ventures that restricts the freedom of Chinese entities, heightened by EU and United States mother-ship control in China: all contributing to the challenges of the localization of globalization.

Quite interesting was the sense of control exerted on the ancient nation that we choose to outsource our operations to. Promotion opportunities are restricted, project involvement is at the latter stages and the freedom to be Chinese is suppressed. Our own worst enemy? After all… when the Chinese are left to their own devices, what can they do other than construct the Pearl River Delta Economic Circle, the $8 trillion Silk Road Economic Belt (largest infrastructure project in history) or the $20 billion Hong Kong–Zhuhai–Macao Bridge?

Supply chain category of determinism: Supply chain industry policy

- E-commerce giants consuming warehouse real-estate; non-licensed exponential logistics companies entering the market, mergers of logistics providers, such as FedEx–TNT, and others forced out of business, such as City Link, due to increasingly outrageous consumer demands; Blockchain: generally lauded as a positive, but there is a risk of hacking and fraud; accelerating force of technology such as near-field communication (NFC), impacting SMEs in particular; ocean alliances and mega-ships resulting in sea-port congestion including inter-modal inbound road and waterway delays; customs documentation restrictions and non-tariff measures including verified gross mass (VGM); containers lost at sea due to rogue weight declarations; slow-steaming and artificial removal of vessel capacity; fuel and bunker surcharges; new limitations set by the Chinese Government regarding dangerous goods processing (directly related to a series of catastrophic explosions in August 2015 at Tianjin); security measures including convoys and restrictions in route-planning (Calais crisis).

Supply chain category of determinism: organizational policy, the TMT strategic renewal process

- Transport and distribution (and thereby) corporate policy-driven *gaps of pain*: Corporate lean inventory holding policies that do not consider supplier events or nuances (no built-in redundancy); failure to plan for CNY; failure to evolve with and adapt new technology advancements, or to consider the people aspect of technology implementations; anti-change culture; failure to engage in the circular economy; failure to adopt the customer-centric Dynamic Alignment™ model; lack of TMT understanding and operational awareness; failure to consider cultural differences in China (indeed Asia), such as the critical need to build *guanxi* and trust in a nation of familistic conservatism, and awareness of contractually dynamic business environments.
- Humanitarian policy-driven *gaps of pain: Top management team decisions*: Delay in decision-making; TMT change in supply strategy; misjudging the scale or nature of the supply chain operation; failure to design and control an appropriate supply chain; failure to appropriately man (experience, education and training) or resource the supply chain. *Management reconsideration*: Changes in financial or operational priorities; changes in manpower or personalities in authority; changes in the end-product, therefore a change in requirements; indirect impact of external pressures;

information flow disruption: failure to communicate effectively and efficiently throughout the supply chain network; failure to communicate internal, external and environmental changes; failure to contingency-plan for potential future disruption. *Unauthorized act*: Deliberate operation of (or permitting the operation of) supply chain assets, such as equipment and vehicles, outside authorized parameters; failure to comply with legislative requirements. *Intentional or incompetent act*: Negligent conduct; failure to control a controllable external force, such as failure of equipment through neglect; use of untrained or inexperienced manpower.

The autonomous supply chain category, impeded by strategic friction

- Supply chain progress is routinely hampered due to relentless and unplannable daily disruptive friction that dooms management to disappointment prior to strategic implementation: An LCL (less than container load) container from Hong Kong is held because it shares another firm's products that are under inspection, necessitating customs negotiation for its release; a second is held by Polish customs because the declared weight on the bill of lading does not match the weight check carried out at the port, and this can only be resolved if the co-loading shipping company in Los Angeles agrees to amend the paperwork.
- Meanwhile, another container, already delayed due to Chinese New Year, is bumped at Shanghai because Apple have just launched the latest iPhone and have taken all capacity at the port; a United Parcel Service shipment arrives at a customer's back-door with missing or damaged boxes, simultaneously requiring a replacement shipment, return material authorization, claim procedure and customer appeasement; a EUR-1 certificate cannot be provided for a shipment to Israel because the manufacturer cannot complete a long-term supplier declaration, resulting in the payment of customs duties that would otherwise be exempt due to preferential origin status.
- Elsewhere, a discovery has been made that a Mexican contract manufacturer has been sending products on pallets (containing as few as two boxes) to US customers by FedEx next-day-air, and separate road shipments are being sent to two US addresses that happen to be within the same building, both scenarios significantly increasing freight costs, for which instructions need to be sent to both the US freight agents and the manufacturer to

implement new procedures; a customer in France has been waiting for products since 7am but the driver has not arrived, and there is a scramble for his mobile number; a truck has come to collect five pallets from another manufacturing site in the Czech Republic, but there was a miscalculation and there are in fact six pallets, thereby requiring the immediate sourcing of a second truck; the 3PL portal crashes just as you are almost finished entering an urgent non-EDI (electronic data interchange) cross-dock shipment, and you have to begin the process again…

- Friction can also arise from discussions with our China counterparts, whose calm and professional exterior may hide an environment of managerial control and an absence of autonomous decision-making, and we ourselves can be responsible for scheduling changes when we do not communicate and re-confirm plans at a deep and robust enough level to prevent face-saving scenarios, or when we do not gain a full understanding of roles and responsibilities, and daily tasks, that could be jeopardized or manipulated by a cultural inability to say no to divisions perceived to be 'superiors'.

It is now irrefutable that since the establishment of modern logistics management circa 1800 policy is the source of supply chain disruption when senior management goals are not aligned to supply chain tactics, thereby causing detrimental *gaps of pain* in response to events across the full spectrum of supply chain domains. The most profound evidence of this was the fact that all of the logistical challenges of two peace-enforcing missions of the Irish Defence Forces, their Nordic Battle Group rotation in Sweden and UNIFIL Lebanon, were caused by senior management strategies and strategic documents, without ever engaging the enemy. Case closed. And the most congruous conclusion as to the reason for this phenomenon is that *'there is no seat at the big boys' table for the logistician'* (David Duddy). A fantastic and defining quote. So what? If both senior executives and supply chain professionals adopt this (validated) theory, then profits can be protected, but, most significantly, global deaths can be prevented.

To determine *how* we can achieve alignment, let me first borrow from dynamic business to information systems strategic alignment literature (a significant body of work) due to the apparent absence of similar research in the supply chain management academic domain, and then return to the original aims and responsibilities of this research.

Dynamic business to information systems strategic alignment: interchangeable with supply chain management

Here the liberty has been taken, validated in the empirical research (such as Esther Lätte and Zoop), to interchange supply chain management with information systems, and this increases the generalizability of the topic. For instance, I am confident that master chefs have been disrupted in their kitchens when not consulted about menu introductions or changes to ingredient suppliers. Restaurant managers could therefore learn from this same concept of alignment.

- Strategic alignment is based on two fundamental assumptions: economic performance, which directly relates to the strategic fit of external positioning and internal arrangements; and that strategic fit is inherently dynamic, and reaching dynamic capability depends on the organization's ability to exploit supply chain functionality on a continuous basis.
- Success depends on the development of a mechanism of shared knowledge integration across the top management team.
- Consider the cross-sectional linkages within an organization and the temporal nature of strategic decision-making. Alignment is a continuous co-evolutionary process that reconciles top management team 'rational designs' and operational 'emergent processes'.
- There is a process of user improvisation and adjustment, due to perception and understanding of supply chain features. Strategic plans are therefore resources for situated action that do not in any strong sense determine their course.
- A supply chain is not an external object, but a product of ongoing human action, design and appropriation, which, over time, becomes imbricated, embedded, entangled and intertwined, subject to social negotiation and sense-making, materializing through anchoring and objectification.
- Alignment must include setting goals, understanding the business to supply chain linkage, analysing and prioritizing gaps, specifying actions, choosing and evaluating success criteria, and sustaining alignment by developing and cultivating an alignment behaviour.
- Alignment can occur through supply chain transformation where the supply chain manager has the role of architect to the top management teams' supply chain vision.

- Supply chain strategy can be the enabler, and has competitive potential, whereby the TMT is the business visionary to the supply chain manager's catalyst role of developing and exploiting emerging supply chain capabilities to impact new products.
- A world-class supply chain organization can be developed if the supply chain manager enacts an executive leadership role, and the top management team accordingly prioritizes the allocation of resources.
- Business to supply chain strategic alignment enablers: top management team support for supply chain; supply chain involved in strategy development; supply chain understands the business; business to supply chain partnership; well-prioritized supply chain projects; supply chain demonstrates leadership.
- The supply chain manager must first and foremost be a business leader and must participate as a real general management peer, displaying such characteristics as a diplomat, visionary, leader, strategic thinker, relationship builder, and reader of markets and the tactics used for influencing top management team members. A close relationship between the supply chain manager and CEO is crucial and this extends to solidarity between the supply chain manager and all functional top management team members.

Alignment inhibitors and challenges:

- Top management team threat rigidity impedes judgement and information-gathering. This impacts strategy itself but also alignment in the sense that often the safest or most dominant cues within their inner circles are settled on.
- The environment is complex, and managers can experience 'bounded rationality' in that they 'cannot comprehensively understand the environment'. Strategy is formed in these situations.
- Strategic formulation and implementation: the simultaneous sub-processes of competence definition, modification and deployment each have a different perspective for the top management team, middle management and operations management.
- Operations managers are positioned to gather new information from both internal and external sources, and the way this information is communicated to the top management team is subject to middle management interpretation, often manipulated due to personal agendas.

- Strategy formulation is a process of political decision-making whereby strategic demands are 'politically feasible only if sufficient power can be mobilized and committed to it'.
- The top management team responds to the tensions of competing demands through their actions, rhetoric and decisions and they must also simultaneously balance strategic exploitation and exploration, profit maximization and social welfare, integrating locally and adapting globally.

Supply Chain Disruption: research

The research asked how supply chain managers engage in the process of dynamic business to supply chain strategic alignment. Arising from this, the research aimed to increase our understanding of supply chain managers' engagement in the process of dynamic business to supply chain strategic alignment, within the context of supply chain disruption, and to contribute to the broadening of supply chain management to an integrated perspective across the top management team rather than a uni-dimensional and dichotomous view. These aims were expanded to include specific objectives, and these can now be probed.

Determine how supply chain managers operationally identify, predict, cope and recover from supply chain disruptions

- The Irish Defence Forces (DF) Nordic Battle Group and UNIFIL disruptions could not have been identified or predicted in the absence of business to supply chain strategic alignment. Strategic documents needed to be re-shaped to situational needs, whilst staying inside the core competencies of the DF. The coping mechanism applied in each case resulted in recovery that was an evolution to a new and more desirable state. The DF pre-positions (prepares) 14 DOS redundant supplies, such as diesel based on average consumption, to mitigate supply chain risk.
- For transport and distribution firms, many events are unpredictable such as factory closures in China, and freight companies are also exposed to client-organization disruptions that are not under their direct control. However, planning for disruption can include:

- *avoidance:* discovery of high-risk goods, gathering of critical cargo information, increased security, preparedness through cargo safeguarding;
- *containment:* indirect insurance investments, inventory redundancy;
- *stabilization:* supply chain design, such as optimizing routes, offering hub solutions;
- *return:* operating flexibility, such as sourcing alternative supplier solutions.

- Structural robustness can help the coping mechanism in humanitarian crises that are unpredictable, contextual and situational. Emphasis should be on having: dedicated personnel in place to manage freight forwarding; procurement planning and tracking that includes agreed-upon thresholds for order increases; well-documented framework agreements that have national and regional consistency; job descriptions that are understood and uniform throughout the organization; all departments should play a role in vendor management, so that the establishment of a 'good name' in the business community would result in more vendors taking part in tenders and providing better bids; technical support must be in place for users of IT systems, including training, and management controls must be implemented such as spot checks in relation to assets and stock disposal, procurement committees, tender standard operating procedures, staff shortages and internal auditing.

- With adoption and compliance to global standard operating procedures, all corporate logistics processes are clearly focused on delivering optimal quality, service and efficiency. 'Logistics control towers' predict, sense, and event-manage the delivery experience for all physical product moves, allowing real-time tactical decisions to minimize negative customer impact. Response to events begins with rapid and effective information exchange, redundant-inventory and dual-supplier sourcing strategies, expeditious quality control and auditing of processes, and continuous market surveillance and technology knowledge acquisition are cornerstones for achieving this particular objective. Gattorna advocates dynamic alignment to customer buying behaviours and the adoption of faster clockspeeds.

- Identification and prediction of supply chain disruption is all but impossible when Chinese Government policies such as the environmental damage-compensation system are enacted. From a Western perspective, identification and prediction comes from understanding the concept of positive energy as the cornerstone of information exchange, appreciating that behind a calm exterior it is important to analyse tasks, roles and responsibilities, the relentless nurturing of *guanxi* and building trust with a culture that values collectivism, almost everything is dynamic, and respecting suppliers as the experts. Demanding relentless cost reductions is short-sighted and ultimately damages relationship continuity when key personnel are forced to relocate.

Identify which phases in the supply chain disruption process require engagement with the top management team to implement strategic solutions aligned to business goals

- DF engagement came during the response phase of the sudden disruptive events, the nature of which were impossible to predict and identify (prepare for) in advance. This response demonstrated a supply chain that was both agile and fully flexible.
- In the case of freight and transportation companies, this becomes an internal business decision on whether to absorb the additional costs of fuel and security or pass them to their clients. Despite the competitive nature of the industry, the growing challenges must be highlighted to client management in order to improve alignment.
- This arises immediately during the humanitarian response phase due to the fact that there appears to be a lack of understanding by strategic managers of logistics functions, processes and procedures. They are *not operationally aware*. For example, the integrated role of procurement as a logistics function is not appreciated. There is a belief that the control of finance is of greater importance than the emergency operations for which the organization exists.
- Schneider Electric sets out its vision in line with corporate change programs. These corporate change programs run from three to five years and are supported by the global supply chain (GSC) strategic prioritization (or HOSHIN) process. They articulate the vision and objectives of GSC, logistics and network design, and of each domain, clearly linking each activity to customer value and company objectives.
- Chinese expertise must be harnessed at the early stages of the strategic renewal process or indeed the design phase of new product introduction.

When we outsource to China, it is critical in the context of *guanxi* to trust that the selected suppliers can add tremendous value if they are involved from the outset of the relationship. Failure to adopt this approach through 'mother-ship control' leads to supply chain disruption.

Consequently, determine whether a categorization of supply chain strategy exists, such as a tier consisting of strategies that can be implemented autonomously by the supply chain division, and a tier(s) that requires 'negotiation' across the top management team prior to implementation

- DF negotiation across the top management team was needed to re-shape the troop profile, or to secure a gross investment for combat capability developments in Lebanon. A sub-tier of autonomous tactical response was found in the context of supply chain friction, such as solutions to electricity provision, robust tent infrastructure, improved container utilization, vehicle movement in Skillingaryd, provision of SUVs, the efficient use of mechanical fitters, and provision of petrol and water.

- Freight disruptions can be light (such as a misunderstanding on fees), which can be responded to autonomously, or severe, which require team-work to solve (such as vessel accidents, or a $5 million case with customs authorities in South America due to wrong documentation). External policies (political, economic, social, technological, climatic) can be placed within the negotiation categorization. Internal policies within the boundaries of supply chain management belong to the autonomous categorization.

- A humanitarian negotiation categorization is impeded by the necessity to continuously educate senior UN managers and directors. This has included improving the procurement process through greater mutual understanding, but in general, given the critical operational circumstances, this is detrimental. Autonomous strategies such as the establishment of asset-inspection regimes need management approval for smooth implementation.

- Financial simulation of various corporate options has been reconfirmed as the vehicle and threshold for engagement with the top management

Engaging in the Process of Business to Supply Chain Strategic Alignment

team in the negotiation category, but this must be combined with market impacts, both of which have been top priorities to consider.

- There is little evidence that such a categorization exists at a local level in China. The calm exterior that we are exposed to in the West hides an environment of managerial control and an absence of autonomous decision-making. Senior executives do not assign much importance to supply chain management, and the failure to promote indigenous supply chain managers, coupled with crippling real-estate costs, suffocates individual growth, perhaps reflected in China being ranked 27 in terms of logistics performance (Germany, Netherlands and Sweden form the top three).

Determine how supply chain managers engage with the top management team in the process of aligning business and supply chain strategies, thereby identifying key enablers and inhibitors

- The military decision-making process (MDMP) is a valuable tool. This analyses supply chain capabilities and tasks whilst simultaneously aligning with top management team strategy (the foremost consideration) and respecting the boundaries of core competencies.
- The transport and distribution threshold for TMT involvement is based on the investment value and therefore the simulated costing of network redesign is critical to engagement. The demonstrable value of people above process is key to negotiation. Supply chain risk mitigation should be built into human resource management.
- The dominant humanitarian conclusion is that senior managers are not operationally aware and that there is *no seat at the big boys' table for a logistician.*
- The top management team must be viewed as a valuable resource of knowledge and experience, and their advice must be consequently sought during key events. Schneider Electric successfully used the sharing of data-analysis and simulation modelling that mapped the benefits to all stakeholders, generated to gain internal functional agreement and alignment, including customer advocacy.
- In addition to contingency plans and SOPs, an SCM law akin to the banking, finance and accounting domain has been suggested by a Chinese professional.

Develop a process model that establishes the phases of supply chain managers' engagement in dynamic business to supply chain strategic alignment

To enhance this objective, the research participants contemplated the best tool, technique, methodology, analysis, etc, to use when attempting to get your strategic point of view implemented with the top management team, and how we can elevate supply chain management to the top management team. Following these empirical discussions, their valuable first-hand views are shared here.

David Duddy, Managing Director, LogAid:

> These final two contemplations sum up in question form the nub of the problem facing logisticians in all areas of business, the military, the public sector and the Third Sector. The core issue regarding getting your strategic point of view implemented with the TMT is that you are trying to get an established management team to implement your world view; and they have a legitimate right to ask you, 'Why should we?' The first thing to do is to conduct stakeholder analysis of the TMT to understand what you are trying to tackle. This will give you a steer as to the best approach to take in each situation because they will all differ. It is your job to convince them that there is a problem; it is their problem and they will suffer if it isn't resolved; and that you have the solution. Only then do you stand a chance of them listening to you. One proven technique is the 'ye olde ownership' ploy: you need to give them ownership of the solution as well as the problem, almost convincing them that the solution you come up with is actually their idea. This will necessitate you taking them by the hand and keeping them engaged at each stage, but don't be surprised if the MD sends his underling as the participating stakeholder. Engagement is critical and if it is the underling, then (s)he needs to be singing your praises at the end of every session and enticing the MD to directly engage.

Regarding the elevation of SCM, David Duddy:

> This is a problem only resolved through education. We can only get a place at the big boys' table when the strategic management level sees us as big boys. That means some of us will have to be trail-blazers. My understanding of the humanitarian environment, particularly in UN agencies, is that if one wants to be promoted beyond P-3 level, one needs to have a master's degree. If one seeks to take up a position at P-5, D-1 or above, a PhD is the minimum qualification.

If you are not sitting with a PhD, they simply don't see you as a big boy, so more of us need to get PhDs! I'm sure the same can be said for many major commercial businesses too, especially where the business culture places great store by titles and qualifications. Let's not mince our words: if you are looking to sit at Volkswagen's top table, or that of Siemens, DHL Deutsche Post or DB Schenker, if you have a PhD, do some visiting lecture teaching at the Kuehne Logistics University in Hamburg and therefore style yourself in the typical German business manner of 'Herr Professor Doktor', you are a big beast indeed. Education is key not just to addressing your own ignorance, but everybody else's too. The fact that the ultimate head of the UN's Logistic Cluster (Head of WFP) has been a succession of US ex-lawyer politicians makes me apoplectic, but they all have PhDs.

Will Holden, Managing Director, Emergency Logistics Team:

Humanitarian TMTs unfortunately only use data that has relevance to the program side and very little to do with operations. Historically this is probably because most TMT members have a development or emergency response background. They come with very different experiences and knowledge, all of which is crucial of course, but the lack of experience in the finer points of supply chain and logistics operations management leaves a big blind spot in organizations. So, taking into account this challenge, I always suggest using 'soft skills', encouraging, coaxing, cajoling, doing whatever works to get your strategic point of view implemented. Coupled with factual and up-to-date data, this gives you at least a chance to convince the decision-makers that your views should be taken into account. Advocacy takes a lot of time but is the best way to bring about lasting change that will result in the elevation of supply chain management to the TMT. Campaigns should be launched through renowned worldwide bodies, such as CILT and CIPS, demonstrating the huge benefits and positive financial outcomes of operational efficiency so that NGOs are encouraged to finally bring the supply chain and logistics experts to the top table. The complete lack of knowledge of freight forwarding, for example, leads to a massive waste of time and money, which ultimately results in people who are in the direst need tragically suffering unduly (*gap of pain*). Supply chain and logistics experts can and do make a profound difference to the humanitarian sector and the sooner that we are at those top tables the sooner that change begins.

Michiel van Berkel, Sales Manager Netherlands, Royal Rotra Group echoes these same sentiments by suggesting 'bold persistence backed by strong evidence and analyses' when negotiating with the TMT, and elevation to the

TMT requires lobby work and media attention for publications on (real and potential) impact of past and future examples.

Paul Aerts, Benelux Logistics Manager, Royal Rotra Group, suggests the 'provision of analyses showing the impact of your view, including scenario simulation to prove what might happen based on strategic decisions' when negotiating with the TMT, and for a seat at the top table, 'we have to show that we are a part of the product value instead of a cost. Logistics more and more becomes a marketing instrument and a value add to the products. For example, the stock quality and the delivery performance are an integrated part of the customer experience and thus the product.'

Ian Truesdale, Global Senior Vice President of Logistics and Innovation, Kuehne + Nagel:

> You have to look at a number of important KPIs and link these directly to an enterprises' strategy, and then how changes in policy and the external factors are impacting these KPIs. So, if the strategy is a growth one into new markets, new channels and maybe also to expand market share, then all customer related KPIs and even end consumer related KPIs are critical. For example, some ERPs don't even measure order fulfilment success, as well as fulfilment lead times, cut-off times, ability to respond to swings in demand, all of which should be wrapped up in some predictive analytics around demand forecasting and overall supply demand scenario modelling. In general, you should be able to accurately measure changes in overall transit times for international and cross-border transport and have a decent control tower that is plugged into news agencies to give the supply chain orchestrators real time status information. Of course, if the strategy is more optimization and cost reduction, then reducing overall total landed cost and overall reduction in working capital should be board level KPIs. All other things being equal, changes in policy can either improve or negatively impact these metrics. For e- commerce organizations such as Amazon, where consumer and retail success or failure is *all* about logistics, then there is a logistician on the TMT! Other sectors will in the end move in the same direction.

Eduardo Vargas, Regional Director Los Angeles, US Southwest and Mexico, Morrison Express Corporation:

> The 'what's in it for me strategy' is very useful (note: 'ye olde ownership'). By human nature we are usually driven by personal context in order to evaluate our environment. We are generally used to a situation or to a routine and for sure we will get used to a new one after a change is implemented (future state). However, the transition to that future state is always concerning, not only to

top management but to everybody. When you ask people to go from where they are to somewhere else, you need to create a vision they can understand and are willing to embrace. Obviously, nobody knows the future, so you would account for deviations (note: acknowledge friction during the strategic renewal process so that it can be triumphed over) and make the future picture as conservative as possible, so that expectations are realistic. Expectations drive future satisfaction and satisfaction drives performance and peoples' attitude facing the new situation. In conclusion, paint a conservative picture, sell your ideas and support them with appropriate numbers (quantitative) and descriptions (qualitative) so it is easier for your management and your team to buy them. The threshold for TMT involvement is based on the investment value and therefore the simulated costing of network redesign is critical to engagement. The demonstrable value of people above process is key to negotiation. Supply chain risk mitigation should be built into human resource management. Life and business are not perfect, but in both cases nothing replaces a willingness and passion to deliver, and an anger to succeed. Detailed standard operating procedures or manuals are not required if people are aligned for success. Personal goals (tuition for kids, car, mortgage, professional growth, etc) must be aligned with company goals (more sales, better service, lower costs, etc).

On the promotion to the top table, Eduardo Vargas:

The difference between supply chain management and logistics is that the former encompasses multiple departments, processes and people across the company. To elevate supply chain management to the TMT requires the 'translation' of supply chain related issues, considerations, pain points, advantages, savings, cost reduction initiatives, etc, into the other departments' lingo. For instance: if I say that reducing our inventory of a specific product is the goal most of the TMT members might not pay much attention, but if I say that I can reduce the company's working capital (to the CFO) or I can reduce obsolescence (to the manufacturing VP) or I can reduce selling price facing our competitors (to the sales VP) then I will get their attention. I think the key is to communicate the initiatives and concerns the right way and word them properly depending on the audience (top management) to finally get the supply chain related ideas across the company.

Stuart Whiting, Senior Vice President, Logistics and Network Design, Schneider Electric:

Use of a tool, such as LLamasoft Supply Chain Guru for network design, removes 'emotions' from the equation and when linked to customer research (buying behaviour) and line of business interviews creates a safe environment in which to simulate alternates together… thus beyond straight facts it helps to draw people into the project and additionally take ownership. In addition, ToolsGroup Multi-Echelon Inventory Optimization (MEIO) truly helps to deliver tangible and logical solutions.

Secret sauce: Stuart provides another defining term when contemplating a seat at the table:

Understand the customer, drive customer centricity through logistics and supply chain and act as a catalyst between commercial and customer demand, demonstrating how we can differentiate product, services and after sales support at the point of sale… essentially become the Secret Sauce.

Jon Bumstead, Director, Nisomar Ventures, suggests:

The old Accenture technique of FUD (fear, uncertainty and doubt). For instance… 'this project is really important, and to you personally, do you really want to cheap out?' (Again, the 'ye olde ownership' technique.) For the promotion of our profession: 'faster supply chains mean faster cash flow and faster cash flow means greater valuation'.

Li (Lucia) Huang, Global Supply Chain and Project Manager, Shanghai, believes:

Everything is about sales, and we as supply chain professionals need to communicate in a way that people can understand what we do and what benefits we can bring. The reason is because supply chain has vast scope and at a deep level can be quite technical, which will be a barrier for people without such a background to understand. Numbers are powerful, and we must project data, such as delivery service level, into profits growth and the benefit of customer retention, competitive advantage, etc, to the TMT. It is critical to have cross-functional thinking – we can only have very good results when we understand what other people care about.

Lucia considers the variability of this topic, suggesting that it depends on circumstances in terms of the industry, stage of company growth, and complexity of the business and supply chain model. This determines the degree of TMT importance placed on SCM.

Heidi Larsen, Global Supply Chain Consultant:

When implementing just about anything with the top management team, one needs to speak a clear financial language, and to back up a given proposal the business case needs to be solid. In other words, you need to be able to speak good maths and to present your message in a convincing manner. Numbers aside, I personally often use the Kraljic Model. Alternatively, I highlight the low-hanging fruit that can be harvested for free, especially for SMEs, using the design thinking innovation model.

Further explanations of these models are given in Heidi Larsen's YouTube videos (Larsen, 2018a, 2018b).

Summary

These learnings and contemplations have concluded the original research objectives and have validated my theory that supply chain disruption is policy-driven. The research aims of increasing our understanding of strategic alignment and the promotion of our profession to the upper echelons can now be expressed in the nascent *Dynamic Business to Supply Chain Strategic Alignment Process Model* on the page, influenced by General Carl von Clausewitz and formed by 21 outstanding participating supply chain professionals. Dwight Eisenhower famously said: 'You will not find it difficult to prove that battles, campaigns, and even wars have been won or lost primarily because of logistics.' So... why are we not at the top table?

Dynamic Business to SCM Strategic Alignment Process Model

Sources of Supply Chain Disruption resulting from no SCM consultation since 1800

External Policy: Political, Economic, Social Exponential Organizations; Accelerating Forces of Technology, Globalization, Climate Change

Internal Industry Policy: SCM self-disruption; Senior strategists *not* factoring in SCM developments

Top Management Team Policy (TMT): (Politics) Strategic renewal (formulation) process

SCM is the management process responsible for identifying, anticipating and satisfying customer requirements, at a profit, through the optimisation of all known channels, by engaging in the process of dynamic business to supply chain strategic alignment

no **Seat at the Top Table** for the Logistician

Needless **Gap of Pain: Supply Chain Disruption**
Lack of SCM operational awareness causes reduced agility: military, humanitarian, corporate, transport and distribution, China (geographical heart of globalisation)

Disruption: Can be the event or the response
Reduction through strategic alignment: thereby balancing hatred, enmity (consumer reaction)

So what? Death and taxes

Become the secret sauce
Faster supply chains
SCM doctorates
SCM: Business leaders
Advocacy: SCM institutions
Media campaigns
TMT education
TMT and Board level KPIs
SCM: Marketing instrument

Supply Chain Management: chance, violence
Strategic implementation

Engaging in the Process of Dynamic Business to Supply Chain Strategic Alignment

Determinism: Strategic Category
Black swan crises and disasters; grey swan breakdowns

Supply Chain Education:
Nurture a shared understanding between the TMT and SCM; TMT authority not diminished by alignment
TMT education: SCM, operational awareness, external and SCM industry self-disruptors, change-adaption
Reconcile TMT 'rational designs' and operational 'emergent processes'; people above process
Cross-functional thinking, speaking a common language, co-evolution

Supply Chain Data and Metrics:
Communication through TMT and Board level KPIs; deploy logistics control towers
Superior data analysis and presentation thereof (translation of SCM technical language)

Supply Chain Simulation:
Scenario planning tools (removal of emotion): gain stakeholder, cross-functional and customer advocacy
Military decision-making process (MDMP); adopt the Gattorna Dynamic Alignment™ model

Supply Chain Mêtis (Rhetoric) and Bie (Strength):
Ye olde ownership technique: fear, uncertainty, doubt (FUD)
Soft skills: encouraging, coaxing, cajoling, persistence

Financial threshold:

– –

disruption then becomes an enterprise-wide event (pre-determined in each enterprise)

Autonomous: Tactical Category, SCM Bubble

Strategy re-shaped to situational needs, whilst staying inside the core competencies of the enterprise

Here, the TMT must not act as swimming masters, teaching dry-land movements, where they have never plunged in themselves

SCM Strategic Friction:
Petty circumstances, blind natural forces

TMT: must factor SCM friction into strategic renewal process in order to triumph over it

HRM policy is critical: SCM team requires anger to succeed, passion to deliver

Seek TMT managerial knowledge and advice

Avoidance, containment, stabilisation, return

Conclusion

Policy conclusively causes supply chain disruption when organizations do not engage in the process of dynamic business to supply chain strategic alignment. This has been academically demonstrated through an analysis of major disruptive events since the Age of Revolution and the founding of economics, modern strategy, modern logistics management and globalization, circa 1800. This was then validated through empirical research across the full spectrum of supply chain domains, such as military, humanitarian, transport and distribution firms and their art of movement, corporate, and the geographical heart of globalization, the People's Republic of China. This phenomenon results in a needless *gap of pain* in response to disruption and in turn leads to significant profitability depletion, and in many circumstances the loss of *human lives*.

The dominant reason for this situation is not just that supply chain professionals are not consulted during the formulation stage of the strategic renewal process, the preserve of the top management team, but that there is *'no seat at the big boys' table' for the logistician*. Without counsel from supply chain professionals, an imbalance in the ancient strategic trinity concept of politics (business, top management team), chance or violence (military, supply chain management) and hatred or enmity (consumer reaction) breeds disruption. Supply chain management can resolve this by *becoming the secret sauce*, and to assist in this regard the teachings of dynamic business to information systems strategic alignment were borrowed. The prevalence of *strategic friction* and a *categorization* of supply chain strategy were also discovered, respectively influenced by Napoleon Bonaparte (via Prussian General Carl von Clausewitz) and God's concept of free will. The categories of *determinism* and *autonomous* suggest that supply chain management is *only* in the business of tactical formulation and implementation, whilst respecting the boundaries of the core competencies of the enterprise.

The nascent *Dynamic Business to Supply Chain Strategic Alignment Process Model* increases our understanding of supply chain managers' engagement in the process of dynamic business to supply chain strategic alignment, within the context of supply chain disruption, and contributes to the broadening of supply chain management to an integrated perspective across the TMT rather than a uni-dimensional and dichotomous view. Strategic alignment does not diminish TMT authority and I am hopeful that this is the spirit in which all senior executives will treat this research. Let me now offer a new definition:

> Supply chain management is the management process responsible for identifying, anticipating and satisfying customer requirements, at a profit,

through the optimization of all known channels, the disruption of which is mitigated by engaging in the process of dynamic business to supply chain strategic alignment.

But this is just the beginning. More inspiration is needed in FOUNTAINSTOWN.

References

Atkinson, AB (2016) Inequality: What can be done? *Panoeconomicus*, **63**(3), pp 385–394

Blackburn, S (1999) *Think: A compelling introduction to philosophy*, Oxford Paperbacks

Davis, HT (1995) *40km into Lebanon: Israel's 1982 Invasion*, Diane Publishing

Freedman, L (2015) *Strategy: A history*, Oxford University Press

Friedman, TL (2016) *Thank You for Being Late: An optimist's guide to thriving in the age of accelerations*, Farrar, Straus and Giroux

Guttenplan, S, Hornsby, J and Janaway, C (2008) *Reading Philosophy: Selected texts with a method for beginners*, Blackwell Publishing

Hayward, J (1995) Hitler's quest for oil: The impact of economic considerations on military strategy, 1941–42, *The Journal of Strategic Studies*, **18**(4), pp 94–135

Heaslip, G and Barber, E (2014) Using the military in disaster relief: Systemising challenges and opportunities, *Journal of Humanitarian Logistics and Supply Chain Management*, **4**(1), pp 60–81

Helm, D and Hepburn, C (eds) (2009) *The Economics and Politics of Climate Change*, Oxford University Press

Larsen, H (2012) *(Easily?) Made in China! From 0 to 100 in cultural understanding*, It's Passion Darling

Larsen, H (2016) *(Easily?) Made for China!* It's Passion Darling

Larsen, H (2018a) https://www.youtube.com/watch?v=1n_vg2q9UlY&t=18s

Larsen, H (2018b) https://www.youtube.com/watch?v=HBuABtrx7so&t=4s'

Luttwak, E(2001) *Strategy: The logic of war and peace*, Harvard University Press

Michie, J (2017) *Advanced Introduction to Globalisation*, Edward Elgar Publishing

Rapport, M (2005) *Nineteenth Century Europe*, Palgrave

Rescher, N (1996) *Process Metaphysics: An introduction to process philosophy*, Suny Press

Schwartz, B (ed) (1998) *The Code Napoleon and the Common-law World: The sesquicentennial lectures delivered at the Law Center of New York University, December 13–15, 1954*, The Lawbook Exchange, Ltd

Sheffi, Y (2001) Supply chain management under the threat of international terrorism, *The International Journal of logistics management*, **12**(2), pp 1–11

Sperber, J (2014) *Revolutionary Europe, 1780–1850*, Routledge

INDEX

3PL partners, e-commerce and 156
9/11 attacks (2001) 12

activities-based view 41
adaptive cycle 17, 41–44
Adizes, Ichak 158
Aerts, Paul 113–14, 232
Age of Revolution 209–12
agile supply chain strategy 8, 159
Airbnb 11
Alexander, Tsar 31, 211
Alibaba 199
all-informed net 137
Amazon 10, 174
American Civil War (1861–65) 4, 33
American Revolution 213
American War of Independence (1775–83) 32, 213
Andrews, Kenneth 40
Ansoff, Igor 39, 40
AP Moller Maersk 106
Aponte, Diego 112
Apple Inc 10, 12
Arab Spring 132
Arafat, Yasser 86
Aramex, disruption management 121–26
al-Assad, Bashar 13, 120, 217
assets, reduced through outsourcing 2
austerity policies 62, 216
auto industry supply chain 200
aviation industry, business-to-supply chain strategic alignment 21–23

Baldwin, Thomas N 6
banking crisis *see* financial crisis (2008)
Begin, Menachem 86
Big Data 11
Bildt, Carl 85
Black Swan (100-year) events 3
  responses to 23–25
Blair, Tony 38, 119
Blockchain 113, 116, 176, 199
Bonaparte, Napoleon 31, 32, 33, 38, 68
  Civil Code 210–12
  defeat and banishment 213
  social and political reforms in France 210–12

Boohoo.com 175
Bradley, Shane 118–19
Brady, Kevin 107–09
Brennan, Kiernan 86
Brexit 5–6, 47, 173
Bumstead, Jon 173–79, 234
Burnside, Ambrose 4
business models, response to changing environments 12
business-to-information systems strategic alignment 49–55, 223–25
business-to-supply chain strategic alignment 207–38
  aviation industry 21–23
  consumer electronics industry 18–21
business-to-supply chain strategic alignment process model 23–25, 93–95, 126–28, 150–52, 179–82, 203–05, 235, 236–38

Calais refugee crisis 119–21
campaign supply chain strategy 7
Campaign Supply Chain™ 159
capitalism 56–57, 62–63, 212, 214
Carey, Paul 80
Chandler, Alfred 39, 40
change-adaption approach 200
  mitigating disruption 122–26
change-adaption culture 156
Chartered Institute of Logistics and Transport (CILT), Irish Defence Forces and 78–79
Chiang Kai-shek 192
chief executive officer (CEO) 44
chief financial officer (CFO) 44
chief information officer (CIO) 44, 49–51
chief marketing officer (CMO) 44
chief operating officer (COO) 44
chief strategy officer (CSO) 44
Ch'in Dynasty 185
Chin Empire 31
China
  ageing population 194
  Belt and Road Initiative (BRI) 113, 200
  causes of the *gap of pain* 196
  challenges of globalization 185–87
  CO_2 emissions 65, 66

China (*continued*)
  contemporary supply chain disruption risks 192–96
  control over foreign subsidiaries 200–03
  Cultural Revolution 191–92
  cyber security policy 194, 196, 197
  disruption from sudden government environmental regulations 198–99
  dynamic business environment 189
  early examples of supply chain management 185
  effects of the social structure 196
  establishing trust 188–89
  'German Auto' Greater China Limited 200–03
  Government of China factory closures 107–08
  guanxi 188, 189
  history of 190–92
  Hukou classification of the population 195
  inequalities within the country 195
  Jin Dynasty 190
  localization of globalization 202–03
  Mao Zedong 191–92, 194, 195, 215–16
  Ming Dynasty 190
  Opium Wars 57, 191, 214
  Pearl River Delta Economic Circle 200
  planning around the Chinese New Year 189–90
  Qing Dynasty 191
  SARS epidemic (2003) 3
  significant dynasties 190–91
  supply chain relational risk (SCRR) 187–92
  supply chain risk mitigation initiatives 199–200
  trade 195
  trade war with the United States 199–200
  understanding Chinese customs to mitigate disruption 196–98
  urbanization policy 195
  Yuan Dynasty 190
Chinese New Year 106, 189–90
Chirac, Jacques 119
Chorn, Norman 157–58
Chunming Gu 198–99
Churchill, Winston 38, 57, 60, 68, 214, 215
circular economy 174
Cisco Systems Inc 4
Clausewitz, Carl von 4, 36, 187, 211, 212–15, 216, 235
  friction concept 34–35
  life of 33
  strategy trinity 37–38
climate change
  disruption of supply chain networks 216
  disruption related to 65–67
  globalization and 63–64
  humanitarian consequences 14–15
  industrialization and 65
  low priority with leading nations 216
  sustainable globalization 65–67
  transport strategy and 63–65
clockspeeds for supply chains 175–79
Cohen, Michael 44–45
Cold War 61
collaborative supply chain strategy 7
Collaborative Supply Chain™ 159
Columbus, Christopher 56
combat service support (CSS), Afghanistan 133–34
comparative advantage theory 212
conclusion 179–82
consumer electronics industry, business-to-supply chain strategic alignment 18–21
Cornwallis, Charles 32, 211
corporate supply chain disruption 5–9, 155–82, 173–79
cost leadership 40
Craigslist 12
Crane Worldwide Logistics, disruption management 118–21
Crane, Jim 118
Cranfield School of Management 19, 187, 188
critical paths in supply chains 9
cyber security 107
  policy in China 194, 196, 197

da Gama, Vasco 56
dangerous goods policy implications 108–10
de Gaulle, Charles 31–32, 68, 215
deforestation 65
Delbruck, Hans 32
Dell, Michael 10
Dell Computers 10, 12, 17, 176
demand risk 19–20
Democritus 39
Deng Xiaoping 192, 195
Depression (1930s) 62, 215
Desert Storm (1991 Persian Gulf War) 4
determinism, philosophy of 208–09
Deutsche Bank 62
developing nations, lack of support from the IMF 217
differentiation and focus strategy 40
disaster management cycle (DMC) 14

Index

disruption management
   planning in the freight and logistics industry 126–28
   responding through the physical supply chain 97–128
   see also supply chain disruption
disruption response, *gap of pain* 29
disruption risk management 8–9
disruptive events in the period around 1800 209–12
DIY Drones 11
Dole, economic impact of Hurricane Mitch (1998) 3
droughts 3, 13
Drucker, Peter 6, 39
Duddy, David 133–34, 138–43, 144, 230–31
Dynamic Alignment™ model 157–60, 177, 179, 213
   Schneider Electric 161–67

e-commerce 173–74
   threat to the 3PL sector 113–14
Ebola virus outbreak, West Africa 135
ecology, supply chain disruption and 15–18
economic impacts of supply chain disruptions 2–4
economic policy, neo-liberalism 62–63
economics, founding of the discipline 56
efficient supply chain strategy 7
Egar, Laurence 78
Einstein, Albert 10
Eisenhower, Dwight 235
emergency planning agencies 13–15
Ericsson 3
Ermattungsstrategie (strategy of exhaustion) 32, 33, 211
European Union 186
exponential organizations 11–12
exponential supply chain disruption 10–12

Facebook 10
Fayol, Henri 45
financial crisis (2008) 5, 6–7, 56, 62–63, 193, 216
Fine, Charles 175–77
fires, impacts of 3
First World War (1914–18) 39, 57, 58, 59, 131, 214–15
five forces model (Porter) 40
floods, economic impacts 3
Ford, Henry 1
Ford Motor Company 12, 58
Foxconn 12
free trade 57, 212, 214

free will concept 208–09
French Revolution 209, 213
Friedman, Milton 62
Friedman, Thomas 10, 63, 116, 126
fully flexible supply chain strategy 7–8
Fully Flexible Supply Chain™ 159
Fulton, Robert 57, 212

Gamelin, Gustave 58, 215
Gao, Raymond 201–03, 204
gap of pain xiv, 29
   causes in China 196
   humanitarian logistics 137, 139, 140, 142, 143
   policy-driven 207
Gattorna, John 7, 16, 53, 198
   Dynamic Alignment™ model 157–60
   on supply chain clockspeeds 175–79
General Motors 58
Genghis Khan 30–31, 185, 190
'German Auto' Greater China Limited 200–03
Germany, rise of Nazism 57–62
global banking system *see* financial crisis (2008)
globalization 56–69
   history of 56–63
   impact on supply chain management 2
   origins of 212
gold standard 215
Google 10, 11
Grant, Ulysses S. 33
Great Depression (1930s) 62, 215
Great Firewall of China (Golden Shield) 194, 196, 197
Great Wall of China 193–94
Greece, effects of imposed austerity 216
Greek empire 30
grey swan breakdowns, responses to 23–25
guanxi 188, 189

Haig, Alexander 87
Hall, Gerry 119–21
Hamilton, Ian 39
Handy, Charles 6
Hanjin bankruptcy 105–06
Harris, Harold 32
Harvard Business School 39
Heraclitus 36, 208
   process method 39–40
Hewlett Packard 12
Hindenburg, Paul von 59
Hippolyte, Jacques Antoine 36
historical context of supply chain management 30–33

Index

Hitler, Adolf 31–32, 58–59, 60–61, 68, 215
Holden, Will 147–50, 231
Holocaust 61
Homer 37
Honda 3
Hong Kong 57
Hoover, Herbert 1
Hourigan, James 80, 84
Huang, Li (Lucia) 196–98, 234
Hughes, Kate 16
human relations model 45
human resources model 45
humanitarian agencies, challenges faced by 131–33
humanitarian logistics 131–52
  compassionate perspective 135–36
  emergency logistics team 143–50
  expected loss of resources 135–36
  features of 150–153
  gap of pain 137, 139, 140, 142, 143
  refugee crisis 131–32
  supply chain design 136–37
humanitarian supply chain disruption 14–15
Hurricane Mitch (1998) 3
Hussein, Saddam 216

Iceland, volcanic eruption (2010) 3
India, CO_2 emissions 66
Industrial Revolution 57
industrialization, climate change and 65
inequality, global and local drivers 217
information systems (IS) strategy 50–55
information technology (IT), role of the chief information officer (CIO) 49–51
innovation, disruptive 11–12
Instagram 10–11
insurgent supply chain disruption 12–14
International Monetary Fund (IMF) 62, 69, 216, 217
Iraq invasion (2003) 69, 216
Ireland, Great Famine (1845–52) 214
Iridium (Motorola company) 10
Irish Defence Forces 77–95
  Chartered Institute of Logistics and Transport (CILT) 78–79
  Nordic Battle Group rotation 80–85
  supply chain disruption 92–95
  UN peace support operations 85–86
Irish Emergency Logistics Team in Yemen 147–50
Islamic State of Iraq and the Levant (ISIS) 13, 120, 143–47, 217
Israel, bombing of the PLO in Beirut (1982) 216

Japan
  atomic bombing of Nagasaki and Hiroshima 60, 215
  economic impacts of the earthquake and tsunami (2011) 3
  Second World War 59–60
Jensen, Bjorn Vang 112
Jia, Fu 188, 192
Joly de Maizeroy, Paul Gedeon 36
Jomini, Antoine-Henri 32–33, 211, 213, 214
Joukov, Gueorgui Konstantinovitch 60–61
just-in-time inventory systems 2

Kehoe, Paul 85
Keuhne + Nagel, disruption management 114–18
Keynes, John Maynard 57, 58, 62, 215, 216
Kilbride, Frank 123–24
King, MA 67
Kodak 10
Kublai Khan 190

Land Rover, impact of supplier insolvency (2001) 3
Larsen, Heidi 187–92, 202, 204, 234–35
last-mile parcel shipments 156
Lätte, Esther 167–73
leagile (lean and agile) concept 137
lean approach, impact of supply chain disruption 2–4
Lean Supply Chain 159
lean supply chain strategy 7
Lebanon, formation of 131
LogAid Humanitarian Logistics Consultancy 133–34
logistics
  definition xvii
  historical context 30–33
Louis XVI, King of France 213
Luftman, J 52
Luttwak, Edward 36, 208
Lynch, Grainne 79

Ma, Jack 199
Macron, Emmanuel 121
Madrid bombings (2004) 13
management information systems (MIS) strategy set 50
management theory 45
Mao Zedong 191–92, 194, 195, 215–16
Marco Polo 190
Marks & Spencer (M&S) 173–74, 175
Marx, Karl 56–57, 212
Materials Management Operations Guidelines (MMOG) 199

Index

McLean, Malcolm 13
Médecins San Frontières 131, 132
Mellett, Mark 77
mergers in the global shipping industry 110–11
Mexican War (1846–48) 33
migrant crisis 119–21
military strategy, history of 30–33
military supply chains 133–34, 137 *see also* Irish Defence Forces
Mintzberg, Henry 39, 41, 45
MIT-90s study 51
mobile phone app industry 10
monetarism 62
Moore, Gordon 10
Moriarty, Robert 80–82, 86, 88–92, 94
Morrison Express Corporation (MEC)
    disruption management 98–106
    lean inventory strategies 99–106
    supply chain risk management 99–106
Motorola Inc 10
Musk, Elon 174
Mussolini, Benito 60

Napoleon Code 210
natural disasters 14–15
Nazism in Germany 57–59
neo-liberal laissez-faire economics 62–63
networked companies 12, 17
New Poor Law (1834) 214
Niederwerfungsstrategie (strategy of annihilation) 32, 33, 211
Nokia 3
non-tariff policy measures 117–18
Nordic Battle Group
    historical context 79–80
    Irish Defence Forces rotation 80–85
nuclear accidents 3

ocean freight *see* shipping industry
OECD (Organisation for Economic Co-operation and Development) 62
oil prices, control of 124–26
Oliver, Keith 1
On War (Clausewitz) 33, 34–35
OPEC (Organization of the Petroleum Exporting Countries) 124
Opium Wars 57, 191, 214
organization set 50
organizations
    characteristics of 44–45
    definition 41
outsourcing 2, 12, 155

Panasonic 3
Pericles 36
Physicians for Human Rights 132
policy
    controlling oil prices 124–26
    disruption caused by 4–5, 18–25
    empirical evidence of supply chain disruption 217–22
    history of supply chain disruption 30–33, 212–17
    source of disruption (examples) 68–69
    war and 57–61
policy schema development 152, 179–82, 203–05, 236
politics, trinity concept 213
Porter, Michael, five forces model 40
power-behaviour approach 40
power relations 41
practice definition of strategy 44
process approach 39–40
process method 43–44
    Heraclitus 39–40
process model *see* business-to-supply chain strategic alignment process model
protectionism 116–17
punctuated equilibrium model 52

Al-Qaeda 12
Quinlan, Pat 86
Quinn, James Brian 39

railways, history of 57
Reagan, Ronald 62, 69, 216
recession, cyclical nature 62–63
redundancy in supply chains 8–9
    effect on resilience 16, 17
refugee crisis 119–21, 131–32
Renault 3
renewable energy 66
resilience
    building into supply chains 8–9
    features of resilient systems 15–18
resource-based view (RBV) 40, 50, 53
RFID (radio-frequency identification) 179
Ricardo, David 56, 212
risk management
    demand risk 19–20
    disruption risk management 8–9
    risk mitigation initiatives in China 199–200
Roelofsen, Hermanus 110
Roman empire 30
Roosevelt, Franklin D 59–60, 68, 215
Royal Rotra Group, disruption management 110–14
RR Donnelley 12

Index

Sadat, Anwar 86
SAM (specify, assess, migrate) model 9
SAM (strategic alignment model) 51
SAMM (strategic alignment maturity model) 52
Santayana, George 95
Schacht, Otto 112
Scharnhorst, Gerhard von 33
Schneider Electric 159, 213
   background 161–62
   business win 164–65
   customer innovation 162–64
   Dynamic Alignment™ model 161–67
   global specialist in energy management and automation 161
   social impact 166–67
   ZOOP Mobility Network Inc 167–73
Schopenhauer, Arthur 208
Scott, Winfield 33
Second World War (1939–45) 31–32, 57–58, 59–62, 215
Selznick, Philip 39
severe acute respiratory syndrome (SARS) epidemic in China (2003) 3
Shakespeare, William 56
Sheffi, Yossi 8, 13–14
shipping industry
   effects of the planned sulphur cap reduction 174–75
   impact of the 2008 financial crisis 6–7
   loss of containers at sea (VGM certification) 118–19
   mergers 110–11
   ocean freight 155–56
   super ocean carriers and seaport congestion 111–13
Smith, Adam 56, 212
Soviet Union, collapse in 1991 5, 47–48
stages of growth model (Nolan) 50
Stalin, Joseph 60–61, 191
steamboats, history of 57
strategic alignment 48–55
   challenges 52–55
   models 50–53
   role of the chief information officer (CIO) 49–51
   see also business-to-supply chain strategic alignment
strategic alignment maturity model (SAMM) 52
strategic alignment model (SAM) 51
strategic exploration 41–42
strategic friction 4, 29–69
   concept of friction 34–35
   gap of pain 29
   historical context 30–33
strategic management
   origins of 40
   as a process 41–44
strategic plans 53
strategic renewal process 41–44
   directed journey 42–43
   emergent journey 42
   facilitated journey 43
   perspectives 42–43
   top management team 218, 220–21
   transformational journey 43
strategic typology 41
strategic uncertainty 47–48
strategike episteme (generals' knowledge) 36
strategon sophia (generals' wisdom) 36
strategos 36
strategy
   adaptive cycle 41–44
   aligning with supply chain tactics 155–82
   definitions 41–44
   disruption caused by 18–25
   evolution of 36–41
   origin of the word 36
strategy as a process 41
strategy as practice 41, 44
strategy set transformation model (King) 50
strategy trinity 37–38
strikes 3
sub-prime mortgage crisis 63
supplier relationships 156
supply base, reduced 2
supply chain, definition xvii
supply chain competition 23, 156
supply chain disruption
   empirical evidence of policy effects 217–22
   impact on lean systems 2–4
   preparing to cope with 8–9
   research questions 225–35
   research studies 2
   responses to 23–25
   sources of 133–34, 138–43
   see also disruption management
supply chain management
   categorizing through the philosophy of determinism 208–09
   definitions 1–2, 237–38
   impact of globalization 2
   origins of 1
   traditional strategies 7–8
supply chain relational risk (SCRR) 187–92
supply chain risk management, studies 2

supply chain strategic alignment 223–25
supply chain strategic management 155–82
supply chain strategy and tactics
    autonomous
        impeded by strategic friction 218, 221–22
    determinism
        external policy, beyond supply chain management 218–19
        organizational policy 218, 220–21
        supply chain industry policy 218, 219–20
        TMT strategic renewal process 218, 220–21
sustainable globalization 65–67
sustainable supply chains 174
Sweeney, Edward 2
Syria
    civil war 13
    drivers of civil war 217
    partition after the First World War 131
    refugee crisis 120

taktike techne (tactics plus rhetoric and diplomacy) 36
technology
    exponential supply chain disruption 10–12
    inequalities created by 217
terrorism, insurgent supply chain disruption 12–14
Thatcher, Margaret 62, 69, 216
top management team 41
    bounded rationality issue 47–48
    composition 44
    lack of consultation with logisticians 237–38
    response to environmental change 46–48
    strategic management and 44–48
    strategic renewal process 218, 220–21
    supply chain strategy 46
    threat rigidity problem 48
Toyota 3, 8, 12
trade wars 116–17, 173, 199–200
transaction cost economics (TCE) 40
transport strategy, climate change and 63–65
transportation and distribution, physical supply chain 97–128

Treaty of Le Touquet 119–21
Treaty of Versailles (1919) 68, 215
Trevithick, Richard 57, 212
trinity concept of politics 213
triple-A supply chain 9
Truesdale, Ian 115–18, 232
Trump, Donald 116–17, 173, 193
Twitter 10
Tyson, Mike xiv

Uber 11
United Nations 62
    UN Interim Force in Lebanon (UNIFIL) 86–92
United Parcel Service 11
United States–China trade war 199–200
United States Military Academy (West Point) 32–33

value chain analysis 40
van Beek, Jeroen 99, 105–06
van Berkel, Michiel 110–13, 231–32
Vargas, Eduardo 99–105, 232–33
variant method 39
vendor-managed inventories 2

Wall Street Crash (1929) 57, 59, 215
walls along borders 193–94
war, policy and 57–61
Waterloo, Battle of 33
al-Wazir, Khalil Ibrahim 86
Wealth of Nations (Smith, 1776) 56, 212
weather
    Beast from the East (March 2018) 2
    disruption related to global warming 65
Whiting, Stuart 161, 233–34
Woodland Group, disaster recovery plans 106–10
World Bank 62
World Trade Center, New York, business impact of the 1993 bombing 3

Xi Jinping 108, 192, 194

Yan, Emily 199–200
Yeltsin, Boris 47–48
YouTube 10

Zara 17, 175
ZOOP Mobility Network Inc 167–73